All
Consuming

Also by Ruby Tandoh and available from Serpent's Tail:

Eat Up!
Cook As You Are

All
Consuming

Why we eat the way we eat now

Ruby
Tandoh

First published in Great Britain in 2025 by
Serpent's Tail,
an imprint of Profile Books Ltd
29 Cloth Fair
London
EC1A 7JQ

www.serpentstail.com

Copyright © Ruby Tandoh, 2025

The essay 'Allrecipes' is adapted from an essay previously published in the *New Yorker*.
'Tonic waters' is based on work originally commissioned by Factory International.

Designed and typeset in Berling by CC Book Production

SRD

Printed and bound in India by
Manipal Technologies Limited, Manipal

The moral right of the author has been asserted.

A CIP catalogue record for this book is available from the British Library.

Our product safety representative in the EU is Authorised Rep Compliance Ltd.,
Ground Floor, 71 Lower Baggot Street, Dublin, D02 P593, Ireland.
www.arccompliance.com

ISBN 978 1 80081 0044
eISBN 978 1 78283 9644

MIX
Paper | Supporting
responsible forestry
FSC™ C104740

Contents

Tastemakers

Everything but the recipe

Impulse buy

Supermarket fugue
Or, an experiential history of four superstores

The ice cream age
Or, how to invent a hit ice cream

Tonic waters
Or, the rise and rise of the magic wellness drink

Fast food

The automat is dead
Or, on the past and future lives of food machines

Wimpy
Or, the good, the bad and the ugly of British American food

Introduction

Our tastes are social. Even when you first drank milk, there was the milk, yes, but there was also the person behind the milk who will have presumably either made or messed up your relationship with food for the couple of decades after that. We learn to eat from our families and friends, at school and in work. A village develops a particular recipe for an apple pie – one that nobody outside the village likes, but who cares? We want these things not just because of what they are, but who we are.

Tastes spread like this, person to person, like viruses, almost irrespective of the qualities of the food involved. We observe other people in their food lives, often judgementally. Nothing turns me off something quicker than the wrong people liking it, by which I mean people almost identical to me in every respect, in a way that doesn't flatter me. I avoided the viral chopped salad moment of 2024 by the skin of my teeth.

Biology has pre-programmed us to crave some tastes, like sweetness, and be wary of others, like bitterness, but these are the broadest brushstrokes. They only count for so much. The most important thing that a few million years of evolution has encoded in us is the ability to be omnivores. Bee Wilson wrote about this in her book *First Bite*. We come into this world wanting milk, but everything else we have to make up as we go along. This is where other people come in. This is where stories come in.

A few generations ago, you mostly learned about food from the people close to you. Your access to food was shaped by forces outside your control, like the climate, or trade, or economics, but the choices you made within those parameters – these would have been intimate and social. Conversations, meals together, some person you want to be more like, some person you hate, a myth about this or that, a recipe taught to you, a story about witches. Not always, not for all people, but as a rule: almost everything you knew about food, you probably learned either in the kitchen or at the table.

All this has changed. In the years since the end of the Second World War, the balance of power has moved from countries to corporations. We've seen the rise of restaurant chains, supermarkets, delivery, fast food, ready meals and industrial agriculture. Migrations have reconfigured the culture. Britain has somehow gone from knowing almost nothing about anything, when it comes to non-Western foods, to being a culinary dilettante. We have supermarkets. We have the Magnum ice cream hegemony. More has changed since the end of the war than changed in the few millennia before that.

In his book *In Defence of Food*, Michael Pollan writes about where some of these new food systems go wrong – the

2

environmentally ruinous stuff, the possible health implications. He explains that for most of human history we didn't
have to worry about the moral and nutritional choices that
have blown up in the last few years. 'To guide us we had,
instead, Culture,' he writes. 'Which, at least when it comes
to food, is really just a fancy word for your mother.' But
what's this capital-C culture that's untouched by society?
You can't separate 'real' appetites from 'fake' appetites
manufactured by industry or media or tech. These forces
aren't tears in culture – they *are* the culture. And besides,
mothers are beholden to them too.

Like it or not, our food culture today is composite and
changeable. It is advertising. It is branding, marketing,
travel and YouTube. Recipes aren't passed from hand to
hand, they come at you from all angles. They're on TV,
on the internet, in newspaper supplements, on YouTube
and in the comments under Instagram posts. Restaurant
trends like smashburgers spread like a rash from New York
to London, Lahore and Tokyo, via the infrastructure of
the commercial internet. We've gone from learning how
to eat from the people around us to learning how to eat
from a few billion dissenting voices across the world via
the global food machine. This expansive food culture is
not, it bears saying, always pure of heart. But it is culture.
And, once you start thinking about these forces acting
on your seemingly personal tastes and desires, you can
begin to look at your own diet with curiosity, rather than
judgement. Why do I want what I want? Now, there's a
question. And I promise you won't find the answer in your
own stomach.

*

This is not the book that I planned to write when I put my mind to it five years ago. Thank god. I thought this would be a definitive guide to why humans want the foods they do. I started at the start, about a few million years ago, when mammals were getting a Swiss army knife set of teeth – incisors, canines, molars – so they could be omnivores. Then I learned about the feasts of Apicius – a Roman epicure who liked flamingo tongues and is a good first-century analogue of unbearable food guys today. In fact, I have just checked and the first chapter I wrote for the first draft of this book started with 3.5-billion-year-old microbial mats. I cannot imagine where I was going with this.

Food culture is always in conversation with the past, but it's also shaped by the economy, tech and changeable social currents of right now. These things move laterally and in feedback loops and pendulum swings and sometimes at cross-purposes. Every time something changes in society, it changes on the plate.

There's a book I found enlightening when I was writing this – *The British at Table, 1940–1980*, by Christopher Driver. Driver writes, from a vantage point in the early eighties, that there were things in food that people even three decades prior could never have forecast: the rise of vegetarianism, the pantheistic diet cults and their demagogues, the invention of cooking as a pastime – not just for real food hounds and hobbyists, but as a kind of factory setting of middle-class urban elites. I've been thinking about the equivalents now, the things that we take for granted in our food culture but that would shock Christopher Driver.

To start with, the anxious energy in our food culture

4

has been redistributed. People who in the eighties would've spent days making fiddly and disenchanting food for a dinner party now commit themselves to breezy, knowingly effortless cooking, but spend loads of time and even more money getting the very best local, heirloom, organic, artisan, PDO, cold-pressed, small-batch ingredients. There's also the health fads – the change of emphasis from health to the more nebulous politics of wellbeing, or self-optimisation. We've managed to fill the Whole Foods drinks refrigerators with hundreds of flavours of woo, from electrolyte elixirs to tummy tonics and magnesium shakes, each of which speaks to a new neurosis.

And then there's the internet – which has replaced farms or factories or supermarkets as the primary food infrastructure of the modern age. This is where I end up ordering food, and booking tables for restaurants, and being bombarded with recipes I never asked for on my TikTok feed. The internet has had a double effect, completely changing how food systems work, but also changing how food culture is created. Old-money food publications like *Gourmet* have gone, and in their place we have Cookpad and Google reviews, which are just as authoritative as the old guard, albeit with a different flavour. When the last issue of *Gourmet* went out in 2009, the food writer Christopher Kimball wrote an obituary for the magazine. 'Is American magazine publishing on the verge of being devoured by the democratic economics of the Internet?' Kimball asked, but he already knew the answer.

These new ways of learning mean new tastes, sometimes broader tastes, often more predictable ones. Different kinds of media – TV, smartphone, books, apps – don't just give us blank space for sharing food, they also change the foods we desire and why. The medium is the message. Food blogging gave us hype restaurant queues of an order of magnitude we'd never seen before. Newspaper colour supplements gave foodie esoterica in Britain a mass readership for the very first time. You can blame extremist pizza cheese levels on a combination of how phone screens are oriented, the evolution of phone cameras, and the birth of high-speed mobile data, all of which have created the conditions for the cheese pull shot.

The point is, if you're reading this, you've probably witnessed at least a small part of a forty-year cultural overhaul that has given us Jamie Oliver, Martha Stewart, Wagamama, the idea of hot chefs, Deliveroo, the sriracha revival, animal fries, Magnums, Resy, Noma and Goop. Just in the time it's taken me to write this book, we've gained Topjaw, TikTok recipes and the kombucha revival. I love it. I love humankind's inexhaustible capacity for nonsense. I love seeing these changes come and go, some of them metabolised into new and equally short-lived trends, others totally overhauling how we eat.

It can get to be too much. Try to keep up with the food discourse – and these days who really has a choice? – and you can end up feeling like you're playing cultural Tetris. It's fun until it's not. And somehow, despite all of this – despite the constant, multimedia discourse around food, and despite the fact that it has never been easier to learn about cooking or find information on restaurants or dig around for nutritional guidance online – nobody seems to know what they're doing. If everything is new, all the time, it can be hard to get your bearings. Harvey Levenstein called it a paradox of plenty – the more we have, the less we seem able to enjoy it, which accounts for diet culture, and the concept of guilty pleasures, and weird culinary nationalism in a time of unparalleled food choice. But you can slow down, and when you do you will see these countless, fractious, prismatic food moments resolve into some kind of shape. This book is partly an attempt to record and decode parts of our food culture at a time of massive structural change – and at a time where, at the snap of a tech mogul's fingers, so much of that culture could suddenly be wiped from the servers. When you work through it like this, you feel overtures emerge, like the way we vacillate between the need for comfort and the desire for change. You start to see the human drives that cause global food system flux. And that's what this book is about.

All Consuming is about food, and the way we talk about food, and the easy, anarchic way that ideas about food are changing right now. It's mainly about modern food culture – the period of whiplash change since the 1940s, during which these systems and cultures have been systemically overhauled. Because I live in Britain, it's mainly about food in the affluent West, but you'll see that modern food culture is most itself when it's online, which means you're never that far from any global food trend.

You'll see a lot of American references here too. There was a point when you could say that French cuisine was the most influential in the world – through colonialism on one hand and the influence of restaurants on the other. Ingredients moved, and people moved, but ideas about food travelled too, and these reproduced French restaurant culture across much of Europe and America. But for the last seventy-five years, the United States has done more to shape global food culture than any other country, for better and for worse. Again, it's about the ways that food stories spread, and this has only accelerated in the age of the internet. For as long as digital culture skews towards the US, those ideas and tastes naturally filter through to us, too. That said, we're beginning to see a shift, across things like TikTok and bubble tea, towards greater East Asian influence on British food, so you'll find stories about this here too. The point is this: social, economic, cultural, legislative and demographic changes have just as much to teach us, when it comes to learning how to eat, as our own families.

The book starts where most food decisions start – at home, with recipes. The kitchen can feel like a refuge from modern, commercial food culture, but of course this isn't the case. Technology, and marketing, and tremors in online media shape the domestic kitchen just like they shape restaurants.

As befits the era we live in, I spend way more time looking at food content on-screen than I do actually eating or cooking. Right now, a huge number of food stories end up, in fact, being tech stories – from the early crowd-sourced internet, to the rise of social media. I've also tackled the important matter of who, exactly, you should trust when it comes to food, now that with Google reviews and TikTok influencers and blogs and Instagram, criticism is the people's art. Then there are all the places we do our food shopping, and the million nutritionally irrelevant but culturally rich things you find on the shelves. We have more choice in what we buy than ever before – packaging and ads and high-intensity trend cycles have evolved to guide us. And fast food – the systems that make it possible, and the tight emotional bonds we form with this super-massive industry.

There's a lot going on out there. This book might be adding to the noise, or it might help you make sense of things. In any case, it's not a book of food ethics, or a polemic, or a practical guide. I don't pretend to offer solutions to systemic problems. There are so many others who have done this. All I can claim to have done is sift through a handful of the inventions of the contemporary food age and try to figure out why they happened, along with how they've shaped our tastes – or, why we want what we want. This is a book about mass change in food culture. It's about the stories we tell about food, and the stories that are foisted upon us.

During my research, I've talked to chefs, restaurant critics, restaurateurs, cookbook authors, editors, food scientists, architects of the early internet, recipe developers, students, critics, historians and friends. People are generous. They came through with everything from the origin story of Cornetto to recipes for buckwheat cookies, memories of being in restaurant queues some twenty years ago, stories about their kitchens, and the kind of litigable industry gossip that I'm sadly unable to repeat. But I have also looked around me at the world as I see it, and wondered what it all means. There's no certainty in appetite – it's the world working through us, but it's also fantasy and desire and imagination. 'Speculative worlds that grow up in the crevices between truths,' Hilary Mantel said, about something completely unrelated. But really this is it.

You can't talk about these things without understanding your place in them. And so I'm limited, and enabled, by my own experience. I grew up in a house where we thought about food a lot. There were experiments with a banana and bean sprout salad. We lived in the aftershock of the beige years of vegetarianism. We did this with not much money, but we were lucky – we were never at the point of desperation where curiosity itself is a luxury. Now, I find myself in the unusual position of not just consuming food culture, but also being part of food media. I've written cookbooks, cooked for a living, and worked for newspapers and magazines. I'm part of the food culture macroverse. But I'm also just another person feeling its shockwaves, and the funny thing is that the latter role has been much more useful for the writing of this book. So much of all of the book has come from simply paying curious attention, as an eater, as a consumer, to the things I used to take for granted. Things like ice creams, and vending machine pizza, and a deluge of viral TikTok videos about chocolate-covered strawberries. I'm in this culture, as are you. This book is my attempt to think things through.

Home cooking

Craving content

Or, the unsubtle art of selling a recipe

Whenever I go online, I can count on being confronted with a recipe that I never asked for and which, the moment I see it, I kind of want to eat. Recently it was 'Herby Chicken Caesar Schnitzel', which was accompanied by the kind of video that's carefully calibrated to stoke a craving. Here's the schnitzel being caressed by soft, amber bubbles in the pan. Here's a money shot, when a knife rasps demonstratively over the crust. Here's a green salad being twisted through a slippery dressing. It is slung on top of the schnitzel like a satin quilt on an unmade bed. 'She's crispy, saucy, cheesy and a little bit spicy,' the recipe developer, Jodie Nixon, explains in the voiceover. It was posted by Mob – a hugely successful recipe platform with an ensemble cast of recipe developers, popular on social media and among younger cooks.

Another day, it'll be an unsolicited close-up of a chicken thigh, fresh out the pan, with tortoiseshell caramelised skin. 'They're crunchy, they're juicy,' Jordon Ezra King – the cook – says on the voiceover. 'Gonna do it with herby rice, and some nice pickle-y fresh crunchy salad.' Again, it was a recipe from Mob. Or how about those few weeks when my For You pages were hacked by an Instagram-famous sausage and gochujang rigatoni? You crumble and fry sausage meat until it's lightly browned, in pieces the size of granola clusters, then add gochujang, cream, shallot, Parmesan, breadcrumbs and a few other things. You can tell it's going to be aggressively pleasing in the same way as a McDonald's double cheeseburger. The recipe developer, Xiengni Zhou, narrates the video. 'It's quick, creamy, and kind of spicy,' she says, and the dish looks so good that you don't even care that you're getting déjà vu. The video has tens of thousands of likes, and it is also, unsurprisingly, from Mob.

Over the last few years, Mob – which was started by Ben Lebus in 2016 – has become one of the most successful cooking sites online. It has released eight cookbooks and counting. As Gen Z's recipe provider of choice, it has 3 million followers on Instagram, 1.4 million on TikTok, and over 100,000 people who pay for their recipes. By the time you read this, it'll probably be more.

Mob is one part of a massive transformation in how we cook. On Instagram, TikTok and even the more sedate platforms like Substack, you'll find searchable, compound-noun recipes like 'sheet-pan miso maple mustard chicken' or adjective-savvy numbers that are 'crispy' or 'chewy' or 'crunchy'. You know these flavours, you can anticipate how this particular assault of umami, salt and sweet will make you feel. They use a weirdly placeless pantry of ingredients, everything from sriracha to miso and cumin. And then there are the visuals – the photos and videos that seem to have been engineered to bypass rational thinking and go straight to the pleasure centres of the brain.

In the last fifteen years, we've seen entire cooking dynasties built on recipes like this. Recipe developers like Alison Roman – 'Slow-Roasted Oregano Chicken with Buttered Tomatoes' – and Yotam Ottolenghi, who puts his name to 'Five-Spice Butternut Squash in Cheesy Custard'. Even *The New York Times*, which used to have buttoned-up, if technically flawless, recipes for things like chicken chasseur, has shifted towards craveable, suckerpunch recipes. Do you want the 1988 hunter's chicken, with a photo of a French country-kitchen-style table, with crystal wine glasses and produce in the background? Or would you in fact prefer 'Roasted Chicken Thighs with Hot Honey and Lime' – which is illustrated with a close-crop photo of the plump, chiaroscuro-rendered chicken thighs, visibly juicy, with lime wedges wrung out alongside? It's about how you market a recipe.

As things happen, I've just seen a new feature on *The New York Times* site. '44 Creamy, Dreamy White Bean Recipes'. They've got 'Miso Leeks with White Beans', 'Refried White Beans with Chile-Fried Eggs', 'Lemony White Beans with Anchovy and Parmesan', 'Baked Mushrooms and White Beans with Buttery Bread'. I don't know if these are the best recipes in the world, but they are unbelievably popular. Except, maybe these *are* the best recipes. Maybe, in an age where most of us get most of our recipes from the internet, the best ones are precisely the favoured few that actually grab your attention.

Right now there are more recipes available to a person than at any other point in history – a number that's increasing every minute despite the fact that most of us will cycle through the same couple of dozen recipes for the rest of our lives. To beat the competition, everything has to evolve along increasingly weird vectors to one-up the recipe that came before. And so 'spaghetti and meatballs' eventually turns into 'creamy linguine alla vodka with crispy cheesy meatball bites', plus a soft porn video of balls getting rolled through a slick of buttery sauce. In a world of seemingly infinite choice, the message is no longer just 'this thing is possible', or 'practical', or 'authentic', or even 'delicious'. It has to be – 'This thing will make you see god.'

In 2002, Yotam Ottolenghi and Sami Tamimi along with a few business partners opened a deli in London inspired by the flavours of the eastern Mediterranean. They called it Ottolenghi, and in 2008 this also became the title of their first book. In the book, there was the same style of cooking as in the deli: lively and self-consciously modern, not beholden to tradition – least of all the English tradition of meat and two plain veg. To a certain extent, they drew on their upbringings in Jerusalem (Ottolenghi is Israeli, Tamimi is Palestinian) but they resisted simplistic readings of the kind of food they cooked. 'Food has no boundaries' – this was the party line. And so there were 'Portobello Mushrooms with Pearl Barley and Preserved Lemon'. 'Roast Chicken with Sumac and Za'atar'. 'Cauliflower and Cumin Fritters with Lime Yoghurt'. 'I want drama in the mouth,' as Ottolenghi put it in one interview. And so they concentrated on high-impact recipes where contrast was prioritised – crunchy toppings, hot drizzles, yoghurt dips and kaleidoscopic salads.

These days, this approach is so ubiquitous that you'd think recipes have always worked this way – that you run through permutations and combinations of ingredients, remixing familiar flavours until you settle on something that feels new. It seems obvious to us that a recipe writer is also a recipe developer. It seems obvious that the entire job is coming up with fresh ideas. But this is not how recipes have always worked. Chefs have been coming up with conspicuously inventive new menus forever, and home cooks have always improvised, building new combinations out of the flavours they already know. But when it came to cookbooks, few had ever done this mix-and-match methodology with the singular dedication of the Ottolenghi syndicate.

In lots of cuisines, dishes are stable entities, with a name and a personality and way of being made. Canard à l'orange, moules marinière, crêpes Suzette. In traditional British cooking, we have something similar. If you started calling Cornish pasties 'chuck steak, black pepper and root vegetable turnovers' or, worse still, riffed on them by adding a chermoula dip, you would be laughed out the door. But in the Ottolenghi universe, cooking is modular and iterative. This was the charm of Ottolenghi, in those early days, and the reason those books shaped the outlook of an entire generation of recipe writers: because people were reminded that you could play with food.

Fusion is crucial. Ottolenghi and Tamimi started with a few flavours loosely drawn from the Levant and twisted them with other ingredients. But especially in recent years, the Ottolenghi Test Kitchen – the group of chefs, recipe developers and writers who jointly create the 'Ottolenghi'-headed recipes – have started working with a broader palette.

In the appendix of *Flavour*, Ottolenghi's book co-authored with Ixta Belfrage, there's a list of 'flavour bombs': fenugreek marinade, sweet tamarind dressing, chamoy, hibiscus pickled onion and date barbecue sauce, each picked from its respective cuisine for some singular property of taste. In what the writer Navneet Alang calls 'the age of the global pantry', all base units of food vocabulary are fair game – you can mix miso with British blackcurrants, harissa with lasagne. This is great news for cooks, but even better news for recipe developers, who are finding that the number of possible recipe formulations has exponentially increased. I know this because I, like so many recipe writers, spent much of the late 2010s trying to repurpose Chinese chilli oil, eventually coming up with a recipe for gnocchi with chilli crisp and Parmesan. A year or two later, Mob kitchen put out their own take on this, and I hate to say this, but it was better than mine.

The Ottolenghi machine got its start at a time before Instagram but in the food blogging heyday – when the recipe world online was competitive enough to demand originality, but hadn't yet raged out of control. Today, things are amplified. The most successful recipe developers are testing the limits of the methods Ottolenghi popularised. When I spoke to Ben Lebus – the founder of Mob – he compared the process to making music. There are countless ways of reconfiguring the notes, most of them exciting. This new influx of recipes can be weird and unexpected, with the compositional balance of jazz. And so, if you go to Mob, you'll find 'Honey Harissa Carrots with Whipped Feta', and 'Chipotle Chicken Mac and Cheese'. There's Sophie Wyburd's smart recipe for

'Squash and Chorizo Orzo with Hazelnut Gremolata'. Subscribe to Caroline Chambers' newsletter, 'What to Cook When You Don't Feel Like Cooking', and you'll get recipes like 'Sheet-Pan Miso Maple Mustard Chicken with Sweet Potato and Sprouts'. Right now, it's the most popular food newsletter on Substack.

In an Alison Roman recipe that did well online a few years ago, you fry the ancient triumvirate of onion, garlic and ginger in oil until fragrant. You add turmeric, red pepper flakes and chickpeas. You take your time here: the skins will tan and crisp; some will burst. Take a few of the chickpeas out of the pan, then bruise the others to help thicken the sauce. Roman will tell you to add stock and coconut milk, at which point the broth changes its character, complicating like pastis in water. You season and simmer. Towards the end, you add sliced greens. When it's time to serve, you scatter mint leaves, yoghurt, those crisped chickpeas and red pepper flakes with painterly flair. You might notice that it looks a bit like Trinidadian channa, South Indian coconut curries, or a particular version of chana dal. Officially this is 'Spiced Chickpea Stew with Coconut and Turmeric'. But you probably know it as it's come to be known online, only as 'the stew'.

Mob operates from a spacious office in East London, along the e-culture corridor that runs from Old Street through Shoreditch and up to Dalston. Ben Lebus – a tall, exactingly casual man in his early thirties – showed me around a while back. The office was lively. People were running data on their laptops and replying to comments online. A group was discussing strategy while picking the leftovers from the morning's recipe tests. Behind a long, glass wall there was a large kitchen with banks of ovens and long, open countertops, with windows looking on to the street below. This is where the team photograph and film whatever they've been working on. Lebus presides over thirty full-time employees, churning out between sixty and a hundred recipes per month. More than a cook, Lebus is a tactician. Increasingly, he's seeing traditional publishers as competitors. 'They are buying recipes and selling them,' he explained. 'And that's what we're doing.'

Lebus started Mob after seeing that his friends at university didn't have the confidence to cook much more than pesto pasta. He worked on recipes that could feed four people for less than £10. He fine-tuned a beetroot risotto, made sesame noodles with sugarsnap peas and hacked homemade fish and chips. He roped in his friends – guys with cameras, guys with a decent suite of Adobe software, guys in bands – to produce the videos. Because it was a brand and not a blog, recipes felt like sneaker drops: teased for a couple of days, then delivered as though this was what you'd been asking for all along. Lebus did market research in the comment section, developing only what he already suspected he could sell. The recipes stacked up, and Lebus got more help. The 'mob' in Mob is the collective of chefs, recipe developers, writers and online-famous cooks – some in-house, some freelance – who create all this content.

What Lebus and countless internet-based recipe developers understand is that a recipe works not just if it works, but if it sells. Here is how things used to work: You bought a one-size-fits-all cookbook. Inside this cookbook, which for some people would be their only cookbook, you'd have a decent selection of day-to-day recipes. Maybe Freda DeKnight's *The Ebony Cookbook*, or Delia Smith's *Complete Cookery Course*. You could get more or less everything you needed from a book like this – a basic puff pastry explainer, a failsafe recipe for roast turkey, chocolate cake, baked Alaska – everything a pre-digital cook could conceivably need, and a few extras thrown in for luck. But even in the biggest book, and some of them were literally called bibles and encyclopedias, the choice was finite. For the most part you would have to take what you were given. A brownie was a brownie. If it was a mind-blowing brownie . . . well, that's a perk.

As I write this, it strikes me that it sounds like a scare story about communist-era grocery stores, with one kind of chocolate bar and one cereal and one state-brand cola-adjacent pop. But with recipes, limits can be enabling. At home we've got a copy of Giorgio Locatelli's *Made in Italy*. In it, there are maybe three recipes that I make, but when I do make them I go for it. I'm not window-shopping for the best recipe for ragù, I'm not 'seeing a few people right now', or cross-referencing with something I saw some nerd on Reddit say. I'm not having to pick out this ragù from a lineup of tens of thousands of possible ragùs, and so it's free to just be itself. Choosing the recipe is easy, because I already chose the book – and the authority of that book, and the author, are the things that have me hooked.

The power of cookbooks is relational. It's about how the recipes are arranged, which things are included, which things conspicuously aren't, the shape and substance of a foreword and how it relates to the text, who wrote it and who they wrote it for. I have cookbooks that map out an entire cuisine, and other ones that are more like memoirs, and some that are just compendia of plausibly helpful kitchen trivia, but in any case, they add up to more than the sum of the recipes inside them. But when a recipe breaks free on to the internet, everything changes, and it has to make it on its own. This starts with the visuals.

There have been photo cookbooks for decades, but if you have any cookbooks from any time before the Clinton administration you'll know that the photos haven't always been enticing. You know the deal – a spiced cider baked ham, cooked in the microwave until shrunken and uniformly pink, then retrofitted with orange segments and maraschino cherries like the back of a nuclear armadillo. To make sure that it pops, this comes on a bed of curly parsley. This is in *Microwave Cooking the Amana Way*, by the way, which was published in 1982. Just in case you need to see it yourself.

I have a copy of the *Hamlyn New All Colour Cookbook* from the late eighties. It is, despite every recipe having a photo and this being the entire point of the book, the least appetising cookbook I own. The three-colour layered moulded vegetable terrine, for instance – a dish that is already, definitionally doing too much – has been flanked with watercress leaves. A carving knife has been placed, slightly askew, at the edge of the plate, in much the same way as you might plant a weapon at a crime scene. The photos do a job, which is to show you – with the orthographic clarity of an architectural drawing – what the dish is supposed to look like. But beyond that, nothing. It's illustrative, and that seems to be enough.

Other cookbooks were more practical, and you'd see how to make something like fondant fancies in a step-by-step photo grid. In higher-end publications the photos could be more evocative, maybe a bait-and-switch photo of a Tuscan hillscape next to a recipe for ribollita, or the uptight set pieces of an issue of *Gourmet* magazine. When you look at these photos, you get the feeling that they were trying to make up for being food photos by putting the focus on the garnishes or the appliqué napkins or the tableware or the view – romanticising everything but the cooking itself. There were beautiful photos, like those by Tessa Traeger, where the food becomes a medium almost like paint or clay.

But in the nineties, paving the way for the transition from Paper Recipes to Internet Recipes, food photography changed. Suddenly it *was* about the food. Take the 1993 *Keep It Simple*, by London chef Alastair Little and Richard Whittington. The photos, taken by David Gill, are . . . kind of sexy. The photo for the ratatouille is a close-cropped photo of a split baguette in side profile. The vegetables – slippery and soft – have been piled into the sandwich, and a drop of olive oil spills over the edge. Or Martyn Thompson's food photographs in *The River Cafe Cook Book*, from 1995. I can't tell exactly how the pigeon stuffed with cotechino is supposed to work, but who cares? The focus is tight on the wine-dark skin. The bird has a deep roast gloss.

We have Nigel Slater to thank for some of the horniest food content. *Marie Claire* magazine, for which Slater was hired to write the recipes, published a cookbook in 1992. The food photographs, by Jean-Louis Bloch-Lainé and Kevin Summers, catch the food in moments of déshabillé:

mussels coaxed open, crust of a cheesy gratin broken by a spoon, juices dripping down a figgy pudding. It was, as Slater put it in the introduction, 'the decision to abandon those props, those traditional scene-setters, and the avoidance of styling and tweaking the food to look good for the camera.' It was the same at the *Observer*, where Nigel Slater moved in the early nineties, with Kevin Summers and then Jonathan Lovekin photographing the food. Everything is burst, collapsed, juicy, swollen or sizzling, and indecently close up. This new kind of photo was composed to make the food look not beautiful, as such, but craveable. It's strange now to think that recipes weren't always supposed to be thirst traps. But the most consequential parts of food culture are often the things like this – things that seem so obvious, so unquestionable, that it never occurs to us that they could be done another way.

Photo-centric recipes translated well to the internet. At the beginning, slow bandwidths had photos loading almost pixel by pixel – the world's dreariest striptease. But once things got going, especially moving into the smartphone era towards the end of the noughties, beautiful food found a natural home on blogs and on Flickr and, before long, on Instagram. Then there was video – and phones with enough storage and mobile data to actually deal with them. And it's here, in the intensely visual, photographic world of social media that this new wave of recipe creation took off. It needed people who knew how to work the algorithms to their advantage.

An Instagram feed is totally visual. Recipes come to you without any context or even a title until you tap through to the caption. In this recipe economy, it's harder to appeal to a person's prefrontal cortex, where the reasoning gets done. You follow a hedonic pathway instead: What immediately registers as delicious? Which arrangement of pixels is crave-able? So, on Mob, there are no world-building photos of figs in a hand-thrown bowl next to an £80 candle on a faux French provincial linen tea towel from Toast. Mob style means shooting against stainless steel and in natural light – an approach that makes the colours pop. Scroll down the Mob Instagram grid and you'll see that photos crop close to the bowl. 'I don't like anything extraneous around the dish,' Lebus told me. 'It's just about the food.'

Even the colours are strategised. Take that sausage and gochujang pasta – when I asked Lebus why he thought it did so well, he just said: 'Orange.' As is traditional in the culture of tech start-ups, he's been listening to pop psychology podcasts. 'Orange is the colour that makes people hungry,' he explained. 'It's why the McDonald's logo is yellow and red.' He added that blue doesn't occur naturally in food – even blueberries are a kind of dusky, purple bruise – which is why it's often used in diet company branding. If you scroll through Mob recipes, the palette is mostly the same shades of sunset, yolk, terracotta, mahogany, vermilion and tar that you'd find in a New York-style cheese slice.

The most important part of Mob's visual presence is the videos: it's here that the craving content comes to life, in close-ups of melted cheese and the soft bubble of pasta. You see fat, slick gnocchi jiggling in the pan. You see Parmesan snow. You see things flow and drip. The sound is important too, weighted towards crunches and crackles and the lubricious squelch of a stirred mac and cheese. It's incredibly sensory, sometimes even whole-body satisfying.

In many ways it's like a cross between the glossy food porn of the nineties, and YouTube-era ASMR. Instead of that back-of-the-neck tingling feeling, you just feel your stomach start to groan.

Because Mob grew up on social media, they speak this language fluently, but all this is becoming standard practice. Even legacy publications are moving towards snappier recipes that can hold their own on the grid. Tell me why, when I tapped through to *The New York Times* cooking pages a while ago, the first thing I saw was a close photo of a grilled cheese and cranberry sandwich, double stacked, with a tongue of hot, melted Cheddar oozing out? Even the language is changing shape. Alison Roman's 'Crispy, Salty Latkes'. 'Crispy, sticky, creamy,' former Mob developer and cookbook author Sophie Wyburd told me, explaining the methodologies behind viral recipes. 'People love those words.'

Only half of a recipe is what it makes; the other half is what makes the recipe – the name, the words it uses, if it plays to the senses, a picture, whether it suggests or demands, the length, the deployment or avoidance of words like *sauté*. How you choose these parts depends on what you want the recipe to do and, importantly, who you want to sell it to. Ben Lebus denies that there's any Mob recipe formula, which I guess is probably true in a limited sense, but you only need to look at the Mob website to see that online recipes have their own syntax and that this is changing how we find recipes, how recipes find us, and even what we crave.

When you talk to Lebus, it can be hard to get a sense of

what he likes – which cookbooks he uses, which restaurants have changed his perspective, what food means to him. I got the impression that perhaps he'd spent too long trying to figure out what other people want to see. Over the last year or so, he's been expanding the Mob vision, figuring out ways to optimise what he sees as the 'recipe delivery ecosystem'. 'There are cookbooks. There are very quick social media videos that are often very hard to follow. There are old recipe blogs that are filled with ads and in no way created with the user in mind.' This seems to mean creating a huge, seamless ur-cookbook, one ultra-craveable recipe at a time.

Mob joins an already crowded field. We have recipe blogs, cooking forums, the online outposts of food maga-zines, YouTube tutorials, TikTok semi-recipes, and the prolific output of places like *The New York Times*, or the *Guardian*, or *Bon Appétit*. Then you've got the Substack-ers, the independent recipe developers, the Instagram queens, and the new-wave brocore set like Bosh or Thug Kitchen. Lots of these recipes were written on the internet, for the internet and, a lot of the time, specifically for social media. Taken together, recipe factories like this contract legions of recipe developers, videographers, editors, photographers, dieticians and cultural advisers, making sure that no matter how many iterations of carbonara there are online, there will always be a new, more clickable one. The paradox is that we've decided that the answer to having too many recipes to choose from is writing more.

On the seventh day, they cooked

*Or, how newspaper supplements
invented British foodies*

I can't remember ever buying a newspaper for the news. As far as I see it, the news sections are fish-and-chip wrapping for the lifestyle supplements inside. Online – where, if I am being honest, I get most of my so-called news – it's the food and lifestyle section that I always navigate to first. Yes, I would like to see a selection of autumn sweaters with statement worm-thick weaves. Now I come to think of it, I'd love to know how to prune the roses I don't have. How do you prepare lips for a matte finish lipstick? What are property prices looking like in Stroud? It makes for a welcome fugue state on a Sunday afternoon. It's also nice to know that, in contrast to the infinite scroll of my Instagram feed, this thing has a beginning and an end.

The best part is the food pages – the photograph-heavy recipes and Christmas pudding round-ups and restaurant reviews that pad out the rear end of the magazine and, sometimes, a supplement of their own. Even when I was a kid I liked these pages. At the time it was Nigel Slater, and it is still Nigel Slater, whose recipes for the *Observer* have been bankrolling the entire paper, it seems, for the last three decades. I liked his recipes before I was even old enough to cook. It speaks to the dreamy, aimless tone of the supplements – the fact that the recipes are as much meant to be read as made. Every week they regenerate, plugging new content into exactly the same, to-the-millimetre defined slots. This puts them in a weird position – formulaic, but committed to novelty, and sometimes pointless novelty at that – like the new ways with asparagus that appear every May without fail, even though you can exhaust asparagus as a concept in ten recipes or less.

Even if you don't get a hard-copy paper, you're part of a food culture they did a lot to create. Delia Smith got her start writing for the *Mirror* colour magazine. Claudia Roden wrote recipes for the *Telegraph*. Ottolenghi and the *Guardian* have practically become binary stars. We've had Prue Leith, Diana Henry, Meera Sodha, Rukmini Iyer, Anna Jones and countless more.

It's impossible to imagine the newspapers without their supplements or the supplements without their recipes. Within the triad of advert, feature writing and lifestyle fluff, at least a few pages will always be given over to food. We're used to ubiquitous food chat, especially now, in a world where Instagram and TikTok will present you with this content whether you want it or not.

Things haven't always been this way. The edgeless miasma of food chatter is relatively new. Paul Levy, one of the three people who have a claim to popularising the word 'foodie' in the early eighties, has said that it was the newspaper supplements that laid the groundwork for a lot of this. By the time the term 'foodie' was coined, there were enough of them that they became a joke. And via the weekend paper, recipes were reaching even more people, expanding the foodie-sphere beyond a cosmopolitan in-crowd and into a generalised suburban mass.

Foodies have infiltrated so much of the culture that the word is almost meaningless. Who isn't a food person these days? The recipe mill, the cookbook mega-industry, the osmosis of food into every conceivable cultural outlet, from podcasts to YouTube and zines ... foodie-ism has become more than just a subculture, it *is* the culture. In barely sixty years, we've gone from being too psychosexually stunted to even get excited about food, to talking about almost nothing else.

The *Sunday Times* published the first British colour news-paper supplement in 1962. The broadsheets were squeezed: tabloids were a fraction of the price and sold millions; on the other side, television – even though it was still a minority pastime – was becoming more widespread. When wartime paper rationing ended, a window opened. The thing that television didn't have yet, and that advertisers needed, was colour. In the supplements, colour ads could reach a huge middle-class audience, especially when it came to people who bought the broadsheets. The papers moved some of their production to the cheap, non-unionised, colour printing plants in the North, and the age of the supplement began. In 1964, the *Observer* and the *Telegraph* printed colour magazines for the very first time. In 1969, the *Mirror* followed.

There had been recipes in the newspapers before, but

they felt like an afterthought. You'd have to work your way through the news, business pages, sports, classifieds, analysis and culture until you got to the women's section – a few greyscale pages covering fashion, advice, parenting and food. The recipes were short and functional, not least because that's what a recipe has to be when it only has a couple of square inches. Even the good columnists were mostly anonymous – the *Observer*'s 'Syllabub' was an intelligence operative before he started writing, and kept a low profile even at his most successful. The supplements gave the recipes room to breathe. The contents of the magazines looked almost like today's: a fashion column, a couple of features, agony aunt stuff, cars, proto-Martin Lewis financial advice, home design, puzzle pages and full-spread recipes.

Towards the end of the sixties, the *Observer* asked Elizabeth David, whose Mediterranean and French cookery books had had the cosmopolitan classes in a chokehold since the early fifties, to write for the magazine. She turned it down, but she recommended another writer, Jane Grigson, who had just written a definitive guide to French charcuterie that, as well as being popular among a pre-foodie community of enthusiasts, was even acclaimed in France. She replaced the magazine's original food columnist, Clement Freud, a man with the offhand confidence of someone who's never had to cook an actual midweek meal. His Christmas dinner menu ran to five days of prep, though in the end this turned out to be the least of his crimes.

Some recipe writers are chefs and home economists: people like Freda DeKnight, Mary Berry and Marie-Antoine

Carême, who come to food writing through the food. The others, a category that includes Jane or Claudia Roden, get to it laterally, through words. Before she started writing about food, Jane worked as a translator. She was the kind of person who got agitated by bad writing, by the tauto-logical implications of calling pizza 'pizza pie'. 'Someone who writes loosely is likely to cook loosely,' she explained, 'and that isn't any kind of cook at all.'

Jane Grigson joined the *Observer* magazine in the summer of 1968. Her first column was about strawberries. She wrote a recipe for strawberry barquettes – small pastry boats filled with fruit and lacquered with redcurrant jam so that they looked like jewels. There was another for strawberry brulée in a sweet sablé shell, and coeur à la crème – a cream pudding set in a heart-shaped mould and encircled with fruit. 'In Venice, in the season of Alpine strawberries . . .' she wrote, and it didn't really matter what she said next, because you were already in.

In most recipes, the introduction serves the recipes. Jane's was the other way around. She wrote about the hybridised origins of modern strawberries in French market gardens, and how they feature in the mythology of the fertility goddess Frigg. After a few lines on the demanding anatomy of strawberry plants, she detoured into Jane Austen, talking about the agro-cosplay fruit-picking of the Regency ball-gown set. She refused to be complacent, especially about the things her readers already thought they knew. 'Strawberries, sugar and cream. The combination allows no improvement, you think?' Well, you're wrong.

None of this would've counted for much if the recipes weren't great, but they really were. One week she'd give you smart alternatives to traditional Christmas cake – rounds of meringue stacked with coffee cream, or Grasmere short-cake with preserved ginger. Another week it'd be the unimpeachable precision of carrot salad, celery soup or a recipe for ice cream flavoured with cooked, puréed apples. The cooking was pantheistic and it dealt with everything from kippers to apples, parsley, prunes and fennel with the same care, even love. We get smug these days about how broad our tastes are, and to an extent we're right. But a newspaper now would never run a double-page spread of recipes for tripe.

The magic of Jane Grigson is that though she was a smart cook, she was really a skilled purveyor of daydreams – even if those daydreams were granular and exactingly researched. 'I sometimes think that the charm of a country's cookery lies not so much in its classic dishes as in its quirks and fancies,' she wrote. This included the esoterica of regional pies and rare apple cultivars. Something could be worthwhile without being useful. 'Walk into the of Château Mouton Rothschild,' began Jane's jellied rabbit, 'and you see a scatter of small fires. Some flare into the sky, others smoke as they are fed faggots of vine prunings.' Noisettes de porc aux pruneaux de Tours, crépinettes with chestnuts, carottes à la Vichy, angel's hair charlotte. She drew from the culinary canon as far back as Gervase Markham's seventeenth-century *The English Huswife*. Like her work in publishing, it was translation – fastidious work in which she had to manipulate the tiniest units of grammar while also understanding, in her heart, what really makes a recipe work.

In less skilled hands the citations could feel defensive,

but when Jane does it you get the feeling of being brought
in on a piece of tenderly embellished gossip. Here's Edward
Bunyard on fruit, or Rabelais, or Hieronymus Bosch. She
wrote lovingly about sixteenth-century monks from the
Abbey of Clairac, who held a small, rural monopoly on
prunes. Nobody wants to give a man any more credit than
is absolutely necessary for his wife's life's work, but her
husband Geoffrey – a poet and repository of literary trivia –
was a huge part of this. When Jane drew a blank on that
first column about strawberries, Geoffrey intervened. 'Find
out what the strawberry has meant to people,' he told her,
and so it began.

A couple of years before, in 1965, Margaret Costa – a freelance writer who'd already written a cooking column for
Farmer's Home and worked on the *Good Food Guide* – started
writing recipes for the *Sunday Times* colour supplement.
Before her, it was Robert Carrier – a former intelligence
turned professional bon viveur. Margaret brought
energy to the job, but less polished, so more
charming. It was a Francophile-lite, sharp, understatedly
glamorous kind of vibe. Look up a photo of her – who else
can get that kind of sweeping, voluminous wave blowout
on a chin-length bob?

Margaret lived in a garret flat in Covent Garden where
the only cooking surface doubled as her desk and the floor
housed her cookbooks. A small sink and fridge with an
icebox were always only a couple of extra dinner guests
away from falling into chaos. If Jane was a romantic,
Margaret was more high-impact – if she wasn't throwing
feasts at the flat, she was at the Ivy down the road. After

working as a critic for *Gourmet* and the *Good Food Guide*, she opened a restaurant, Lacy's, which closed down after a karmic run of bad reviews. Food writers still haven't learned their lesson on this particular count, and I'd like to clear things up: it is much easier to go from restaurateur to cookbook author than the other way around.

At home, though, Margaret was a great cook. She also had the gift of being a great shopper. She frontloaded the effort so that when she got into the kitchen, she could focus on the basics of the cooking itself. You could say she wrote a template for bougie cooking culture today, where it's about the produce stores you go to, as much as what you do with the ingredients at the end. One of her columns was all about black pepper, mustard and salt. Good pepper steak will have the aromatics of cathedral incense – a warm anchor note, a resinous edge, harmonic iterations of spice and musk, and a more piquant heat laid over the top. If you're going to cook, you need to consider the geometry of Maldon salt and learn how to deploy French mustard correctly in lapin moutarde. The average British cook at the time was probably using pre-ground pepper and a reflexive pinch of table salt.

Nobody did an opening gambit like her. 'No self-respecting sardine would dream of being seen more than twenty miles north of Cherbourg,' she'd write. 'There has been a ridiculous rumour around for some years that puddings are out of fashion and likely to stay so,' she wrote. 'Nothing could be further from the truth. It is simply wishful thinking on the part of housewives and slimmers.' You see it from Laurie Colwin, who also wrote for *Gourmet* later on. With the exception of a few food writers, people have mostly forgotten her. Unlike Robert Carrier, who had the job before her, she didn't become a celebrity. And she never got a big, belated posthumous reappraisal of her work. But her legacy, like Jane's, would end up being more diffuse, and I guess – in a way – more profound.

For any recipe writer, the mark of success isn't teaching people how to cook well, it's showing them how to *think* well about food, of which 90 per cent is just about having the confidence to disagree. Margaret got into the history of things, explaining that flummery – a jellied fruit cream – used to be set with the shavings of the horn of a young deer, and then was made using the gelatinous powers of simmered calves' foot, and then with isinglass – a collagen derived from the swim bladder of a fish. In the end, she gave you a more down-to-earth raspberry syllabub recipe with Sauternes, rosewater and cream. Margaret could give a detailed appraisal of tinned foods or she could convince you – like she convinced me – that a cheese soufflé isn't just a reasonable proposition but in fact an easy midweek lunch. 'Why *should* people enjoy cooking?' Margaret would say, because she knew it was her job to put forward a case.

'Let's face it,' the journalist Derek Cooper opened his 1967 book, *The Bad Food Guide*, 'food is not something you talk about.' I'm probably not telling you anything you don't already know here but – British food really could be horrible back then. The war was twenty years over, sure, but something had been lost during the rationing years – a mixture of small, diverse farms, and cooking know-how, and access to fresh ingredients. Cooper's book was a polemic. He wanted to expose this culture for what it was, and to make people care, kind of like a proto-Michael Pollan, if a little more . . . parochial, let's say. And so he wrote about the problems with food hygiene, ingredient adulteration and messed-up labour practices. But his real beef was with something bigger – a British culture block that was stopping us even thinking about improving our food. People seemed to have given up. 'We've learned to live with our food,' he wrote, 'by laughing at it.' This was two years after Margaret's column had started in the *Sunday Times*, and the year before Jane. It puts in perspective what these writers were writing within – and writing against.

The supplements got their start at a time when supermarkets were choking the British grocery market, but you don't see any praise for self-service Sainsbury's superstores, or recipes with American-ish imports, or sliced white bread. That's why people read them. 'It's odd to reflect,' Jane wrote in her second column, 'that although millions of us eat tomatoes, few of us ever eat a good one.' The ones we get are 'moneymakers to the last pip, sprouting productively even on the sewage farm'.

The recipes in the supplements got to people when they were at their most receptive, relaxing at home with the Sunday paper. And so tens of thousands of people were exposed, week after week, to low-level deep knowledge about prunes or syllabub. You didn't have to go to a bookshop. You didn't have to make any effort at all. No medium has swerved the course of British food culture as sharply as those columns. They were an invitation to turn food from something you just did, to something you thought about in your spare time.

I keep thinking about a story that I heard, which isn't

about a Sunday supplement specifically, but goes to show the reach that newspaper recipes could have. In one of her early columns for the *Mail*, Prue Leith – who was hand-writing and then mailing in her recipes, at the time, made a copy mistake. She forgot to cross a T, and so '2 Tbs black treacle' became '2 lbs'. I don't know why cooks didn't clock that this was a mistake, but so many people ruined their pans with this stuff that Prue Leith had to go to the switch-board and field the complaints. A couple of weeks later, during the IRA newspaper bomb scares, she got a parcel to her desk. It had a soft centre and an orbiting jumble of wires which is exactly, by the way, the morphology of a bomb. And so the *Mail* offices were evacuated, and when they opened the parcel, what they found was a set of dental braces set into a rock of toffeed marmalade.

Jane and Margaret were both popular among a new generation of bookish, offbeat, middle-class chefs. You can't understand Simon Hopkinson's former restaurant Bibendum – or his and Lindsey Bareham's cookbook *Roast Chicken and Other Stories* – without understanding Margaret Costa. Jeremy Lee, Alastair Little, Rowley Leigh, Margot and Fergus Henderson have all been, in different ways, more influenced by food writing than by the ecosystem of other chefs. A lot of modern British food is about restoring a culinary heritage, using British ingredients, paying attention to the seasons, taking on the role of a cultural custodian. At the same time as Margaret and Jane were writing, Britain began to revive its cheesemaking culture. Before long, farmers' markets – which had pretty much become extinct by the sixties – were coming back.

The point is this: these recipes had legs. Some of the

most treasured recipes in ordinary kitchens aren't housed in cookbooks, but found on a slip of paper pinned to a noticeboard, tucked into a ringbinder, scavenged from a magazine circa 1974. In the late eighties, Claudia Roden – who is most celebrated for her books about Jewish and Middle Eastern food – wrote a series about regional Italian food for the *Telegraph*. There was supposed to be another series, about regional British food, she told me, but it was impossible. People were cooking the same things in Truro as in Coventry. Everyone was making the same food, because they were reading the same recipes – and they were all from the newspaper supplements.

Their recipes didn't speak to everyone. Margaret and Jane didn't really *get* non-European food, even at a time when cooking from former and contemporary colonies – India, Hong Kong at the time, Jamaica, Trinidad – was working deeper into the canon. And they could be out of touch – Margaret's bon viveur lifestyle, Jane's cottagecore cave house in rural France. Like a lot of food writers, Jane was interested in a fantasy kind of peasantry, but not the actual realities of shopping in a Tesco now. They did speak to the white middle classes, though, and in their own language. The recipes, all the smart and ambient and dreamy food noise around them, resolved an old anxiety – a Victorian hangover – about whether it was menial to spend time at the stove. They showed people of all genders that cooking didn't have to come with all the baggage of being a homemaker. They established supplements as a part of British food culture that has been as influential as cookbooks, almost as tastemaking as TV. Food could be a pleasure, and there was an entire set of people, with time and money and ambition, who started defining themselves by it. In many ways, the foodie was a character the supplements dreamed up.

Recently on a train, I was reading a Jane Grigson book – *Food with the Famous*, for what it's worth. Someone leaned over to tell me that they loved her recipe for trifle. This trifle is an exactingly extra recipe that uses dessert wine (she recommended muscat-flavoured Frontignan), brandy, macaroons, Elizabeth David's everlasting syllabub, a pint of cream made into a thick custard, raspberry jam and candied peel. Then, someone across the carriage said their uncle was a chef and was obsessed with Jane Grigson, and used to quote passages from her *Observer* recipes to the butcher when he came to drop off meat. This was an insufferable conversation, and if I had heard someone else having it I would've hated them. Diehard food people are easy to laugh at – this is karma's way of beating the earnestness out.

But then, elsewhere in the carriage, there were probably people scrolling the recipes on the *Guardian* lifestyle pages, or watching some unsolicited video about the proper way to peel garlic. There will have been ordinary, non-Grigsonheads on their way back from a fashionable restaurant run by some actual Grigsonhead. There will have been people reading *Crying in H Mart*, or *Butter*, or *Lessons in Chemistry*, or any of the other bestselling books of the past decade that are not recipe books or even food books, but are all about the connective power of what we eat. There will have been people with too many opinions about coffee. People who are swimming in food discourse and don't even realise it, because this is now just the way things are. Because you don't have to go looking for ideas about food any more – from the supplements onwards, it has simply come to you.

Jane's final project for the *Observer* magazine was six columns about processed foods. She invoked John Ruskin, a cookbook from eighteenth-century France and a short history of American soda fountains. Lacking a feel for the mechanics of American fast food, she filed her draft of a hamburger recipe with a hand-drawn Venn diagram showing how the circles of bun, hamburger, onion, tomato and lettuce could be arranged. The series started on 11 March 1990, the day before she died of cancer at the age of sixty-one. The remaining columns were published posthumously.

After Jane died, it took a couple of years for the *Observer* magazine to find a new voice – somebody who could speak to liberal, mostly middle-class readers who had got their spiritual sustenance from the Sunday morning recipe columns in the same way that people used to get it from going to church. In 1993, they hired Nigel Slater. Nigel had been to cooking school and worked in restaurants, but really he got his inspiration from words, and he had a copy of Margaret Costa's book that was broken at the spine and a ream of Jane Grigson clippings that he'd refer back to in times of need. He picked up the thread, and others followed. Some people ended up reading his supplements and writing recipes of their own. Later kids would end up on the food-flooded internet for which the supplements paved the way, filming the cooking videos that nobody ever asks for but everyone seems to want. You don't stop thinking about food just because you're done eating. Cooking is a connective process – or at least Jane thought so. 'It gave me a chance of relating cookery to life beyond the kitchen, which is what, in the end, I think cookery should do.'

Allrecipes

Or, the chaotic recipes of the realist's internet

There are other routes through the online culinary morass. A few months ago, I found myself in possession of a bag of apples and craving an apple pie, of the archetypal cooling-on-the-window-ledge variety. I pictured a double-crust flaky pastry around apple and cinnamon – not too complicated to make on a weeknight, but robust enough that I'd be able to slice a clean, thick wedge. Despite knowing how to make apple pie, I wanted the peace of mind that can come only from following a trusted recipe. I have more cookbooks than my bookshelves can support, including at least a dozen that could've proffered something reliable and extensively fussed over. I ignored them and Googled 'apple pie recipe'.

The search engine quickly returned some options. First was 'Homemade apple pie', from Good Food, a British site. (The algorithm tends to meet us where we are, which in my case is London.) Next, from the more boutique recipe sites, a run of superlatives – 'Best Apple Pie Recipe We've Ever Made', 'My Perfect Apple Pie', 'Apple Pie Recipe with the Best Filling', 'My Favourite Apple Pie' – laden with Byzantine, keyword-riddled preambles. I stopped at the eighth result: 'Apple Pie by Grandma Ople', from Allrecipes.com. It showed up next to a thumbnail photo that I probably could've taken on my phone. The preview text cut straight to the ingredients list, whereas other recipes had started with more of a hard sell. ('The pie crust is perfection and the filling will surprise and delight you.') Grandma Ople's version seemed low-key, amenable to the ordinary constraints of my kitchen and my patience. It had more than 12,000 ratings, Google told me, with an average of 4.8 out of five stars. I clicked on through.

If you have searched online for any classic American recipe at any point in the past twenty-five years, you will almost certainly have encountered Allrecipes. This is the everyperson's cookbook, the search engine democracy – in other words, the opposite of the super-niche, stylised food content of the homemakers over on Instagram. This is, for better or worse, the real cooking of a great many people, many of them housewives who would die before they pulled a Nara Smith. Feed the Google search bar 'best chocolate chip cookies' and an Allrecipes version, submitted by a user going by Dora and with more than 14,500 almost unanimously glowing reviews, will probably come up on the first page of results. The site lacks the gravitas of *Bon Appétit* or *The New York Times* cooking section; instead, it falls into the category of sites you never really intend to end up on. Like the internet itself, Allrecipes suffers for its ubiquity. You might not recall that you've used it, even if you've cooked Grandma Ople's apple pie every autumn for the past decade.

The recipes on Allrecipes are nearly all user-submitted. This gives it an aura of shambolic good will, a cross between a church cookbook and a fan-run Wiki. The site has a 4.5-star mac-and-cheese recipe posted under the username g0dluvsugly. One of the most popular recipes on the platform is John Chandler's 2001 upload 'World's Best Lasagna', which could be called the most popular lasagna in the world: more than 20,000 ratings, nearly 15,000 evangelical reviews, and more than 7 million views per year. In 2013, Chandler was invited to talk about it on *Good Morning America*; when he died, in 2022, he was eulogised on Allrecipes.

The site's anarchic tendency can be charming. It also evokes the cautionary 'too many cooks'. Take the messy roster of carrot cakes: one anonymously authored carrot cake is a traditional version; 'Best Carrot Cake Ever', by Nan, involves precooking the carrots; 'Carrot Cake XII', made with canned, puréed carrots, is unfortunately a dud. Because the site relies mostly on targeted searches, the recipes that do well tend to be the ones that people already know they want: meat loaf, Cinnabon dupes, seven-layer dips. Often, the best-performing recipes have a smart but subtle hack. In the case of my apple pie, it was simmering butter with sugar first, then pouring the mixture over the lattice crust before baking, letting it glaze the crust and trickle down on to the fruit. This isn't the traditional way, but it results in a richer pie, with a crispy, caramelised crust.

Since it started, Allrecipes has become a repository for more than 113,000 crowd-sourced recipes. Irma S. Rombauer's *Joy of Cooking*, perhaps the most influential

American cookbook of all time, has more than 20 million copies in circulation, since it was first self-published a century ago; Allrecipes.com reaches somewhere in the neighbourhood of 40 million home cooks each month. You won't see intricate methods or nerdy adventures in technique here – just recipes, backstories, transparently bad ideas, homespun strokes of genius, delicately Midwestern one-upmanship, and, collectively, one of the greatest archives of American food culture the country has produced.

What is now Allrecipes began with a crew of archaeology students at the University of Washington: Tim Hunt, Mark Madsen, Carl Lipo, Michael Pfeffer and David Quinn, along with Dan Shepherd, a Web-designer friend of theirs. Dan ran a scrappy Web company called Emergent Media making sites for a range of customers (the Illinois Department for Natural Resources, Microsoft), using a shared internet line and a few servers in an office cupboard. Domain names were abundant at the time, and the group wanted to start a site of their own. They tried out a few concepts: ultimatefrisbee.com, roadsidereviews.com, beerinstitute.com. Porn came up as one possibility, although when it went to a secret ballot the vote returned unanimous nos. They took a chance instead on something else they could bank on bored, internet-surfing Americans seeking out, and registered the domain Cookierecipe.com.

The site, created by Hunt and co-created by Shepherd, with the others as business partners, went live on 28 July 1997. The guys seeded the site with a few cookie recipes from family and friends, but the idea was that the contributions would ultimately be crowdsourced, with visitors uploading their own. They'd wondered whether people would bother typing out their recipes for no money or measurable reward, but they found themselves quickly inundated. Cooks sent in their recipes, emailed their entries to friends, bookmarked them, and printed them out in what amounted to an accidental guerrilla marketing campaign. There were Beatrice Savitz's 'Apricot Cookies', posted by her granddaughter; lemon bars submitted by Ingrid, from a German lady she met in Indiana more than twenty years prior; a chocolate chip cookie recipe attributed to Hillary Clinton. 'There's always somebody in a friend group who goes, "I hate their cookie recipe – my cookie recipe is better,"' David Quinn, one of the co-owners, said, recalling the site's early days. And besides, he added, 'Every American wants to be famous, right?'

Hunt, who was understood to be the Emergent team's database genius, realised that if a digital recipe archive was going to be successful it'd have to offer more than just straight instructions. Tech has been trying, and mostly failing, to improve on traditional cookbooks for a long time. The Honeywell kitchen computer, which debuted in the late sixties, was a paper-tape-reading meal-planning system that required the homemaker to code. By the eighties, home computers were being advertised as recipe-storing devices, but people seemed to spend more time on them making spreadsheets or playing games. The nineties saw the emergence of CD-ROM recipe books like the *MasterCook* series. All things considered, it was probably easier to just use a book.

With the growth of the internet, people could finally

start to exchange recipes rather than just hoard them. Usenet, an all-purpose mega-forum, had recipe-sharing message boards, but they were clunky and difficult to search. For a more comprehensive resource, you could go to Epicurious (tagline: 'The taste of the web'), which scraped recipes from across the Condé Nast stable of magazines. There was also the more grassroots SOAR – the Searchable Online Archive of Recipes – built by a student at U.C. Berkeley. It was thorough, esoteric, and incredibly hard to follow.

Cookierecipe.com had to be different. Hunt built in features that allowed users to search not just by ingredient but by multiple ingredients, and by ingredients they wanted to avoid. Users could convert from imperial to metric measures. Before Cookierecipe.com, most recipes online were just facsimiles of those offline – blocks of static text. But, over the first few years of the site, Hunt created a recipe matrix, where if you entered, say, your grandmother's chocolate chip cookies it would be broken into discrete units of data. Instead of 'a cup of flour', the database would place 'one cup' in one column and 'flour' in another. This made it possible for users to scale a recipe up or down in a single click. Before the advent of Google, Hunt and his team anticipated perhaps the biggest transformation in cookery of the past century: that once you had access to all the recipes in the world you'd need help finding what you were actually looking for.

Cookierecipe started with a couple of dozen recipes; by January 1998, it had nearly 800. The team expanded their territory to encompass Chickenrecipe.com, Cakerecipe.com,

Pierecipe.com, Thanksgivingrecipe.com, and more. In 1999, at around the time these sites hit a million users combined, the group consolidated all the sites under the übergeneralist banner that they still use today: Allrecipes.com.

I came across 'Banana Cake VI' (Allrecipes has many) while looking for a dressed-up alternative to my usual dowdy, loaf-tin banana breads. The recipe was uploaded to Cakerecipe.com in 1999 by Cindy Carnes, a licensed nurse living in Iowa. It was a large, tray-bake-style banana cake with cream-cheese frosting and a preternaturally moist crumb – a recipe given to Carnes by a friend she had gone to visit. Buttermilk and lemon juice add gentle acidity, sharpening the banana flavour and keeping the fruit from browning so much; baking soda – rather than baking powder – gives instant lift. The real trick, though, is the technique. You cook the cake in a low oven, lower than most people would trust is going to work, but for a very long time. Then, you put it into the freezer for forty-five minutes, right after you've pulled it out of the oven, to arrest the cooking process. It's a smart idea, especially for a large cake, given how often the edges get overbaked before the centre is set. Carnes told me, of the friend who gave her the recipe, 'her son worked in a bakery in St Louis, and he said, "That's what we do with all of our cakes." I told her, "We need to share this with the world."'

Today, Carnes is in her late sixties and lives in Iowa. Her mother ran a small restaurant called Val's Cafe. Carnes helped with making pies there, and still considers herself a baker. About twenty-five years ago, she was given some particularly great peanut-butter fudge, and when she asked for the recipe she was told it was online – somewhere called Allrecipes. 'Back then, I wasn't on the internet much,' she said. She tracked down the recipe and found 'Creamy Peanut Butter Fudge', uploaded by a user named Janet Awaldt. That fudge, and Allrecipes, has been part of Carnes' cooking ever since.

Carnes is pretty typical for an Allrecipes user. Most visitors to the site are women, with an average age in the fifties. She tends towards everyday recipes. Carnes lives a forty-minute drive from the nearest decent grocery store, and she benefits from the skew towards recipes that don't involve too many from-scratch ingredients or, indeed, too many ingredients at all. When I asked Arie Knutson, Allrecipes' senior editorial director of features, whether any city or area is a particular stronghold, she stressed that the site is borderless, but anyone who has spent even five minutes on it will notice that it has a Midwestern lilt – to start, there are at least 180 Jell-O salads. In a food-media world largely defined by the coasts, it is one of the most important sites cataloguing the culinary proclivities of the country's middle tranche.

Like lots of Allrecipes users, Carnes has little time for the preciousness that establishment food media can sometimes promote. Take Martha Stewart: 'She's telling us about the Madagascan vanilla beans.' Carnes' voice, an Iowa singsong, can wend from weary to impassioned in the course of a single thought. 'Well, honey, Martha – I'm going to break this to you gently. I'm not going to pay eight hundred dollars to make my own vanilla. I can get it for seven dollars at the grocery store.' She looks, instead, for simplicity. Her Allrecipes uploads tend towards low-prep classics: a family-favourite olive cheese ball, a simple yet kaleidoscopic taco dip, and no-bake peanut-butter cookies. 'I don't want to make my own sauce,' she told me. That night's dinner was cabbage rolls from an Allrecipes number from a user going by Judy. In this preparation, the ground-beef filling is wrapped in a delicate cabbage-leaf caul, and then braised in canned tomato soup.

In 2009, Christopher Kimball, the co-founder of America's Test Kitchen, wrote a eulogy for the late *Gourmet* magazine, the one-time home of such revered food writers as Ruth Reichl, James Beard, Laurie Colwin, M. F. K. Fisher, and Jonathan Gold. Kimball mourned it, and saw the loss as part of a bigger problem in American gastronomic life. It's a common complaint that, in the age of the internet, everyone's a critic; the other side of this is that everyone's a chef. 'Google "broccoli casserole" and make the first recipe you find. I guarantee it will be disappointing,' Kimball wrote. He didn't mention Allrecipes by name, although he didn't really need to. The site has always championed the expertise of ordinary home cooks. An early staff T-shirt depicted a wooden spoon in an upraised fist, with a slogan about 'breaking the hegemony of tyrant chefs'.

Allrecipes exists in a long line of collectively authored recipe projects, which reflect everyday cooking in granular and occasionally unflattering detail. Community cook-books circulated by rotary associations, Girl Scout troops, synagogues, churches, sororities, and military wives' circles are perhaps the most prolific expression of American culinary thought; from the 1850s until the end of the century, recipes in *The New York Times* were crowdsourced, and collected in a drab if effective home-economics section called 'The Household'. Amanda Hesser, the founder of Food52, curated an extensive selection of the recipes for the 2010 edition of *The Essential New York Times Cookbook*. Among them were broiled steak with oysters and Boston cream doughnut. She told me, 'It was a very candid look at: What were people thinking about? What were they needing to know?'

In a 2002 article for *The New York Times*, under the headline 'America's Real Foodie Bible', Regina Schrambling reported on the cultural heft of *Taste of Home* magazine – a publication that almost exclusively features reader-submitted recipes, and which, in 2002, many cooks outside the Midwest had never heard of. It was, at that point, the most popular cooking magazine in the country, its circulation of nearly 5 million more than that of *Bon Appétit*, *Food & Wine* and *Gourmet* combined. Carnes vaguely remembers one of her recipes being printed there. It's the only food magazine that she ever subscribed to, until it got too expensive. By that point, she'd set up an Allrecipes account instead.

By 2001, Allrecipes was the most popular recipe site on the internet. A couple of years before, the co-owners had brought on a new CEO, Bill Moore, who had conceived and launched the Starbucks Frapuccino and, as it happens, oversaw the *MasterCook* CD-ROMs. As food businesses took note of the site's some 3.5 million users, ad revenue increased, and brands like Hershey's and Quaker Oats began posting advertorial recipes. Before long, Allrecipes was being courted for a buyout by precisely the establishment media that it had tried to disrupt.

Although the site continued to grow, it never quite

resolved a dilemma that had beset it from the start: does an autarky of passionate home cooks need an editor? When you give people the freedom to upload the recipes they love, you can bank on many of them being average and at least some of them being bad. Even a great cook may be inept at recipe writing, a complex exercise that involves carefully recording your work and anticipating any of the million places where an amateur might slip up.

Early on, the co-owners developed a system for moderating the recipes as they were sent in – checking whether they were plagiarised; scanning for any glaring errors, like tablespoons of baking soda where it should have been teaspoons; adjudicating whether a submission was a recipe at all. ('Somebody tried to tell us to heat up a burrito and add a bottle of taco sauce to it, and nacho sauce, and add cheese and put it in the oven. This is not a recipe,' Quinn recalled. 'But I immediately went home and I was, like, "This is awesome."') So long as the recipe made sense, it was good enough to allow on to the site – and that's how something like 'Carrot Cake XII', the dud with the canned carrots, passed muster.

But it quickly became obvious that the best approach was to let the cooks be the judge: it's the reviews, even more than the recipes, that make the site. Look at its all-time top recipes today – 'Good Old-Fashioned Pancakes', 'Easy Meatloaf', 'Taco Seasoning', 'To Die For Blueberry Muffins' – all vetted by tens of thousands of home cooks, and all uploaded in Allrecipes' golden age, between 1998 and 2002, when there were comparatively few other resources for finding recipes online. It's hard to imagine John Chandler's 'World's Best Lasagna' doing quite so well if it were uploaded now, to a busier and more cynical internet.

In 2006, Allrecipes sold to *Reader's Digest*, and within a couple of years all the original co-owners had left. Six years later, Allrecipes sold to Meredith (now Dotdash Meredith), the media group that owns *Food & Wine*, The Spruce Eats, Serious Eats, and *EatingWell*. In the years since, the site has taken on the mannerisms of establishment food media, in which editorial content is pushed to the fore. Go on Allrecipes today and you will see a selection of highlighted user recipes, but also more carefully vetted pieces such as 'Chef John's Best Recipes for When Summer Tomatoes Are at Their Peak' and '8 Essential Tips for Summer Hosting (and Actually Enjoying Yourself)'. The potential liabilities – recipes with the energy of your drunk aunt at a party – are sequestered in the almost unnavigable depths of the site.

It joins brands like Food52, which Amanda Hesser established with Merrill Stubbs after she left *The New York Times*. 'We were trying to create an alternative – a complement to the kind of resource that Allrecipes was,' Hesser explained. They envisioned a website with its foundations in community-submitted recipes, but that foregrounded its own editorial content – explainers about how best to microwave a corn cob, lifestyle content that works hard to promote the pans and table linens in the online store. It's a compromise between the freedoms of a completely unregulated system and the technocracy of somewhere like the modern *Times*. 'This wasn't just a recipe search engine.' Allrecipes seems to be looking at sites like this, and wanting in.

As a compromise, in the past few years, Allrecipes has appointed about a hundred 'Allstars' as the face of its relaunched site. These users submit regular reviews and recipes for a small amount of money, often picking from a selection of ideas supplied by the editorial team. One Allstar is Shelia Johnson, a social worker from Kansas City, Missouri, who got the gig after she was spotted doing a cooking segment on local TV. Until then, she'd been one of the majority of Allrecipes users – a digital lurker, visiting to cross-check an ingredients list or get some inspiration, but never adding recipes of her own. She tends towards healthy food, like a summer-leaning white bean and tomatillo soup, and West African dishes like chicken yassa, or a Pompano fish stew flavoured with red palm oil. Her favourite recipe is an ingenious fusion snack: geometrically precise, crisp-shelled collard green wontons. Still it's on her own platform, a YouTube channel called Gangsta Goodies Kitchen, where Johnson comes into her own, as a multi-hyphenate interviewer, cook, host and entrepreneur. 'I figured Rachael Ray can do it,' she told me, 'I can do it.'

Curation has its upsides. For most of its time at the helm of the internet, Allrecipes has not really been *All* recipes but something more like All-American recipes, All Midwestern Recipes, All Heartland Recipes. This was never what Hunt intended – in the early days, staff supplemented the dozens of chocolate chip cookie recipes with a more pointedly diverse selection of their own, including ghraybeh – a Middle Eastern cookie with the texture of shortbread. When someone submitted a recipe for crockpot squirrel to Allrecipes, they were relieved to be reaching beyond a very specific kind of middle-class crowd-pleaser. But on Allrecipes, it's always seemed like an uphill struggle to make it in any way diverse. Looking at the recipes, you'd think that the average American was from Italy via Des Moines. The trouble is that although it reflects American society, it doesn't actually reflect the richness of American life. It reflects the market forces that have turned the internet from a plausibly common resource, to a place dominated by a small number of massive companies. It reflects what happens when recipes become things you sell, rather than things you share. It naturally reflects who gets to play around in the kitchen in the first place.

As for the old, more chaotic Allrecipes, it survives in the archives but is increasingly hard to find. Of the 113,000 recipes on the site, some 55,000 are actually accessible by search. Many older recipes have been suppressed, and new ones now undergo a more rigorous vetting process. 'The submissions go into a queue that our editorial team reviews for publication,' Molly Fergus, the site's senior vice-president and associate group general manager, told me via email. 'Recipes are only searchable on-site (or on Google) once they are accepted and edited by our recipe team.' In some ways, it's a more reliable site now – curation means that the test-kitchen-approved recipes tend to rise to the top of the search page, and those with bad reviews can be found and re-evaluated by the editorial teams. Yet it feels less like a place for home cooks to gather and experiment than it used to. And certain tools that Hunt put in place in the early days – searching by multiple ingredients, scaling recipes up or down – are gone. Carnes told me that she's had recipes languish in the backlog for years. In striving to professionalise itself, the site has lost the often troublesome entropy that once made it so fun.

Tim Hunt left Allrecipes shortly after the sale to *Reader's Digest*, and hasn't used it as much since then, except for cookie recipes. He hardly cooked when he first engineered the site, but he's now a proper culinary nerd, smoking chillies and making his own cider vinegar from the fruits of an Asian-pear tree in his garden. On the phone, he enthused about the chef Derek Sarno – 'a vegan, but not a fascist vegan' – and told me about a Sarno-inspired sandwich he'd recently made for dinner, with blocks of fried, spiced tofu and really good barbecue sauce. Hunt also grows buckwheat, a favourite ingredient of mine, and after we hung up we exchanged recipes: he sent a link for buckwheat crinkle cookies that he and his wife make each Christmas; I sent a recipe for buckwheat shortbread in return.

At its best, this is how Allrecipes worked – as a kind of culinary hive mind, a place that understood that the only thing people like more than making recipes is comparing them. (My buckwheat shortbread was caught up in the purgatorial Allrecipes queue for a few months, but is now finally online.) One of Cindy Carnes' most treasured contributions is called 'Mary's Meatballs', named for a nurse Carnes worked with in the nineties. You take a jar of chilli sauce, a cup of brown sugar, a sixteen-ounce can of whole cranberries, and a can of sauerkraut, put it all in a pan, and heat over a gentle flame. Once it's simmering, you pour it over three pounds of meatballs, and bake for an hour in an oven at 350 degrees. 'She brought those all the time to everything, every potluck and everything at the hospital,'

Carnes told me. People seemed to love them. Mary handed over the recipe after she was diagnosed as having terminal breast cancer. 'She said, "Please make my meatballs. And remember me."' She died in 1995.

Right now, Carnes is in the middle of putting together a family cookbook, using an old collection of her aunt's as a scaffold for her own additions – clipped from copies of *Taste of Home*, printed out from Allrecipes, or kept on a scrap of paper, then painstakingly typed up. So far, she's collected more than 1,000 entries; 'Mary's Meatballs' is among them. Now she's got to find a way to actually print and share the volume with her family. If only there were a place for all this – a forum big and lawless enough to host several generations' worth of eclectic culinary lore. 'Well,' she said with a sigh. 'That's the bugaboo.'

Tastemakers

The critic hits the road

Or, real influencers and where to find them

In December 2022, a fan messaged the former MMA fighter Keith Lee about a small restaurant, Aroma Latin American Cocina, in the suburbs of Las Vegas. It was their parents' restaurant, and it was struggling. They knew they had the goods: on the lunch menu there was a churrasquito plate with grilled steak, beans, fried plantain, a half-moon quesadilla and chirmol. Or you could get enchiladas with beef picadillo and pickled beet, the flavours pulled into focus with crumbled cotija cheese. But getting people through the door was hard, especially such a long way from the Strip. And so, they became the first to do what countless small American food businesses have done in the few years since – they sent out a bat signal, or at least a DM, asking for Keith Lee's help.

Keith Lee, who was twenty-six years old at the time, already had a moderately successful TikTok account. During the pandemic, he'd film himself cooking for his family. Or he'd sit in a parking lot, reading messages from his pregnant wife, Ronni. Things like: 'If I don't get wings you better grow wings, because I'm throwing you off the building. I love you.' People liked this amiable guy who'd drive around at 11am on a Tuesday hunting down wings for his wife. He filmed motivational talks in the car. There were Trader Joe's shopping haul videos. He was sweet and disarmingly goofy, and had a gift of really connecting with you through the screen. Before long, Lee was a minor TikTok celebrity, with about a million followers there. But you could almost see the thought process in real time: What if he used that power for good, and not just for a paid partnership with Wingstop? And that's when he got the message about Aroma Latin American Cocina.

One evening that December, Lee drove across to the restaurant and got two huge bags of food: litre cups of hibiscus agua fresca and horchata; tostadas; beef enchiladas with lightly pickled beets; a skillet meal with fried eggs, grilled picanha, beans and plantains; three tacos – pork, carne asada and fried avocado; an enormous sandwich. He dumped it all on a low table in a room lit like an interrogation chamber, and apologised for how he was going to pronounce things wrong. 'I got it, let's try it, and rate it one through ten.' And so he began. He would've liked the steak less well done. The hibiscus wasn't for him, but the plantain was unreal. Then there were the enchiladas. 'I've never had food like that,' he said. 'The beets are acidic, the beef itself is spicy – not too spicy but it's got some heat on it.'

When you write it down, Keith Lee doesn't seem to say anything all that profound. But he isn't a written-down kind of critic – the meat of what he says is in the way he moves, the snap cuts that he edits into the videos, the carefully constructed facial expressions, the well-timed eye rolls. When something tastes good, his jaw slows to an almost frame-by-frame slo-mo as he takes it all in. His signature move is a hard, deep zoom on to his stunned face, when something really is too good to capture with words. You need to see it for yourself: how contagious his enthusiasm is, how masterfully he works the crowd. And so when he says 'This is the best sandwich I've ever had in my goddamn life' – insistently hammering the sandwich with his index finger to push home the point, you believe him. 'This is a ten,' he said, and held up the sandwich to the lens so you could see the strings of melted cheese. Other things did less well: the fried avocado taco got, under the baseless precision of the Keith Lee vibe scale, a three out of ten. But all in all, the review was a rave. 'Las Vegas – you've got a goldmine on your hands and nobody knows about it? That's crazy.'

He posted the video and left it at that – a late-night, ad hoc restaurant review by somebody whose mainstays had been pro fighting and cooking content. In no time, the review went viral, tapping into a hunger for relatable, feel-good and – crucially – honest restaurant commentary. Within a few days, Aroma Cocina had queues out the door and hundreds of new, sub-Keith Lee TikTok evangelists ready to rave. The business completely turned around. The video was favourited over 5 million times on TikTok alone.

Looking back on it now, this was the Keith Lee origin event. Afterwards, he started travelling around to more small restaurants – fast-food joints, drive-thrus, pizza places, everyday kinds of food – and giving them as thoughtful a read as if they had a Michelin star. He laid down the germs of his ethos: he wanted to support family-owned businesses, he would never charge for promotions and he would always – even when it was difficult – be honest about what he thought. He reviewed anonymously, with standards of critical impartiality that even the newspaper critics don't always bother to uphold. He treated the work like a civic duty, the patron saint of restaurants without a marketing budget. He is a restaurant critic, through and through – he just happens to operate on social media.

There are countless people trying to do what Keith Lee does – to leverage online popularity into real-world influence – but nobody has his special sauce. Restaurants pray for a good Keith Lee review to keep the lights on. If he gives a rave, people come in swarms. There was a time when only a legacy media critic could pull these kinds of crowds, when only a *New York Times* or a *Guardian* review had the power to actually shape rather than just document restaurant culture. But social media has blown all that apart. Here's the thing: Keith Lee does not, by his own admission, know all that much about food. Whether this matters really depends on what authority means to you. Are you going to trust a traditional restaurant critic – a gavel-banger whose taste is definitionally better than yours and therefore, possibly, different to yours? Or are you going to trust this guy – one of the most likeable guys that TikTok has ever thrown up, with the baby-face and the natural camera command of a boyband member, in a freshly laundered sweatshirt, trying not to wake up the toddler? The people have spoken. Keith Lee now has over 15 million followers on social media. He is, in his earnest, understated way, the most powerful restaurant critic in America.

*

Restaurant critics are strange people and sometimes hard to like. They have become bogeymen in the minds of restaurateurs, and gods in the minds of restaurant fans. We're ambivalent about them. They're cruel, they can be wise, they can make or destroy a place. But even when we hate the people, these are characters that we are drawn to. It's no surprise that in the film *Ratatouille*, the Disney Pixar movie about a rat who ends up working as a chef, the meatiest character is in fact the coffin-headed critic, Anton Ego. In an age when more people are going to more restaurants than ever, influence – whose opinion is trustworthy, who can deliver a truly reliable recommendation – is power. And so it matters who the critics are, and whether we chose them or not.

One of the earliest restaurant critics was Alexandre Grimod de La Reynière – an early nineteenth-century nepo-baby and gourmand who was born into a wealthy family in France. He had that critic's touch, which is to say the confidence of a young man with an allowance and no job. He went out a lot, then started publishing his opinions on the food. He put himself at the centre of the French dining scene, with a secondary industry of hangers-on who turned the great restaurants of the time into engines of unmediated hype. This is the blueprint for at least 90 per cent of all professional restaurant critics since.

In the late 1950s, Craig Claiborne started covering restaurants for *The New York Times*, and in May 1962 he wrote 'Directory to Dining' – a lean, unillustrated column with recommendations for five New York restaurants. There was the platonic ideal of a seafood restaurant, with excellent broiled lobsters, seabass and wine. Tien Tsin in Manhattan's

Chinatown got an unequivocal rave. There was a Middle Eastern restaurant in Greenwich Village and a Northern Italian place. To appease the Manhattan food cultural overseers, there was also an upscale restaurant in Midtown. A year after the first column, he started using star ratings – a system that nobody, least of all the critics who use it, really understands, but which adds a certain spice.

This was the beginning of restaurant criticism as we know it today – a field where a person might look at a carrot with the same intensity as you'd review a theatre show. Food moved, in the papers but also in the discourse more generally, out of the lifestyle ghetto and into the world of deep culture. The next four decades were a critical golden age, and the cult of the restaurant critic became almost as intense as that of the chef. The restaurant industry is locked in battle with them, but the reality is they're part of a symbiotic – or mutually parasitic – whole.

As for the methods of these critics, they were diverse. Some of them ran with Claiborne's approach, others took a more poetic line. Ruth Reichl's personal Battle of Austerlitz was a review of the upscale Le Cirque, a double-pronged attack in which she went once undercover, once as the undisguised critic for *The New York Times*, and wrote about the different meals she received. In the UK we've had a more bombastic line of critics – people like Giles Coren, whose TV show *Million Dollar Critic* tells you everything you need to know about who the main character of a review really is. You've got the proclamations of someone like Jay Rayner, restaurant critic for the *Observer* and now the *Financial Times*. At the other end of things, the lyrical and down-to-earth reviews of someone like Jonathan

Gold – the critic for *LA Weekly* and then the *Los Angeles Times* – who in 2007 won a Pulitzer Prize for his writing. His influence is so great that he's changed the very tenor of restaurant criticism, forcing critics, at least some of them, to look further than fine dining, and celebrate the skilful cooking that threads through everyday kinds of places, from taquerias to people selling Brazilian cakes from their homes. For all these critics, what matters though is their authority and their expertise, gained through a lifetime of sometimes monomaniacal food research. You listen to these people because they know more than you.

But Keith Lee is different. There are parts of his work that connect with the chaotic, cult-of-personality methods of someone like Grimod de la Reynière. And when it comes to his anonymity and his adherence on an otherwise lawless platform to journalistic ethics, he shares the diligence of modern newspaper critics. But there is a third lineage, Keith Lee's closest spiritual analogue: a pre-Claiborne tradition that thrived during the mid-nineteenth century and fell out of fashion when the 'serious' critics stepped up. Now, it's being revived in the internet age. If you want to understand the cosmic influence of Keith Lee, you need to look at Duncan Hines, and Victor Hugo Green, and the long, under-respected tradition of hypemen eating on the road.

Duncan Hines was born in Bowling Green, Kentucky, in 1880, died there in 1959, and spent nearly all of the intervening time in his car. He expended equal energy on his two true vocations: being a salesman and being a semi-professional Wife Guy. Both involved a lot of travel.

Once he bought his first car, the United States seemed to open up – the excitement of movement and the inevitable anxiety of finding decent food. He came to it with the pragmatic enthusiasm that would come to define his entire body of work. 'My interest in wayside inns is not the expression of a gourmand's appetite,' he wrote, 'but the recreational impulse to do something different – to play a new game that would intrigue my wife.' They travelled, eating barbecued buffalo in Colorado and North Carolina country ham. Both seemed to enjoy it – Hines was jovial in the way you'd expect from a man whose only real problem, most days, was finding a place to eat.

Over the next few decades, Hines visited inns, restaurants, hotels, tearooms, drive-thrus and cafeterias across most of the United States, treating the country and its cuisines like a kind of analogue Pokémon Go. He kept notes, filling hundreds of pages with verdicts of the food, the decor and the people. His criteria were broadly relatable: he didn't want to waste his money or disappoint his wife, he disliked pompous service and appreciated the kind of details that seem to come into particular focus when people hit their middle age – natural coloured knotty pine, meals served on English Wedgwood plates, reservations not required. 'I would like to be food dictator of the U.S.A. just long enough to padlock two thirds of the places that call themselves cafes or restaurants,' he wrote. It wouldn't be long before he did actually have this level of clout.

Travel has long been the foundation of restaurant writing. The *Michelin Guide* was commissioned by a car tyre manufacturer for places to eat in the likely eventuality that their 1902 Renault Voiturette broke down. Over the years – and especially as road networks expanded – there would be more crossovers: the American Automobile Association's restaurant directories; the critic Egon Ronay's *Guide to British Eateries*, which was eventually sold to the AA, while Ronay himself consulted for Welcome Break motorway services. The road became an attraction in its own right, a site of potentially limitless leisure – at least in theory. It's incredible just how much of American dining in particular was shaped not by taste, but by cars. The mainly white, middle-class people taking to the road needed guidance from someone they could trust. Travel anxiety usually crystallises around one of three things: being robbed, getting lost, or getting food poisoning. A good recommendation can save you from all three.

Friends came to Hines for a lunch recommendation for Cleveland, or somewhere with good lobster rolls. He indulged them and then he indulged their friends, and then the strangers who wrote him letters. If he'd belonged to a different time, he almost certainly would have set up a Substack, but as things happened he typed up a selection of his recommendations, printed them and mailed them out with his Christmas cards in the winter of 1935. The next year he started compiling a more formal guide: a few hundred recommendations, organised by state, with notes, opening times, meal formats, addresses and price points. It would be a small red book, just about the right size to fit in a man's jacket pocket. He self-published it, and called it *Adventures in Good Eating*.

In Lincoln, Nebraska, Hines recommended a tearoom where you could get a double-crusted chicken pie with pastry made from lard. He wrote that the dining room was both air-conditioned and sound-proofed. He mentioned a restaurant in Ridgewood, New Jersey, which had no special dishes but Italianate architecture copied from a building in Pisa. He told readers to go to Stoddard's – a rooftop restaurant in New York, run by the inventor of US Pneumatic Mail Tubes, with the slogan: '16 floors above the average food level'. Hines loved regional American foods, breaking the monotony of roadside chicken and steak with Creole gumbo, soft shell crabs, Mississippi River catfish, Montgomery lemon pie, Nebraska corn fritters, black-eyed peas. For a time there was a Hines-branded line of Kentucky country hams. You could count on finding listings for the classics – places like Manhattan's Delmonico's or the Brooklyn steakhouse Peter Luger – but you were just as likely to be taken off the beaten track to Ham-That-Am-Ham, a ham specialist upstate.

Hines was a natural salesman. He interspersed the restaurant recommendations with reader testimonials – not for the restaurants but for the book itself. 'Most valuable book for travelling I ever saw,' from C.A.T. in New York. Some editions of the book had cut-out recommendation postcards, addressed to the Hines Institute. Others had autograph pages, where you could collect the signatures from the featured restaurateurs. Hines reminded readers at the start of every edition to spread the word about the book by telling friends – a pre-internet 'like and subscribe'.

The book sold out quicker than he could reprint it, each edition incrementally more ambitious. The book was dense with particulars, but there was an almost accidental romance, too. Fried chicken, fresh channel catfish,

cinnamon rolls, brook trout, homemade cherry pies –
pedestrian and beautiful lists that made *Adventures in
Good Eating* a cross between *The Pillow Book* and the
Yellow Pages. Readers became fanatical about the guide.
They were, as a report put it at the time, a freemasonry
of motorists – but also gourmands, busybodies, retirees,
servicemen, empty nesters, travelling salespeople and every
other middle-class white American who staked a claim to
the road. When a restaurant got a Hines recommendation,
they could lease a sign to put in their window, the same
way as a restaurant might put a Zagat decal on the door.
Over the next twenty-five years, *Adventures in Good Eating*
sold over 4 million copies, making it the most influential
restaurant guide of its time.

Duncan Hines was not, by modern standards, a serious
critic. He mainly stuck to a WASP-inspired culinary
canon – lemon chiffon cake, lamb chops in the English
style. He found almost nothing he enjoyed when he went
to Mexico and the south-western border states. He occasionally mentioned Chinese restaurants but never seemed
to know what to say. He was even sceptical of what he
considered to be European affectations: 'Baby beef, baby
lamb, baby lobster, baby chicken. Who wants to eat babies?'
He was easy to laugh at. 'Reno is a fine town to eat in,' ran
a profile in the *New Yorker*, 'although no Reno restaurant
is mentioned in Duncan Hines, possibly because none
features popovers or peppermint ice cream.' A satirical
poem – 'Memo for Duncan Hines' – repeated the words
'cottage cheese' as a kind of rhythmic anchor.

Most of the few thousand entries in *Adventures in Good*

Eating are fastidiously boring – specifics about price and opening times plus a word on whether a place was friendly or well-maintained. He shared the ordinary worries of ordinary American tourists. Was there parking? Was the place clean? Before he went into a restaurant, he would leave his wife in the car, cut through the parking lot and see what was up with the bins. If the garbage left a good impression, he looked through the kitchen doors to check for pests. He performed a kind of olfactory diagnostics, smelling for rancid cooking fats and old food and making a decision about whether it was worth seeing a menu. 'I've run more risk eating my way across the country than driving the highways, dangerous as the latter has become.' Hines' informants – a hypochondriac pan-American Neighbourhood Watch – reported on whether the knives were buffed and the tables clean. As the influence of the guide grew, restaurants started dramatising sanitation. Some installed glass panels so that you – a Hines-affiliated narc – could look into the kitchen yourself.

Duncan Hines liked anything that seemed to profes-sionalise cooking, even if it sometimes risked standardising taste, and Fred Harvey chain restaurants appear in the guidebooks with depressing regularity. The guide was exacting without being high-minded, discerning but never with any more moral or historicising complexity than you could stomach while on the open road. Hines tapped into the desires of the risk-averse, majority white American middle class, the most potent of which was the desire to avoid risk. When he died in 1959, obituaries read like testimonials to a particularly good insurance salesman. *Adventures in Good Eating* was a bible for people who, as

John Steinbeck put it, 'had no interest in what they ate as long as it had no character to embarrass them'.

Hines had wanted to critique restaurants in the same way as the newspaper critics wrote about films and theatre. But he was a different kind of critic, and all the more influential for it. What he really created was more like a prototype for Yelp – a connective link between restaurants and diners, between the culture and the discourse it creates. You could recommend a restaurant to him and he could recommend it to the hundreds of thousands of readers of the book. Reputable readers were inducted into an unofficial cabal of informants, and prolific contributors got a shout-out. The only qualification that anybody needed to be a critic was to be a consumer, which put Duncan Hines – a man born a century before Google reviews – aeons ahead of his time. *Adventures in Good Eating* was *the* American restaurant book, loyal to the everyday American arts of eating, driving, and spending.

Every edition of *Adventures in Good Eating*, which was printed until 1962 – two years before the Civil Rights Act was passed – came out during the era of segregation. A restaurant which refused to serve Black Americans was named 'one of Baltimore's very finest'. Earlier editions spoke highly of restaurants where Black waitresses doubled as a kind of minstrel show. Maybe it's asking too much to expect Hines – a white man born in the nineteenth century – to ask why some of the only Black people he saw were the staff who he called mammies.

None of the millions of copies of *Adventures in Good Eating* was useful to Black diners. At points during this time, there were fewer than twenty cities in the United States where Black Americans could realistically enter a white-owned restaurant. If Hines was useful, it was only through the meanings he never meant to convey. To Black diners, an old inn serving 'satisfying New England country dinners' might have struck an ominous tone, just like the 'old-time' costumed waiters of tearooms in the South. It was better to travel with lunch packed in the trunk of the car or even drive through the night. When travellers couldn't be sure who a 'Rooms Available' sign was really for, they tapped into word-of-mouth networks instead. Black Americans had bought vehicles to avoid segregated public transport, but it was a freedom with nowhere to go.

Victor Hugo Green published the first edition of the *Negro Motorist Green Book* the same year as Hines started selling *Adventures in Good Eating*. Green was a postal worker and, like Hines, began mapping restaurants while on the job. On his meandering routes through Manhattan, he made note of restaurants where he, as a Black man, could count on being served. He collected the names and addresses of beauty salons and auto repair shops, taking tips from the extended community of Black postal workers in the city. The list eventually grew into a booklet covering the whole of New York. He self-published the first national edition in 1937 – a listing of everywhere a Black American could safely travel in the continental United States, running to just sixteen pages long. All Green promised to do was 'give the Negro traveller information that will keep him from running into difficulties, embarrassments and to make his trip more enjoyable'. Both guides came down to risk management, except for Hines' readers the risk topped out at whether you'd be given stale dinner rolls. Eventually, the *Green Book* was selling about 15,000 copies each year.

Green's guide covered motels, gas stations, hotels, cafeterias, liquor stores, golf courses and grills, interspersed with advice on car maintenance, pre-empting every reasonable need of the American traveller. There were some moments of levity, but even these feel like they could be *Top Gear* lines. 'Never stop, look or listen at railroad crossings. It consumes time.' In a twist on the food-vehicular accord of the *Michelin Guide*, Green entered into partnership with Esso gas stations, who agreed to stock the book – at least in part because over a third of their franchisees were Black. He had help from the Negro Affairs consultant in the US Travel Bureau, and his USPS whisper network eventually covered much of the United States. The guide ended up being published annually – with the exception of the wartime years.

Green didn't get into the ambience or vouch for the quality of the meals, and many restaurants paid for ads. In Hines' world, trust came from feeling that this was somehow a civic project, made in the same spirit as when he sent out those first Christmas cards. In the *Green Book*, trust was maths: restaurants wouldn't pay to advertise if they didn't want you to come. Despite the breadth of its remit, the book always ran short, with one restaurant in the whole of Oregon, four in Oklahoma. James Baldwin described being turned away from multiple restaurants one night in Princeton, New Jersey, during the early 1940s. An edition of the guide from around that time lists only one safe restaurant in town. It speaks to the impossibility of travel in certain states – the listings almost perfectly overlaid the areas where Black Americans already lived.

There is no world in which you could properly describe Green as a restaurant critic. He was, however, a restaurant influencer, with greater sway over the dining habits of ordinary Black Americans than anything that someone like Clementine Paddleford, the manic pixie restaurant correspondent for the *New York Herald Tribune*, could drum up. The guide was a complement to *Adventures in Good Eating*, the green book to Hines' red. There was almost no overlap between their readerships or the restaurants they covered. If somewhere got a glowing write-up in Hines' book, you could guarantee that it wouldn't show in the *Green Book*; and Black-owned restaurants had no place in the particular America that Hines mapped out. In their different ways, the two books wrote the blueprint for a new genre of American service journalism written by non-experts and couched in everyday language – a peer-review recommendations engine.

By the time of the 1960 lunch counter sit-ins, sales of the *Green Book* started to drop off. After the Civil Rights Act, it went into free fall, and in 1966 – a few years after Victor Hugo Green died – his widow published the last edition. Green had predicted and even hoped for this. 'There will be a day,' he wrote, 'sometime in the near future when this guide will not have to be published.' *Adventures in Good Eating* also died in the sixties. More people started travelling abroad and once you've been to Paris, you can't help wondering whether 'Recommended by Duncan Hines' is not, in fact, such a high bar. The chains expanded too.

If you could drive across the entire American Midwest without ever leaving the care of the Fred Harvey group, you no longer needed Duncan Hines. The last edition was published in 1962. The same year, like a cosmically ordained changing of the guard, Craig Claiborne wrote his first review in *The New York Times*.

Sometimes, critics get so caught up in their work that they forget that restaurant criticism, like restaurants, is fashion. Restaurant guidebooks, reviews, recommendation engines, critics, influencers – each of these addresses a different need in the culture at a moment in time. It's as messy down here in the restaurant discourse trenches as in the actual kitchens. Cars invented Duncan Hines' book. Civil rights ended the *Green Book*. When cities got richer and bigger and more cosmopolitan, that set the scene for big, serious newspaper restaurant critics. The very idea of what a restaurant critic is supposed to do, supposed to mean, is constantly changing. And now, they face a new upheaval – not a change on the ground, but in the cloud.

Just like Green and Hines passing the baton to Craig Claiborne forty years before, in the noughties food blogging took off. Influence moved into the hands of many people, instead of just three or four unelected tastemakers-in-chief. In 2010, the year that Instagram debuted, an article in *The New York Times* warned about a particularly engaged community of restaurant goers operating out of New Jersey. 'People come in with iPhones,' one restaurateur explained. '[It] seemed strange at first, but now we're used to it.' The car overhauled American dining in the Duncan Hines era. Now it's the smartphone reconfiguring how we learn and think about restaurants. Travel is opening up to more people than ever, except this time you can do it from your home.

The most famous newspaper critics still had cultural prestige, but this isn't always the same as influence on the ground. The thing that gives a newspaper critic power is the newspaper – the reputation it has and the readership it brings you to. But online you have to tell, and sell, a different story. You give people not what you think they ought to know, but what they want to hear. You're a representative of the people who follow you. Eventually, if you're doing it right, people follow you precisely because you don't know anything more about food than they do. And so we have Topjaw – a British double-act who are 'charming', I've been told, in a hollow ex-private school kind of way, and who pretend to know less about restaurants than they actually do. Or Eatingwithtod – Toby Inskip – who seems to want to be the London Keith Lee and has accumulated millions of followers to his gross-out, cheese-in-the-beard, sauce-down-the-T-shirt Instagram account of facile restaurant recs.

I once met a restaurant critic who put finger quotes around 'internet'. And it's easy to see why, when you're looking at the worst of it. But then, you have to filter out the noise – maybe we need a critic of the critics – because if you sift through enough Topjaws, you do eventually find a Keith Lee. The thing is, critics don't like these threats. I'll tell you this: you didn't see Craig Claiborne referencing Duncan Hines. And when the blogging revolution started, establishment food writers weren't excited – they were worried. Would society fall apart? People have bristled at this new wave of professional influencers, paid partnerships, mukbang, meet and greets at pop-up food festivals, performance eating – an ungoverned community of hobbyists, marketers and ordinary people who believed in the power of their taste. Almost as often as anyone writes a review, someone will say that criticism is dead.

But then, remember the moral of the story in *Ratatouille*? If you say that anyone can cook, it's not that *everyone* can cook. It's just, as the critic comes to realise, that 'a great artist can come from anywhere'. If a rat can become a chef, why can't a travelling salesman, or a postman, or an MMA fighter become a critic? Victor Hugo Green had to graft to get partnerships with Esso to distribute his self-published guide. Duncan Hines self-published *Adventures in Good Eating* too. Eventually it was so popular that he got offers from publishing houses, but he turned them down – he knew that he was successful, at least in part, because he hadn't come through the establishment.

Keith Lee is also a self-platformed man. And he had to be. How often are we allowed a Black critic? In the UK, pretty much every major restaurant critic we have ever had has been white, and nearly all of them – and I need to stress this – went to private school. Several went to Eton. One is King Charles' stepson. Jimi Famurewa was the first Black critic ever given a position of power – as restaurant reviewer at the *Evening Standard*. And then, he got laid off, and his editor – who is white, and who I wish I could describe, but who I really couldn't pick out of a line-up of one – took his place. Things are better in the US media landscape, but not by much. And this is where Keith Lee comes in – the people's champion, a Wingstop-sponsored Diana, Princess of Wales.

When she became *The New York Times*' restaurant critic in 1993, Ruth Reichl said this: 'You shouldn't be writing reviews for the people who dine in fancy restaurants, but for all the ones who wish they could.' Well, Keith Lee has followed a different path – a more *Adventures in Good Eating* path, in which if a critic isn't intensely useful to either the reader or the restaurant, and ideally both, then they aren't doing their job. Seventy-five years after Hines' relentlessly practical guide, Keith Lee's calling card is a keen interest in restaurant ordering systems. In Atlanta, he went to restaurants with weird opening hours, restaurants that only accepted orders through Doordash, restaurants where the wait for a table was an hour, restaurants where the wait for a table was five minutes if you were Keith Lee, restaurants that didn't allow takeout, restaurants where you couldn't get water, brunch restaurants with the door policies of Studio 54. The video reads like an episode of *Curb Your Enthusiasm*. Cardi B posted a reaction video; the story went viral. Everybody could believe, but nobody would accept, that in America's Black metropolis, the world's most famous Black food critic couldn't even get brunch.

Lee is lucky to have entered the game at a time when nearly all of us navigate restaurants through websites, restaurant ordering platforms, menu screens and third-party apps. For someone who is both famous and committed to journalistic impartiality, it's a gift to be able to order facelessly, pick up with the minimum of human contact and eat behind the tinted windows of his car. The old-fashioned restaurant drive-thru seems almost quaint when so much of eating out these days is vehicular by default. But the way the Atlanta series resonated showed that things weren't really working. Post-pandemic, power in the restaurant industry no longer lies with the consumers or the producers but somewhere in the transactional middle – in all the places where money changes hands. Costs of living are high, the ordinary luxury of sitting in a roadside restaurant – the kind of thing that the Hines-era middle classes could take for granted – is moving out of reach. There's a huge market for takeout food, and an equally big secondary industry of people making fast-food review videos from the front seat of their car. Keith Lee's videos are about good food, but they're also about what happens when the system falls apart.

When he visited San Francisco, Lee's videos showed a city running on and riven by tech money. He didn't get too deep into the economic fractures – he only noticed that homelessness was a huge issue, and he found good food hard to come by, and that the city didn't seem like much of a place to visit as a tourist. He upset San Franciscans, and accidentally revealed the sketchy logics of the travel-critic role. In his choice of foods, he accidentally reveals the shortcomings of both mainstream criticism and the TikTok influencer economy. The staples are burgers, milkshakes, a restaurant called Heart Attack Grill, giant versions of normal foods, the marketability of a fast-food brand. The fact that he takes these foods seriously is why Keith Lee has been a success – he shows respect to a side of American food culture that serious criticism rarely touches. But you also see the limits, when the only videos that the algorithm rewards are the ones that show us the foods we already know we like. Somehow we're back with Hines, in the noose of super-mass-cultural appeal.

Like Jonathan Gold at *LA Weekly*, Lee recognises places that aren't usually awarded by mainstream criticism. He goes to mom-and-pop shops, holes in the wall, food trucks, street vendors and any other small treasure in the expansive, infinitely diverse world of everyday American food. He asks for recommendations via social media, for the kind of places that a Google search might not throw up. On a follower's recommendation, he'll go to a community takeaway spot, or a family restaurant that doesn't know how to cultivate an avatar online. His intentions are good, but in many ways he's held back by the platform that's made him a star. Everything has to be the best and biggest. Some reviews feel like episodes of *American Idol*: you need a compelling sob story for the narrative to really work. It's easy to mistake this for giving someone dignity.

When people don't want to call stars like Keith Lee critics, sometimes they'll call them influencers. Of course nobody cares about the difference except critics themselves. What matters is the same thing that has always mattered – the simple, impossible question of where to go to eat. Critics might covet a Pulitzer, but the truest test of success has always been influence – the ability to shape the restaurant industry by talking about it – and this is what Keith Lee has.

*

At the very start of January 2023, barely a couple of weeks after his first huge review, Keith Lee got an email from an employee at Frankensons, a family-run pizza shop in south Las Vegas, saying that the food was amazing but business was slow. A minor social media celebrity had tried to charge them $2,600 for a good review. Lee decided to go. He uploaded a video with the caption 'Frankensons pizzeria taste test. Would you try it? #foodcritic'. Sitting in a quiet corner of his home, he pulled out a stack of takeaway boxes. He started off with the garlic knots dusted with red chilli flakes – a 9.2 out of 10. Next, peach chutney wings. 'That's a delicious wing. It's sweet, it's salty. That's a 9 out of 10.' The Frankensons classic Italian sub was outstanding, a 9.6. There was a burger, fries, a garlicky thin-crust white pizza. A pizza with full-moon circles of pepperoni. 'Boy, I swear this is why I started making videos, because of places like this,' he said. The ranch sauce wasn't great, but when it came to the lemon pepper sauce wings, he added a freeze cut and a bass tremor in the edit. 'This is one of the best wings I've ever had. It's a 10.'

In twenty-four hours, the Frankensons TikTok account gained 70,000 followers. The shop had been empty when Lee went. Now it had a line out the door that wouldn't let up for days. In the week that followed, local news crews started showing up, then national ones, reporting live from the queue that Lee had summoned. People called it the Keith Lee Effect – one guy's ability to make a restaurant or ruin it. Lee posted update videos about the news coverage, feeding remorselessly into the hype hall of mirrors. He went back, took pictures with the crowds. The visitors took pictures of the queue. Lee reshared them. The internet always finds ways to regenerate.

'It's a blessing,' the owner, Frank Steele, said. 'This restaurant has been a dream of mine for thirty years.' People planned road trips from other cities and even other states, using Keith Lee's TikTok feed like a modern astrolabe. In the two days at the height of the furore, Steele made more garlic knots than he'd made in his entire career until then. They took on more employees. 'It wasn't me,' Lee said. 'It was the food, and it was God using me as a vessel.' Except it was Keith Lee, and it would be Keith Lee again, and again, and again.

About eighteen months after the buzz, Frankensons fell on hard times. 'I was hospitalized for over 3 weeks,' Frank Steele wrote on a GoFundMe page that his supporters encouraged him to create. 'The medical bills are far beyond the means of what I can afford.' It was a choice between asking for donations or closing the doors. Right now, it has donations of just under $9,000. In an update video, Steele thanked everyone who'd turned out to order the specials or sent money from afar. He talked about the trouble with the big franchises and how hard it was to run a small restaurant. 'You know we're all trying to live the American dream.'

At the time of writing, Frankensons is still going, though the restaurant business is never easy. They want people to keep talking about the restaurant – both locals and the Keith Lee wannabes who proselytise about the pizzas online. Restaurants need their influencers, and the influencers need the restaurants. A lifetime ago, Frankensons would have been casting around for a nomination to *Adventures in Good Eating*, putting a 'Duncan

Hines recommends' sign in the window. But things have changed, beyond recognition and not at all. Keith Lee's review video is pinned, in perpetuity, to the top of the Frankensons Instagram page.

Anatomy of a queue

Or, the pleasures and pitfalls of hype restaurants

As soon as I saw the TikTok videos of the chocolate-covered
strawberries, I knew two things: that I was going to buy
them, and that it would be a mistake. They'd shown up
on my feed while I was busy avoiding writing this book:
effusive videos about completely average strawberries half-
drowned in chocolate fondue. The videos were all pretty
much the same. 'People travel all over the world to get
these chocolate-covered strawberries,' a disembodied voice
would say over a pan shot of London's crowded Borough
Market. And then the camera would sweep across a queue –
an ultra-concentrated throng of bodies, the line bunching
up and coiling round. 'This vendor uses milk chocolate to
cover the freshest strawberries you'll ever try,' the voice
would go on. And then you saw the rows of clear plastic
pint cups filled with strawberries, and there'd be a close-up
as the cup went under the fondue tap, and the milk chocolate cloaked and pooled.

The money shot was the twist – rotating the cup for
the camera, showing the cross-sections of chocolate and

strawberry, something like the swivel and glance-back of a runway model. 'The result,' the voice would say, 'is ooey, gooey, delicious warm chocolate over cold straw-berries, which is why' – and this is where TikTok loops the video – 'people travel all over the world to get these chocolate-covered strawberries.' It was an obvious thing to do, a time-tested combination of ingredients, executed without any particular flair. In a food culture of almost mandated novelty, maybe this is why it worked, even though it costs – and I need to stress this – nearly £10.

The algorithm brought these videos to me tenderly but insistently, the way a cat drops a dead mouse on the carpet. I was hooked. The viral strawberries, people were calling them. Some people made videos like game walkthroughs – routes, menu hacks, prices and ways to beat the queue. Others gave hard data: twenty minutes to find the stall, forty people ahead of them in the queue, no more than a few minutes before reaching the front, overall 9/10 rating. The videos were mostly American or Australian, but there were splinter factions from Germany and the Netherlands. Some had voiceovers in Arabic and prices converted to UAE dirham. The wilder the ratio of effort to payoff, the better. 'I flew eight hours to try the most viral strawberries in the world,' they said. Or 'pov: u saw the tiktok so you came from Australia for the strawbs'. Depending on the whims of the algorithm that day, a video like this could get anywhere between just ten and ten million views. Have I mentioned that the strawberries looked, at best . . . fine?

In the olden days, you needed a newspaper critic to pull a crowd like this. How else, except through a write-up in a paper with a few hundred thousand daily readers, could you create a scrum for something like fruit in a cup? And then, demagogues like Keith Lee perfected a different kind of hype that was more relatable and tapped into appetites of the novelty-seeking internet. The foods and the style were radically different, but both ways of talking about restaurants ultimately relied on the cultural heft of whoever was doing the talking. It could be Lee, or Claiborne, or the general seriousness of a masthead like that of *The New York Times*. In any case, somebody has authority – innate or bestowed, soft or absolute – and this is all that counts.

But the strawberries were different. There were no reviews or write-ups in the Best Of lists or *Time Out* clippings to tape up in a shop window. Restaurant critics weren't writing about the strawberries – and why would they? This was unserious food for unserious people and tourists and suckers and kids. When I talked to friends who are food writers and semi-pro opinion-havers on the London food circuit, none of them had tried the strawberries and some didn't even know they existed. I had heard about the strawberries, but only through the splintered channels of my social media algorithms – random videos from people I didn't necessarily trust and usually didn't even know. Hundreds of thousands of customers, millions of strawberries, tens of millions of video views – the strawberries were an internationally famous, runaway success of the London food scene for about two years – and not one authorised tastemaker was involved.

The whole thing, it seemed to me, worked like a murmuration of starlings – the crowd following a logic that nobody inside of it fully understood. Each video was the impetus for more pilgrimages, many of which ended up on social media themselves. Who knows what inspired it, or who exactly it inspired. It doesn't matter. Things here proliferate in a non-linear way, spreading exponentially and beyond the facts. 'After seeing these viral chocolate strawberries, I had to see if they were worth the hype,' someone will post. This is it – the surge, the quantum mechanics of hype.

I thought this was insane. But I had a book about modern food to write, so I joined the other hundreds of people going to Borough Market that day with the strawberries in mind. I did this while feeling superior, and then I worked my way through the same congested market as everyone else, and went through the democratic embarrassment of queueing for a TikTok-viral food. I paid with the same pounds sterling. Then I found a spot next to a bin, where a few other strawberry people had come with their cups and their wooden sporks. It was hard to tell who was there for real and who was a hater stress-testing the hype. People took a few videos, which I'm sure they ended up posting online. We ate, and spilled chocolate down ourselves, and rubbed the chocolate deeper into our clothes with ineffective paper napkins. I probably don't need to tell you that the strawberries were average, but what difference would it make anyway? At the time of writing, the strawberries have been viewed over 150 million times on TikTok alone.

It should be obvious by now that appetite is social – that we rely on the judgement of people who've been there and eaten that before us. Maybe what's less obvious, or at least what we're less willing to admit, is how often these people whom we trust are . . . just some guys, people who know as little as us and sometimes even less. People like our parents. And if it wasn't your parents, it was your friends, or the ambient pressure to eat the same things as the other kids at school. As an adult with disposable income and an intense interest in food, a lot of my decisions come down to nothing more complicated than – what are they having over there?

You see it in restaurant queues. Go to a tourist area in any city in the world and you'll see people deciding which restaurant to go to not by looking at the menu but by sizing up the line. This is the paradox of queues: the longer they are, the more people want to join them. You have to factor in the number of people in the line, how fast the line is moving, and how sensible, on average, the people in line seem to be. You may want to adjust to account for the unaccountable taste of Americans, or based on location or time of day. The calculations are delicate, but the basic principles are simple: if all those people are doing it, then it must be good; and if it's good, then I should be doing it too.

A queue, in its most basic form, is an expression of supply and demand. But recently queues have mutated. If you've been paying any attention at all to restaurants in the last thirty years, you'll know that there are now two main characters in every hit restaurant story: the chef, and the queue, and often the queue has the more personality of the two. In London, in just the last couple of years, people have talked about the strawberry queue, the Toad Bakery queue, the Knoops hot chocolate queue, the queue for loaded chips at Camden Market, the Dishoom queue. These queues aren't just collections of people – they seem to have acquired sentience. They are organic entities, with a will and a way of moving. Forget critics or influencers or PRs – the best representation a restaurant can dream of is a line. And the more that people hate the line, the more they complain about it, the more powerful it becomes.

Hype hasn't always been this visible. In the eighties, say, chances are that you'd have to call to make a booking for a buzzy restaurant. Whether or not you got the table, that was your business, but you certainly never had to do anything as conspicuous as standing in a line. But in the nineties, an emerging genre of restaurant pivoted towards a more casual way of doing things with no-frills service and, crucially, no reservations. Taste seemed to settle on an egalitarian-feeling type of casual, middlebrow restaurant – even if the prices weren't. Everyone is equally welcome here, they said, by which they meant that everybody is welcome to join the queue. But it was fun, feeling a part of the buzz. One of the first of this type of line in London was for Wagamama, a noodle bar which opened in 1992 and which people mainly remembered for the casual, no-reservations communal tables. Before the reviews or the write-ups in the guidebooks, the first big advert was the line trailing down the street.

Still, it's New York that does this best. Manhattan in particular – a borough built on over-concentrated human ambition – has produced some of the most hated but popular queues since Depression-era breadlines. In 2001, Shake Shack opened as a summertime hotdog cart in Madison Square Park, and gradually built the kind of queues that would have you thinking, if you didn't know better, that it was hard to find a hotdog in New York. In

2004, the business settled into a small purpose-built kiosk in the shade of an old elm tree, and expanded the menu to serve burgers and shakes and crinkle-cut fries. Over the next couple of summers, the queue started to develop a personality of its own. People were queueing from 11am, hovering near the kiosk, pretending to read a paper or wait for friends. It had energy. It was the rare line that people were happy, even eager, to be in.

By 2006, the word about Shake Shack had spread and the queues – for what was still just a summertime, lunchtime burger place in a small public park – could stretch a hundred people deep. Management was required, with A lines, B lines and signs directing people through the route. The queue no longer just had a personality, it had a reputation – and a crew of minders and managers and a cult following of its own. A fan site, Shackwatchers, was set up to monitor the line. You could, in the most mid-noughties internet transaction imaginable, take a blurry photo of the line with your BlackBerry phone and upload it to Flickr with the tag 'shakeshackline'. These photos were shared on the site, the most recent first, making it a kind of manual webcam.

And then the actual webcam happened, on the official Shake Shack website: a feed that refreshed every five to fifteen seconds, showing the line in real time. At first, Shake Shack management thought it was a horrible idea. If they see a line, they said, people won't go there. But the cam got tens of thousands of hits each week. 'It was meant to be a service,' Pete Wells, until recently the restaurant critic for *The New York Times*, told me. You could check the webcam – presumably on your office computer, because realistically who had a phone that could handle this much data – and then go when the line was short. 'But it was also,' he added, 'the beginning of the celebration of the line.'

It's strange to think that the blueprint for the Borough Market strawberries was set way back in 2006, a year before the first iPhone. But this was it. A simple food, marketably unpretentious, just doing a basic thing reasonably well. The burgers were good, but of course they could never be a ninety-minute-wait good. The point was that there was this line, and you probably wanted to be in it, and you probably didn't want to be seen in it, and so you tried to game it. 'West Coast casual', they were calling the burgers. But here Manhattanites were, sweaty-palmed, refreshing a webcam feed at their desktop Apple Mac for a burger halfway across town.

'Lines are so central to the Shake Shack experience that they have symbolic overtones,' Wells wrote, a few years into the Shake Shack era. 'The line is democratic . . . It is a signal of freshness: everybody waits, because the food is cooked to order. It is the people's endorsement: everybody waits, so it must be worth it.' This mattered, for a vernacular American food that couldn't bank on receiving a serious *New York Times* review – until Wells did it himself. Things like this got mentioned in diary pieces sometimes and burger round-ups, but they were never given the critical close-read of, say, a midtown, sit-down restaurant. And so the queue became the critic, and the internet spread the word.

There was one more thing. In the mid to late noughties, food blogs started to grow. A whole ecosystem of mostly hobbyist food bloggers started talking about restaurants online, cross-referencing each other and competing to outpace the hype. These bloggers – who nobody was really paying, by the way – did the combined job of newspaper gossip columnist, restaurant critic, local reporter and opinion writer, and at breakneck pace. At the same time, online food publications were having a miniature golden age, and there was also the piecemeal user-generated content of sites like Flickr or the message boards on Chowhound. Where once you'd have to buy the newspaper and search for the microprint restaurant review, now you had a constant stream of food media content and, naturally, everyone was writing about the line. By the end of the noughties, there was the line, and there were people writing about the line, and people writing about people writing about the line.

By 2013, these feedback loops had been expertly calibrated to create hype. When Dominique Ansel developed his recipe for the cronut – a deep-fried doughnut ring, but made of croissant dough – people were reporting on it, and anticipating the appetite for it, before it even launched. It wasn't just the line, which started forming from 6am, two hours before the bakery even opened, or the scalpers, who queued for hours and resold the cronuts for profit to 'I'm not a morning person' people. It was the media – Grub Street, Eater, *The New York Times*, the *Village Voice*, the *Week, Huffington Post*, the *Atlantic*, all of them feeding the ego of the queue, and all of them, in a weird way, dependent on it.

Cronuts became, in the end, the most famous hype food of the 2010s. A lot of it was timing: they came at the height of super-intense restaurant coverage, but also at the dawn of a new, more adaptive, more instinctive kind of media. Instagram was launched in 2010 and had expanded to Android phones in 2012, and by the cronut inception event it had around 100 million users. On Instagram, you shared a photo of the food with an explanatory caption, rather than a blog post about the food with an illustrative photo. This allowed you to bypass thinking altogether and just look: burgers, hotdogs, fries, pizza, ice cream, cake, bubble tea – all those foods that instantly register as delicious.

'What we're talking about,' Pete Wells explained to me, 'is a shift from talking about places, venues, establishments and addresses, to a single experience.' Nobody was talking about Dominique Ansel's bakery, which would have involved thinking about what kind of place it was and how it dovetailed into the New York scene. People just shared the cronut, a platonic torus of golden dough with a sugar–salt–fat ratio to please the gods. The cronut – a singularity. Instead of spreading person to person through word of mouth, it spread exponentially, like a contagion, and the template was laid for the next fifteen years of viral restaurant trends.

Since the cronut, we've been living through an age of serial virality. We find ourselves now surrounded by lines, usually for inexpensive, seemingly democratic foods in the Shake Shack kind of mould. I say in the Shake Shack mould, but maybe that's talking around the point. In the last decade in London, nearly all of the runaway, social-media enabled success stories have been for some version of the meat-in-bread format. Burger vans; deep-fill sandwich places; a pop-up of the hugely successful West Coast burger chain In-N-Out, but for reasons unclear to anybody at all, in Hendon. In the last year alone, two new smashburger places have opened. Both have a knockoff, Shake Shack-style burger-modernist vibe. And I've been to both, spending cumulative hours waiting for the archetypal fast food.

In the last few years, TikTok in particular has become *the* platform for viral food. It's all in the details: the way that the app knows how long you linger on something, how many times you let a mac and cheese video loop before you swipe away; the way that before you even see the name of the uploader or the caption of the video, you see how many tens of thousands of views and likes it has. I guess this is the digital version of the long, snaking queue – a conspicuously visible way of quantifying hype.

Traditionally, social media platforms emphasised the social. This meant following friends or family or celebrities, and mainly being shown their content. Restaurant influencers became a thing, and people trusted in their authority the same way as they used to trust the critics. TikTok, and the apps that have followed its lead, is different. The beat falls on the media, not the social. The For You page is an algorithmically curated scroll of videos. It doesn't matter who posted something or how many followers they have or whether you even know them. The important thing is the content – does it make people linger? Do people send it on? Does it do its job? Its job, by the way, is to keep people scrolling the app, not necessarily to lead them to good food. This recommendation algorithm accounts for over 90 per cent of everything you see on the app. It is the first thing you see when you open TikTok, and maybe the most powerful tastemaker in the world right now.

Some of the most viral foods in London in the last couple of years include a foot-long croissant, a brick of honey butter toast and cookies thicker than the average burger. A more-is-more principle is in effect. It has led to mash-ups like birria ramen, cheeseburger tacos, cruffins, crookies, brookies and cereal milk ice cream. When something goes viral on here, it reveals something about the things we really want. And what people want, it turns out, are easily digestible food ideas – things they already know, like the burger, hybrids that they double know but that are also novel, like the 'Yorkshire pudding burrito' I got last year, on TikTok's recommendation, which was exactly how you would imagine it would be.

We have got to a point now where even restaurant critics follow the queues, following the lines of people, who themselves are following the online hype. Influence is being broken, or it's being fixed. The balance of power is moving towards the simple rubric of likes, sends, hearts, forwards, views, head counts in a queue. This is the maths of the Fear of Missing Out, and it's responsible for 80 per cent of my biggest food mistakes.

But, I can't help myself. As much as I like to complain about queueing and viral mash-ups and circular hype, the truth is that a person can't ironically queue. I had to admit this to myself a few months ago, voluntarily in line for the worst sandwich I have ever had, designed by a man I don't trust, for which I paid £16. You're either in line, or you're not. Mild humiliation kink is one of the big drivers of restaurant culture right now.

A while ago, inspired by a slew of TikTok videos, I went to another place that I knew I'd hate. In Camden Market, which used to be a semi-countercultural punk ghetto and is now the visiting French teenager's Winter Wonderland, there is a stall where you can buy loaded chips. The people in front of me were there thanks to TikTok. The people behind were too. We all waited there, in the queue, watching videos of queues strikingly similar to the one we were stuck in. And then, after what felt like a week, I got the chips, which had been tossed with mayonnaise, grated cheese, a spice and herb mixture, chilli sauce and jalapeños. They were terrible, but then you already know that. I complained about the chips and the line to anybody who would listen, including my dry-cleaner – and as it happened, he had gone there too. Never again, I said. Never again, he agreed. And I left the shop, and opened TikTok on my phone.

Author's note: As I was finishing the edits on this book, something happened. In the online food media crossover event of the century, Keith Lee – *the* Keith Lee – came to London and got the Borough Market strawberries, having seen them go viral on TikTok. His conclusion? 'It's a strawberry.'

I like bubble tea

Or, the cultural ingredients of a global mega-trend

There's a bubble tea store I go to in London – a small Taiwanese place that always has a queue out the door. The infusions tend towards grounded beiges and browns: bu zhi chun oolong tea; over-steeped Ceylon tea with milk and dark sugar syrup; an Earl Grey latte. One of their signature drinks is based on lei cha – a Southern Chinese blend of tea, roasted nuts and seeds and herbs – except here, they make it into a latte and marble it with sesame cream. If you get your tea with tapioca bubbles, you'll find they're made to a diameter of precisely 85mm, which is exactly the right width to slip through the straw. My order of choice is the milk tea with roasted buckwheat – a Ceylon blend that's rounded out with soft, nutty undertones of soba. I get it with extra tapioca pearls, standard ice, standard sweetness.

Sometimes, instead of going for coffee, I take friends here. For the people who don't know how much they're going to love bubble tea, it can be a lot. Bubble tea isn't one thing but an umbrella term for a miscellany of Instagrammable drinks, many of which don't have tea, milk, or even tapioca pearls. They can be fruit-based, or blended milk with chestnut purée, or high-concept versions made from scratch with oolong and hand-rolled pearls. You choose a base tea, add-ins, sugar and ice levels, milk types and whether or not to get a top of sweet-salty cheese cream – a thick, plush foam head, which gives black tea the visuals of a pint of Guinness. Depending on the drink, you can choose hot or cold. The permutations are seemingly endless – even the most seasoned off-menu Starbucks drink aficionados can get overwhelmed by up to a thousand possible routes through the menu.

So, when they want to play it safe, I tell my friends to get the brown sugar boba milk tea – the archetypal bubble tea, the bubble tea emoji bubble tea. The milk tea is brewed to the colour of a manila envelope. It is, I will explain to the first-timers, served cold. Inside you will find the plump, brown-black tapioca pearls – also called bubbles, or boba – that have become the drink's leitmotif. You can see them through the clear plastic, slipping around in the dark sugar syrup at the bottom of the cup, then heaving up through the straw, punctuating sips like fat cartoon full stops. They have a texture called QQ, a kind of dense bounciness like fish balls or firm mochi. Once people try bubble tea, they tend to like it, if for no other reason than they can customise it to almost atomic alignment with their tastes. I explain all of this gently, like the elder statesman of bubble tea, as though I did not in fact start drinking it five years ago.

Until 2010, Britain didn't have a standalone bubble tea shop. But here we are – there are a dozen bubble shops within a ten-minute walk of my usual place. In fact, there's one fifty metres away. And a new branch of my usual place has just opened around the corner. There are more good places to get bubble tea in this area than there are to get good coffee. We have bubble tea in Huddersfield, Portsmouth, Guildford and Leamington Spa. Southend-on-Sea, where I grew up and which still doesn't have a Pret, has six. Walsall has a combination bubble and smashburger dark kitchen. By the time Costa started selling a 'tropical mango bubble frappé' in 2022, it was clear that this thing – which before you could've said was a city thing or an Instagram thing or a Taiwanese thing – had become an unignorable part of British food culture. Bubble tea is so big among Gen Z and Millennials that for the first time in my lifetime, there's a genuine challenge to the supremacy of coffee shops. It's a generational shift. The last time a food took off this quickly in Britain, it was the fifties, and it was hamburgers.

When it comes to the British bubble tea boom, there are two obvious questions. The first is – how did we come to love this so much? The second is – why now? Some foods evolve incrementally, over generations. A new ingredient is discovered or a technique is perfected through countless iterations of a single, everyday dish, like risotto, or roast meats on rice. Things slowly work their way into the culture: people make them, more people eat them, and eventually people start telling stories about them, which is the point at which you know a thing has really laid down roots. It's unusual to be able to pin down exactly when a food was invented, and even rarer for it to be in living memory. They're just there, units of cultural vocabulary with hidden roots and circular systems of meaning.

And then, there are zeitgeist-seizing foods – the foods that spread at lightspeed, becoming not just a food but the food of a generation. Usually, they're invented by accident, but there's something about the way that they dovetail with the culture at that moment. Burgers, customisable coffees, sliced white bread. The economics are right, the cultural plexus is ready, the networks of trade and agriculture in place. Most importantly, there's an appetite for it. You can call these crazes or trends, but there's always something deeper than fashion. These foods don't just find a place in the culture, they have the power and the momentum to totally rearrange food culture around them. In recent years, there have been flashes in the pan – like avocado toast or cupcakes – but nothing has done it quite like bubble tea.

In Taiwan, where bubble tea was invented, people have been drinking Chinese tea styles with milk since Dutch colonisation in the seventeenth century. But milk tea – specifically, Indian black teas where milkiness is as important as the tea – arrived late, some time around the Second World War. As the story goes, a former bartender, Chang Fan Shu, thought to serve it cold, and shake it like you would a cocktail. When he did this, the fats and proteins in the milk allowed it to form a foam, and he made what people started to call bubble tea. Some shops started serving iced versions, shaken like a cocktail. And then in the eighties, in a Taiwanese tea shop – and nobody can agree which one – someone had the idea of adding chewy pearls of tapioca starch to the bubble tea, making bubble tea-squared. New variants quickly appeared. Earl

Grey boba tea. Milkless jasmine green tea or osmanthus versions. A lot of the time the tea was lost completely, most notably in the crystalline pop fruit flavours such as lychee or mulberry, although also in milkshake-like blends like lilac taro. It took centuries of culinary negotiations for milk tea to become A Thing, in any meaningful sense. And then it took a couple of years for the bubble tea Cambrian explosion to blow the whole thing apart.

Within a decade, bubble tea was huge in Taiwan, and not long after in Hong Kong. By 2002, Singapore had 5,000 shops. Some places, like Japan, were more ambivalent. But it caught on in mainland China – particularly in the South where tea culture was most robust – and it was helped by the fact that tapioca was already part of dessert culture. Today, there are nearly half a million bubble tea stores in mainland China, where bubble tea is a bigger market than coffee. It went to California in the nineties, via Taiwanese American families, and there it was known as boba tea. Bubble tea was, and mostly continues to be, a young person's drink. Within a few years, boba shops were to West Coast Asian-American kids what soda fountains were to white American teens a couple of generations before.

Even by the standards of wildly successful foods, bubble tea has been a sensation. There is no practical reason to drink bubble tea, no culture to which it is truly traditional. In fact – in most places, the point is exactly that it's fun and unserious. Even in Taiwan it doesn't pass the Michael Pollan 'don't eat anything your great-grandmother wouldn't have recognised as food' test – creamer-based tea came to Taiwan after the war, and the actual boba add-in idea is from the eighties. Still, in the past few decades it has become a global export, and a reminder that when you're talking about the terroir of a food, you're not just talking about place, but about a moment in time.

The 'first' bubble tea shop in the UK, Bubbleology, opened in 2011. It was on the edge of London's Chinatown. In the window, there was all the paraphernalia you'd expect to find in a meth lab: a display of Erlenmeyer flasks, test tubes, beakers and snaking glass pipes. Inside the shop – a chaotic, cave-like space with a few small tables and molecular diagrams on the walls – the staff wore lab coats and worked through the orders as fast as they could, while the queue stretched out of the door. You could get kumquat fruit tea, or almond milk tea or taro or plain Assam. For some reason, you could also get customisable cruffins.

I say all this as though I was there when it happened, which I was not, but my friend Kaila was. She was a straight-edge punk with a sweet tooth and a nebulous interest – like so many British teens at the time – in East Asian culture. She was a dream customer, not least because she had nothing to compare these bubble teas to. Kaila has this beautiful capacity to be delighted by things that a more cynical person would dismiss out of hand. It is the best thing about her. And so one day she was walking by the shop, and saw the high-concept set-up and the neon colour scheme, and she went on in. Her entry point was the fruit flavours. She also experimented with the popping bubbles – a squishier, juice-filled, jelly-based alternative to the bouncy tapioca, making it a drink, inside a solid, inside a drink. She showed her friends, and they showed their friends, and eventually they tried other shops, stalking through Chinatown, going to new openings in Islington or Camden when they got the word.

Around this time, in the early 2010s, lots of people who hadn't grown up with bubble tea were suddenly 'discovering' it. White people started talking about it, coy but kind of self-satisfied, comparing the QQ-ness of the boba at Cafe de HK and at Candy Cafe, or saying Bubbleology was overrated, which it was. Taiwanese bloggers wrote with delighted bafflement that this drink – which was beloved but really not that deep – had become a focus of food-crowd hype. Bubbleology opened an outlet in Harvey Nichols, and more bubble tea chains like Mooboo and Ci-Tea opened up.

In a strange kind of way, British people had been primed for this. Britain has had a tea culture for hundreds of years. Or maybe it's better to say Britain has been a tea culture: the rituals of tea are so embedded that it's become a point of identity. It has this in common with Taiwan, Hong Kong and mainland China. Catherine of Braganza married into the British royal family in the seventeenth century and popularised drinking delicate Chinese teas. Within 100 years it was everywhere, helped by the mystical, Orientalist ideas that British people had about culture in the East. Tea was invented again in the nineteenth century when imperial Britain started cultivating astringent, high-tannin varieties of tea in India, to break China's monopoly on the tea trade. You don't counteract or even complement this tea with milk – you complete it, and so tea as we now know it in the UK was born. 'There is no English history without that other history,' the cultural theorist Stuart Hall wrote, and he was right. Talking about tea means telling a thousand other geopolitical and economic and imperial stories.

But you can't understand the bubble tea explosion by looking at historic British tea culture, really – just like you can't understand Hulk Hogan by looking at Olympic wrestling. To start with, a lot of the bubble tea that British people were buying in those early days in the 2010s was fruit-based and milk-less. In East Asia, bubble tea started from sensible milk Assam tea, and got methodologically weirder, all the way through to monster crème brûlée brown-sugar hybrids.

But we began at the postmodern end, in late-stage bubble tea – with super sweet, syrup-based drinks targeted at, if not children, then at least every adult's inner child. If Brits were primed for the taste of these early neon bubble teas, it was probably by something more like Robinsons fruit squash.

What bubble tea did benefit from, however, was the growth of coffee culture. In the nineties, coffee evolved past being a semi-medicinal sludge. Some baristas put their time into sourcing the great beans and perfecting the specific roasts that would end up being integral to second-wave coffee. And in other coffee shops, like Starbucks, people took a different path, making coffee not better, but just more fun. The American chains sold pumpkin spice lattes and eggnog cappuccinos and coffee-flavoured frappés. They gently suggested that it was OK, actually, for adults to go into a coffee shop and leave with a grown-up triple-XXX version of a milkshake. Suddenly, you could customise your coffee – single or double or triple shot, a choice of six kinds of milk, hot or iced, any one of a dozen flavours of syrup.

None of us realised this at the time, but in a way we were being groomed for bubble tea. The market research process for Bubbleology included going to Taiwan for taste tests and getting equipment from East Asia, but it also involved – and I am serious – staking out branches of Costa.

There were hurdles, not least the best part – the tapioca. Or, as I've seen it variously described in the British press: 'mysterious black lumps' or 'gummy globules'. I don't know what these people are talking about. But then again, it's not new – Brits talking about Asian food like this. In lots of East and South East Asia, tapioca is appreciated for its textural assets, as a sweet soup and an add-in to drinks and shaved ice. But for most pre-Millennial Brits, tapioca means tapioca pudding – a famously hated dessert in which small tapioca pearls are cooked in milk to a porridge with a texture that people usually liken to frogspawn. People don't have a convincing precedent for this kind of chew. It's not even just the particular, supercharged QQ bounce of tapioca that people get weird about: it's also the popping pearls, the grass jelly and the slurpable coconut pudding.

The year after Bubbleology opened, 2012, Instagram launched in the UK. Maybe this is an understatement. Bubble tea *needed* social media platforms like Instagram and TikTok. Bubble tea is engineered to look great: rainbow gradients, jellies, a high-contrast head of cream, bouncy dark boba. Images started coming in from boba culture in the US and Singapore, which made people curious. And then British young people started making their own bubble tea content. These days, the close-up cup-in-hand shot is so ingrained in the culture that when you go for bubble tea, it's pretty much a prerequisite that you get your nails done first.

If you work on your TikTok algorithms even the tiniest bit, you'll see how quickly all this lends itself to hype: launch events of new flavours, and limited-edition cups, and new-wave bubble tea store openings, which can get a queue around the block. I was in Wandsworth a while back, in a tired, one-drag shopping centre, and there was a new bubble tea place – people were lined up halfway down the mall for it. Word gets around online, through photos and videos of people holding the cups – always the same shot, the same half-pan and gentle wiggle. The most consistent feature is probably just the cup, which is made of transparent plastic so you can appreciate the best angles of the drink, which is every angle, by the way. In Taiwan, where people know what bubble tea is and like it for what it is, the cups aren't usually see-through. They're opaque, decorated with the branding of whichever shop they're from.

Timing was everything. Bubble tea could never have taken off in Britain in the nineties, say. Everyone was still too deep in the tapioca pudding years, and besides – you can't go from never having had anything more exciting than a Maxwell House instant coffee, to choosing a micro-personalised bubble tea order. There are intervening stages we had to live through. You have to wonder whether part of the answer to the why now? is just that a new generation has aged into spending power, and they don't remember tapioca at its worst.

The stores also worked the novelty angle. It wasn't 'this is traditional in Taiwan' or 'these are great ingredients' but – 'Isn't this wild?' At Bubbleology, that meant rebranding ordinary bubble tea as some kind of molecular break-through. And it was about aggressively branding and repacking, from the very start. The early 2010s wave of shops concentrated in and around central London, where restaurateurs often come to test-drive fad foods with the shelf life of a pint of milk – things like half-pound soft-bake mega cookies or a new mutant subspecies of smashburger. Not long after Bubbleology, the franchise Mooboo was founded in Camden. Now they're the two biggest bubble tea brands in the UK, and between them have hundreds of stores.

But Bubbleology was not, in fact, the first bubble tea shop, even though this story is the one that's stuck and it works well for Bubbleology. Back in the noughties, you could find bubble tea in food courts like North London's late Oriental City. There were Cantonese restaurants selling it, and dumpling shops and diners. Hardcore boba fans posted leads on the nerd-moderated backpages of the internet, but casual drinkers could plausibly just stumble across a shop. In Glasgow's Savoy Centre – a shopping arcade where you could also go to buy a kilt – there was a Taiwanese tea shop called Easy Way, which sold sour prune black tea, and green apple with boba or grass jelly. By 2004, *Time Out* was publishing articles on how bubble tea was the next big thing.

At that time, bubble tea was mainly popular among people who already knew what it was: students from China, Taiwan, Hong Kong and Singapore; East and South East Asian tourists; British-Asian kids. Even in the early days of the big chains, a comparatively small percentage of the customers were outsiders to bubble tea culture. But I guess this was the problem, or at least this was what business savvy people saw as the problem – here was this product, which is unbelievably marketable and which you can sell with decent profit margins, and it was mainly the preserve of family-run shops.

What if, instead of just one part of a varied Taiwanese food culture, you made it A Thing? The founder of Bubbleology, Assad Khan, was a banker working at J. P. Morgan before he got into the bubble tea business: he'd seen it selling well in New York; he imagined there was money to be made here, too, and he'd wanted to do something entrepreneurial for a while anyway. 'I was too young to take advantage of the coffee boom in the 1990s, and didn't understand technology to take advantage of the dotcom boom,' he said in one interview. But this was an opportunity. 'Bubble tea businesses have largely been either small hole-in-the-wall outlets or Asian-inspired brands,' he went on, 'but I see Bubbleology as the first true global brand.'

For all the excitement of going into a bubble tea shop and all the seemingly limitless possibilities you find there, the rise of bubble tea in the UK was never just about taste. It wasn't just down to the person-to-person, or Instagram-to-Instagram, transmission of culture and ideas. It always comes back to bigger, colder forces: business, the economy, import–export, property. It's here, in the devil's details, that bubble tea was made.

There are words that people use when they're deciding which food businesses get financed: scalability, overheads, franchising, labour costs. So long as you don't think too hard about the quality of the tea itself, bubble tea shops do well on all counts. Unlike a restaurant, you don't need to hire trained chefs – the work is skilled but formulaic. The machinery is inexpensive, especially compared to large coffee machines, which can run into the thousands. You just need a fridge, a couple of tea urns, a machine to heat-seal the cups, something for cooking the tapioca, trays and storage and cups and straws.

And so chains and franchises dominate bubble tea. Unlike the independent places that were selling bubble tea in the 2000s, these shops are completely standardised. A Mooboo franchise in Portsmouth isn't much different to a Mooboo in Southend. Considering the dizzying number of choices required to order just one bubble tea, it can help newbies if they at least feel like they know the shop itself. It removes one variable, even if there are still ninety-nine left. Plus, this is sad but I have to say it: according to those who remember, the very early nought-ies bubble teas could be inconsistent. And so you ended up in a situation where a Taiwanese blogger trying London bubble tea had headlines like 'dreams broken at Jen Café' and 'the horrifying HK Diner' but said Bubbleology was actually pretty good.

There's also the question of property. Chains and franchises have name recognition and capital, which makes them safe prospects for landlords looking to lease a shop. Are you going to give it to a family restaurant, with slow tables and a big kitchen and all the usual inefficiencies? Or are you going to divide it up and rent it to money-printing national chains? You see it in action in London's Chinatown in particular: since 1986, the Shaftesbury property group has bought up a huge amount of real estate here, and businesses don't own the buildings they occupy. As a result, rents keep climbing, and the ecosystem keeps being squeezed towards maximal profitability, even if this comes at the cost of genuine community or diversity of offerings. This got worse around the time of the pandemic – restaurants shut, and delivery and takeout business gained ground. There are twenty bubble tea shops in Chinatown, spread across just a few streets, and they're all chains.

And yet, people do still matter in this story. For culture to move, you need real people – people who already hold and cherish these ideas. Sometimes this means importing a certain set of tastes, and recreating them as well as you can from the materials you now have. It can be the skills that move with you when you go elsewhere to work: an understanding of wok science, or the know-how to grow kai lan on an allotment, or the social networks you need to properly staff a dim sum restaurant. This was what the early bubble tea stalls did, in the noughties, before the more corporate boom. And it still happens now: Taiwanese people in Britain opening independent bubble tea shops, someone in a Cantonese restaurant working a particularly good boba milk tea on the menu.

There have been various waves of migration from East Asia to the UK. There were seafarers in the late Victorian era, who set up Chinatowns near the ports, in Liverpool and London. Then there was a small cohort of students in the early 1900s. The biggest influx started in the fifties, when migration laws were changed to add to the workforce after the war. Men came to Britain from poor and rural areas of Hong Kong. They set up restaurants serving people-pleasing incarnations of Cantonese food. When the economy tanked, lots of restaurateurs pivoted to a more casual model, and the British-Chinese takeaway was born. Right now, there are two migrations from East and South East Asia to the UK. One group are mainly middle-class migrants from Hong Kong. The other group are students, mostly from mainland China. This second group is a vital part of the bubble tea success story. As far as food and taste in Britain go, it's one of the most important migrations of people in recent times.

It started in 2012, when tuition fees were raised and university funding was cut. The smart thing to do was to encourage international students to enrol – universities could set the fees higher, subsidising the whole thing with the money gleaned from comparatively wealthy kids from other parts of the world. China was an obvious site for recruitment. There are around 150,000 Chinese students in the UK today – almost three times as many as in 2011, and the same as the total number of Chinese people in the UK back in 1981. They make up the biggest proportion of international students in the country.

Unlike the people who arrived in the UK from around Hong Kong in the fifties and sixties and popularised British-Chinese takeaway, these students are not the creators of bubble tea culture. They're consumers of it, and great ones – the kind of clued-in, internet-viral, quick-tap, online-order customers that restaurants have come to rely on these past few years. Most are young, most are living in student flats where the kitchens are small or useless. Many have spending power. And so they eat out, and order in, and a whole secondary industry of restaurants, dark kitchens, takeaways, cafes and shops has grown around them. There are now entire, multifaceted Chinese scenes in towns that used to consider themselves lucky to have a single Chinese restaurant.

The universities were seed crystals for British bubble tea culture. My usual bubble tea shop is in the middle of London's university district. Nearby UCL alone has almost 10,000 international students from mainland China, many of whom know bubble tea well and grew up drinking it. Nowhere in the UK has such a concentration of students, and specifically those from East and South East Asia. Near here you'll find dozens of bubble tea shops, an entire secondary industry of omnitextural fun. It's not just London. If you look at the cities with the highest concentration of bubble tea shops per person, they're university towns, and ones with above-average numbers of students from mainland China – like Glasgow, Edinburgh, Oxford, Cambridge and Manchester. Durham, a small city in the shadow of its university, has five bubble tea stores within five minutes of each other. Universities advertise bubble tea societies during freshers' week. You can pretty much faultlessly overlay British bubble tea with where international students live, study and work.

The franchises and chains organised themselves with this in mind. Companies got on the student-favourite delivery apps like Hungry Panda and Fantuan, one foot in the physical shopfront but another in the digital convenience economy. I talked to the owner of an independent bubble tea shop, Dragon Cat Café in Hammersmith, whose market research included searching Google for halls of residence in their area. When Happy Lemon first opened in London in 2015, almost all their customers were Chinese international students.

But as the number of international students grew, bubble tea started diffusing into mainstream culture. Over the last fifteen years, bubble tea filtered into British tastes as quickly as Chinese takeaways did a few decades ago. In both cases, one small expression of East Asian food has found its way over here and become wildly popular at breakneck speed. In both cases, the food has entered the culture from the bottom up – the food that ordinary people eat or drink every day, instead of top-down from luxe restaurants or because the critics said so. At the point of entry, both are inexpensive and flexible – the pick-and-mix proteins and sauces of a Chinese takeaway menu and the customisable bubble tea ordering screen today. Fifty years apart, a similar migration of taste. Except this time, with fun-first, photogenic bubble tea, the people spreading it are students.

Usually there's a grey area, when it comes to how foods hit the mainstream, but with bubble tea in the UK you can pin down the 'why now?' with uncanny accuracy. The balance tipped – and the chains entered the market – over a couple of years in the early 2010s. It happened because this is when Instagram, the digital conduit for all things bubble tea, launched in the UK. It happened because this is when tuition fees tripled, and universities started recruiting for students from abroad. It's strange just how much of the roll-out of wild, postmodern, excellent Taiwanese bubble tea comes down to the nuts and bolts of business, tech and policy. Right now it's hard for working-class people to come to Britain through legal pathways, and it's difficult for Chinese restaurants to hire chefs. And so the foods that are most free to move are the ones that anybody, with a bit of light training, can make. The power balance tips towards delivery chains and convenience franchises – places which, even if they're geared towards Chinese students, can fall back on tight, impersonal food prep systems more than individual skill. Look at things from this angle and you see the conditions for diaspora restaurants, whether they're Chinese takeaways or bubble tea shops, are set in Westminster, in the hands of the small group of people who write policy, draw up budgets and set migration laws. Who is allowed in? Under what conditions? At what income threshold? To fill what economic gap?

By the late 2010s, bubble tea had reached ubiquity. Most of the customers at shops like Happy Lemon are now Londoners from across every cultural and ethnic group. Bubble tea does well with Muslim teens and students, stealing customers from South Asian chains like Chaiiwalla. In the absence of alcohol, these shops are meeting points, just like the first wave of diaspora bubble tea places were for California kids in the nineties. 'Now, more than half of our customer base are from British, Black and Asian backgrounds,' a Gong Cha rep told food writer Angela Hui in 2022. 'There's a newfound enthusiasm from people wanting to try new things.'

In the last couple of years, Chinese and Taiwanese chains have arrived, too – following the international students but ending up with cult followings among terminally online British teens too. These are megachains like T4 and luxe places like Heytea, selling teas made with real fruits, fresh milk and house-made add-ins. This is the luxification of a drink which, barely ten years ago, British people could only get in about six fluorescent shades. My tea shop – and I need to stop calling it my tea shop, although I am fond of it – is one of this new wave of high-craft bubble tea stores. The chrysanthemum and buckwheat and osmanthus and special oolong – this isn't Build-a-Bear bubble tea. There's another new chain, with a bank of Teaspresso machines firing like the Flying Scotsman. Through the steam, you can see the tea canisters on the wall – Da Hong Pao oolong tea, and a silver tip jasmine green. I took my friend Oliver here, and we got a cold Ceylon tea with grapefruit purée, and with an aloe vera cream top.

Over the last few years, a British accent of bubble tea has started to creep in. When I spoke to Eric Khaw, the founder of Mooboo, he mentioned that green apple, strawberry and mango flavours are unusually popular in the UK compared to other countries. And so I am vindicated, the way I see things, in my theory about the British precedent for bubble tea being not tea, but fruit squash. There's a shop in Sunderland selling an Irn Bru bubble tea – an unstable isotope that goes to show how far we've strayed from nature's path. To a certain extent, bubble tea is being taken out of its original cultural context. But then, if we know anything about tea, it's that the entire story has been about displacement, ruin and growth. The culture adapts. New ideas come out of left field. I mean, barely a generation ago, the very idea of a tapioca-centric tea drink was left field, even in Taiwan.

You have to wonder if bubble tea will exhaust itself – if

it's an intractable part of the culture now, like English breakfast tea, or whether time will show it to be a fad, a reflection of the particular economic and social circumstances of our time. But for now, it's still going strong. I went to a food industry trade expo a while back, and salespeople were demoing robotic bubble tea machines with the soft but deliberate arms of a ballerina. There were special biodegradable straws, bubblegum-flavoured popping bubbles, talks with titles like 'Breaking the Bubble: Boba Stories from the Greater Manchester Area – Utilising AI in Direct Marketing for Franchisees'.

Go to any bubble tea shop, anywhere in the country, on any weekend, and you will find bubble-tea-literate non-Asian parents ordering drinks for their kids. They'll be practising the same diplomacy you used to need when a kid wanted blue and red and chocolate sauces on their soft-serve ice cream. No, you cannot get the extra-large cup. One flavour of popping jelly pearl is enough. As well as international students, here's a family of German tourists getting caramelised brown-sugar milk tea from a Taiwanese store in Soho. Here's a crowd of schoolgirls sharing lychee Yakult special with passion fruit popping pearls, which don't even go with the drink, but that isn't the point.

Recently I saw a video from one of the worst food accounts on YouTube – a 4.5-million-follower duo of Brits whose mainstay is videos of people trying new foods. You know the vibe – perky white guys who, before the collapse of mainstream broadcasting, would probably have been kids' TV presenters. 'British Taxi Drivers try Bubble Tea for the first time!' the video was called. One of the younger cabbies had tried it, but nobody else had. One of them nearly choked on the pearls, someone else had trouble latching on – he couldn't actually figure out how to suck the boba up through a straw. There are two lessons you can take from this. Firstly, that Brits continue to moan, and will probably always moan, about tapioca. But also: look at where we are, look at the change that fifteen years can make. It really says something about Britain today that you have to survey a bunch of white guys, mainly in the fifty-to-seventy age bracket, to find someone who hasn't tried bubble tea.

Everything but the recipe

Dream home

Or, fantasy and feeding, from magazines to
Instagram

Last year I came across a video on Instagram. There was a voice, low and feminine and with the texture of brushed cotton. 'When I asked my toddlers what they wanted for lunch they both said grilled cheese,' the person said, 'so that's exactly what I got started on.' The woman was young and beautiful in the orthographically exact way that rules out having a single bad angle. She started with the bread, mixing flour, yeast, salt and water, and put it aside to rise. Then she turned her attention to the mozzarella – warming milk with rennet and citric acid, then cutting the curds, draining it, stretching the cheese and rolling it into balls.

There was more. 'My kids love pesto,' she said. And so she made that, too, with fresh basil and pine nuts. By the time it got to the butter, I knew the routine. She said: 'You always need butter for a grilled cheese,' and I said – because this is the script – 'You wouldn't dare.' But she did. She beat heavy cream until the fat separated out, then mixed the pliable gold butter with parsley, garlic and sea salt, and rolled it into a log. You could do some rough maths about the time all this would've taken, in the window between toddler breakfast and lunch, but that's beside the point. She did all of this with nail extensions and a cute, chin-length, *Matrix*-sleek bob.

Nara Smith was brought up in Germany and was scouted to be a model as a teenager. In 2020, when she was eighteen, she married one of the most famous male models in America, Lucky Blue Smith. Within a few months, they had their first child. Now the Smiths have three kids and are living in a roomy starter home in a family-friendly neighbourhood in Texas. In many ways, the Smiths are the average American family, just uncommonly good-looking. Until a couple of years ago, Nara's posts were what you'd expect: fit checks, makeup explainers, mood videos overlaid with soft music. But then she hit on a formula. She began doing lo-fi stunts, like making a dupe of Dairy Queen-style Oreo blitz soft-serve ice cream, and starting by baking the Oreos from scratch. When she realises she's out of condiments, she does a 'restock' by making ketchup, ranch dressing, hot sauce and barbecue sauce, in one session, while wearing a red polka-dot, frill-trim off-the-shoulder dress. Since she started posting like this, her Instagram and TikTok accounts have gained millions of followers. It's addictive – the low-stakes suspense of seeing just how much Too Much she's going to do this time.

There's a cottage industry of videos online where people reverse engineer Pop-Tarts, or say they're making a pizza but then start by grinding the flour themselves, or growing tomatoes, or milking the cow for the cheese. And there is a healthy market for mom content – meal prep, toddler-friendly meals and relatable lifestyle tips. But Nara Smith is a singularity, somehow absorbing both expressions of the moment but becoming something bigger and weirder than either. It's all about the delicate absurdity of the framing. 'My toddlers were playing in the backyard,' she says, over a video of her chopping fruit in a pastel yellow dress with gauzy, pleated balloon sleeves the size of accordion bellows. 'They asked me for a Capri-Sun. Since I had all the fruit at home to make some, I told them to give me a minute while I got started.' There's something about the way Smith moves, like if you programmed a Stepford Wife in the *Sims* game. The expression on her face looks passive but is clearly micromanaged. A lot of the time, these videos start with a craving, although it's rarely hers. 'My husband mentioned that he was craving Coca-Cola the other day' – you know where this is going.

Naturally, she has been a fulcrum for discourse. Some people say she's propaganda for big, eerie Mormon families (Lucky Blue was raised in The Church of Jesus Christ of Latter-day Saints). For other people, the whole thing is just depressing – a woman in her early twenties, doing so much, deliberately moving through the gender ruts that plenty of people fight to leave. Smith seems to oblige, even live for, her husband's requests. She is also Black – her mother is Mosotho, her father is German – which complicates how all this comes across. I'd like to believe in the obscure and plausibly masterful motives of Nara Smith, method-acting the extremist American housewife: she delivers a deadpan line with a comedian's touch; she's a master of irony – the coy set-up, the labyrinthine joke. But who knows. So far,

Nara has been evasive about her motives, except to say that she likes this life.

Nara Smith is part of a bigger cultural switch-up. Traditional homemaking inspo – usually by and for women – is blowing up online. In the past, you found dreamy, inconsequential content like this in women's magazines. This is where you learned about flower arranging, and economical ways to deal with leftover turkey, and how to unmould a decorative terrine. These days, this stuff is moving on to social media where, like a plant repotted in a far larger vessel, it is rooting outwards, in a thousand directions and at speed. Sometimes you come across genuinely useful tips, like how to measure honey without the spoon getting sticky (you press the back of the spoon into the flour or sugar, creating a tablespoon-sized hollow which you can then pour the honey into), but the real substance – and the discourse – is in the weirder things. Acts like Nara Smith, or the content creators working the 'come pack my husband's lunch box with me' beat. There are card-carrying tradwives – mainly young women who grew up in a culture where uber-traditional views about motherhood and wifedom aren't just outdated but actively discouraged. There are the obsessive organisers, who compose the contents of their fridges as though it's a nativity scene. There are the conspiracy-leaning health-food nuts who feed their kids blue steak for their birthday instead of cake.

Each of these subcultures has its own figureheads and food and social codes, but what they have in common is that they're not about generalised home cooking but a more pointed, purposeful kind of cooking *for* the home. Home could be Lucky Blue Smith and the kids. It could be the home of the Mennonite homesteaders, or it could be the flawless type-A vision of a stay-at-home twink preparing their partner a four-course breakfast each morning. It's about the food, but it's also about who the food is for, who's cooking it, and where the balance of power lies. If the comments or the column inches are anything to go by, it's contentious, this fifties-coded backslide, but as my social media For You pages go to show, it's also weirdly compelling. People who grew up generations removed from women's lib are playing around not just with cooking, but with their identity as feeders, asking what it would mean to just, maybe, possibly be the world's most perfect cook.

When your back is against the wall, you don't think about what kind of a homemaker you are. You just do things. Go to Tesco Express, mop the floors, clean that air fryer, make a soup, save the leftovers, get the kids to bed, and then the next day, and the one after that, until there's no one left to feed. This is how people, mostly women, employed or with the kind of multi-kid, hard-graft household that takes all day to upkeep, have always done things. It's exhausting but straightforward. The work is just what it is. If it's special, it's because caring for people just *is* special. That is what caring is.

But the moment that people have a choice in things, the simple calculation of jobs to do, and time to do them in, and energy and effort and money and space – it breaks down. For the last 200 years, since the modern middle class was born, people have been looking into a freakier, non-Newtonian kind of household physics. In this world, what you do isn't just about what needs to be done. It's about what kind of a person you want to be. You start with reputation and social standing and you work from there. Sometimes this means spending as little time in the kitchen as possible. But often, it means making cooking more work than ever before, which is how, in the age of supermarkets and Deliveroo, the biggest flex a girl can perform is making her own hotdogs.

There's an idea that the kitchen is a sanctuary, but of course it isn't, and if you've ever spent even five minutes in a kitchen you will know this. Homemaking is sensitive to changes in politics, because changes in politics are ultimately changes in how people are accorded value and power. You feel this even in the kitchen, maybe *especially* in the kitchen, where household power gets hashed out. And so the perfect homemaker changes, depending on the times. In the nineteenth century, the time when all this kicked off, the middle class as we know it today was reasonably new – an expanding group of people who weren't poor, but also weren't rich enough to own land or have household staff. Some families were lifted out of the working class and became comfortable, but lots had started higher and settled down here. In Victorian England, many women were clueless about cooking, because nobody in their family before them had ever needed to care and people were still holding out hope that one day soon, nobody would have to care once more. Writers wrung their hands about how everyone, over the course of a generation or two, seemed to have become incompetent. This work is too valuable to be half-arsed, they said. No woman should consider herself above it, although you have to wonder why, if it was so skilful and vital and beautiful, the men never stepped in to fill the gaps.

If you want people to do the work, to start with you have to show them how. But you also have to sell the idea. You can imagine them, the Victorians, workshopping ideas over coffee in a WeWork conference room. Cooking? Too pedestrian. Catering? Too commercial. Housewifery? Been there, give me something new. It needed a new spin. In her cookbook *Modern Cookery for Private Families*, Eliza Acton called this kind of work 'domestic economy'. 'No longer sneered at as beneath the attention of the educated and accomplished,' she wrote, domestic economy was as dignified a vocation for an educated woman as doing charitable work or speaking French. Mrs Beeton called it 'household management'. Maria Rundell's book was called *A New System of Domestic Cookery*. On both sides of the Atlantic, women established schools and women's groups and federations. They came up with other euphemisms, like home economy. It was partly about morals – if the home was society in miniature, then a healthy country had to start with a well-run house. But when you systematise domestic work, when you make it part of a curriculum, you also make it credible as work.

Once you've got to the bottom of how to keep a good home, the next question is – whose? In the late nineteenth century, the majority of Black women in the United States were domestic workers. Even if you kept a beautiful house, it might not have been yours. Home, household, work; mother, mammy, mom; servant, servers; kitchen, dining, cook, cuisine; lady, woman, mistress, girl; domestic the adjective, domestic the person – even the words slipped around. The contradictions are thrashed out in the character of Aunt Jemima – a racist chimera made up to sell pancake mix. A high-end restaurant chef cooked by learning every point of culinary grammar, then internalising everything, and channelling as culinary elan. But people like Aunt Jemima? As Toni Tipton-Martin writes in *The Jemima Code*, they were 'ignorant figures, incapable of creative culinary artistry'. It was a necessary fiction for white Americans, and maybe even a hopeful one – that if cooking was grunt work that was below you, and if someone else was going to have to do it, then wouldn't it be nice if they just kind of . . . loved it? They believed in Aunt Jemima the same way that kids believe in Santa Claus. It's a backhanded compliment for the ages – you're a wonderful cook, because it's what you were born to do.

Cookbooks by Black cooks told another story. Carrie Alberta Lyford's *Book of Recipes for the Cooking School*, published in 1921, was a beginner-friendly but methodical guide to everything from meal planning to how to make creamed leeks. For the upwardly mobile housewife, how about coquilles of sweetbread, from the 1910 *Federation Cookbook*, compiled by Bertha L. Turner? *The Southern Cookbook* was by a man, S. Thomas Bivins, for a more cheffy readership of caterers and hotel keepers – recipes for larded quails, Charlotte russe and English plum pudding. Around the same time, Mary McLeod Bethune set up a school for Black girls – the Daytona Educational and Industrial Training School – in Florida, where cooking was on the curriculum along with Bible study and dressmaking. It was the same drive as the Victorians, just in a different context, teaching people that homemaking could really take you places. 'Cease to be a drudge,' McLeod Bethune said. 'Seek to be an artist.'

As a small Black middle class started to form, recipes changed tone. You've seen it – as soon as you settle into your life, you find ways to make it complicated again. What if, instead of just making a note-perfect casserole, you took a more baroque approach? 'At the close of the honeymoon –' wrote Leona Eldridge Porter, the domestic science editor of *Half-Century Magazine*, in 1916, '– comes a realisation to the bride that she is soon to become mistress of the lifelong dream – her own home.' And so in *Half-Century* – half-century since abolition, that is – there was a recipe for 'surprise potatoes', which turn out to be croquettes stuffed with leftover cold meats. After-dinner cheese puffs. Carrot marmalade. Raspberry vinegar. Cheese soufflé. How many full-time housewives were there, really, at a time when a majority of Black women were still working in other people's houses? It didn't really matter. 'Mistress of the lifelong dream' – this is the thing that counts.

There is a finite amount of good homemaking advice – you can fit most of what you'll ever need to know in a decent-sized book, and still have pages to spare for things like etiquette and animal husbandry. If you really want to be inspired, you're better off doing what daydreamers have been doing for generations, which is to buy a glossy magazine. Magazines have almost nothing to do with real life. This is why I have always been fond of them. I started at fourteen with *Cosmo*, which misled me about how big a role feathers and ice cubes would play in sex. I've gone through *Vogue* and *Lucky Peach* and *Bon Appétit*, each of which was unhinged in its own special way. Recently I bought a load of *Martha Stewart Living* magazines from

2001 – a time capsule which included a recipe for chicken livers with shallots and marsala, tips on how to handcraft a dreidel case from felt, and an op-ed about 9/11.

Magazines are about lifestyle. And not just that, but a lifestyle that will sell advertising slots, perfume fold-outs and whole-page product placements from homeware brands. They're for finding things you never knew you needed and will probably never think of again, which makes them the perfect place for people to hash out the aspirations of the average cook. They bear witness to the neuroses of their time. Of course you don't see this in the moment. You just skim *Saveur* or the old *Marie Claire* food pages while you're in a waiting room, or in the bathroom, taking a break from your actual life. But I've been looking back through a lot of magazines while researching this book, and they can tell you about the pressure points in food times gone by. They do this, because instead of showing food culture as it is, they show it how people dreamed it could be.

In the fifties, soldiers were back home after the Second World War, and the economy was decent, and some of the women who had entered the workforce en masse during wartime now realised that they didn't have to work any more. On top of this, with money and paper and factories freed up after the war, magazines got more serious – which is to say more serious about producing more unserious lifestyle content. They had glossier pages and full-colour photos, and these things lent themselves to beautiful food photography, yes, but also beautiful adverts and these were the real point. The perfect fifties housewife – an archetype we're still fighting about today in the comments under the videos of Instagram Mormon sister wives – was finetuned in these pages.

There's a feature I came across a while ago, while kicking back with a 1947 issue of *Ebony* magazine. (You know how it is.) It was a photo spread for the *Ebony* magazine food column, 'Date with a Dish', and there were recipes for some relaxed, low-key luxurious coffee cakes that you could make on a Sunday morning. In the photos were Dorothy Dandridge and her daughter, Harolyn. Later, Dandridge would be the first African American actor to be nominated in a leading role for an Academy Award, but back then she was a homemaker baking with her toddler. Obviously, she is gorgeous. She strikes a pose like a domestic goddess marionette – like Nara Smith. Banana bread, cinnamon buns, cinnamon date braid, laid out on beautiful china, at an impeccable table, decorated with a flower arrangement as big as a roman urn. 'Perfect for a busy career girl like Dorothy –' the column's author, Freda DeKnight wrote, 'a perfect mother and a good housewife.'

Ebony magazine was relatively new. The first issue was published just a couple of months after the end of the war. The publisher, John H. Johnson, already had a portfolio that included *Negro Digest* – a breezy mix of celebrity gossip and political news. But things were different for a lot of Black Americans after the war. People who had arrived in the cities a few decades earlier, during the Great Migration, started thinking about the suburbs: a horizontal topography of driveways, porches, lawns, ranch-style houses, highways, a bigger sky. There were Black suburbanites before – working-class Americans who wanted affordable housing, big enough for their extended families, and maybe a garden for growing food – but the post-war exodus was different, more than the inevitable diffusion of people into space. If the first wave came to suburbia to have a shot at survival, this new wave came when survival was no longer enough. 'We were going places we had never been before and doing things we'd never done before,' Johnson wrote. 'We wanted to see that.' So *Ebony* was born.

There were puff celebrity pieces, news items about achievements in the Black America, behind-the-curtain features on people's home decor. It was mostly upbeat. It was filled with adverts that spoke, many for the first time, towards this new Black market. Life is passing time; lifestyle is how you spend it. *Ebony* imagined how these new iterations of a Black lifestyle could look. Naturally, they started printing recipes. The first 'Date with a Dish' column was a smart recipe for no-barbecue barbecue chicken. You started by jointing the chicken and seasoning it well with a dry rub of garlic, hickory salt and paprika. Next you put it in the fridge, giving the bird a few hours to acquiesce to the rub. On to the most important part – a barbecue sauce to spoon over the chicken while it cooked. It was a stable isotope: fourteen ingredients, each too much in its own right but de-escalated when you mixed them together. The meat tenderised and the chicken skin, lacquered with sugar and spice, came up in blackening welts. 'Brown as a berry with hickory flavour cooked in,' promised Freda DeKnight, who headed up the column for more than fifteen years.

Freda's recipes ran towards the back of the magazine. Her job was to show you that you could aspire to a better kind of home life, while preparing you for the worst.

She could tell you how to master pie dough or talk you through the process of arranging a platter of canapés, but she was attuned to the emotional plasma of the kitchen, too. 'Monday morning's refrigerator,' she wrote, 'dotted with small cups of leftover vegetables, congealed gravy, odds and ends of Sunday's roast, is a sight to make inexperienced housewives burst into tears.' Then again, she'd also give you a recipe for tuna and apple salad with celery and olives. 'Just the thing for that bridge party.'

There were geometrically demanding side dishes like green beans and diced onion made into the shape of a Horn of Plenty. A recipe for Swiss steak supreme in which green beans were stacked like logs on top of the braised meat. And Freda wanted to be clear – Black cooking is as diverse as Black cooks. If you found Southern-style recipes in *Ebony*, you also found shish kebab, sweet and sour spare ribs, French-inspired chicken in wine and rose petal pudding. There were cameos from people who were richer than you. A marketing executive, the wife of a defence attorney, a district judge in the Virgin Islands. These weren't people you knew but, as always, whether this is relatable is not the point.

Ebony was the first Black-owned magazine in the United States to have traction with white advertisers, so alongside the ambitious recipes there were advertorials for cheap, almost anti-luxe foods. Cheeseburger loaf made with Carnation evaporated milk, a ten-minute pizza made with tinned tomato sauce, 'Fancy Frank Fry'. Not that it's a contradiction – what we want to see in recipes is usually the things we don't yet have in our lives, precisely because we don't have them. It's always been ambivalent, this kitchen climbing. You browse the magazines, and then you – by which I mean I – put a ready meal in the oven.

I keep thinking about that Dorothy Dandridge photo-shoot, like I keep thinking about Nara Smith. I have a weakness for domestic, even tradwife-coded content. After seeing *17 Kids and Counting* at an impressionable age – the show about a Christian mega-family in Arkansas who, by the time they got to *19 Kids and Counting*, were on the cusp of a public sexual molestation scandal – I briefly decided I wanted to be a serial mum. I have a light interest, if I am being honest, in the Women's Institute, although in a detached kind of way, like how people are curious about what goes on in a Masonic lodge. Still, I've got to my early thirties without yet having children or learning to drive or moving to the suburbs or voting Conservative, for which I'm glad. There's no accounting for why I'm so interested in these women, I tell myself, but then I know that's not true. There are things about Nara Smith that I see in myself – there's something about the vanity of mixed-race women choosing where to stack their bets. And there are things about me that I don't see represented in those pointedly non-queer worlds.

Dandridge has also been on my mind because around the time of the *Ebony* feature, it became clear that her daughter – the co-baker of those coffee cakes – had brain damage. The next year, her marriage broke down. She pulled things together, and then she gave Harolyn over to a full-time carer. She worked her way through racist Hollywood. She pulled things together again, and got an Oscar nomination, then surrendered all her parental rights. She went bankrupt. She went on talk shows. And she died, seemingly of an accidental overdose of antidepressant medication, at forty-two. This isn't a cautionary tale about not believing everything you see, because honestly who does? But you have to wonder who's allowed the beautiful life, when you really get down to it. If good homemaking is about perfect homemakers, that sets you up to fail.

In the pages just before Dandridge's recipes, there was an essay – an appraisal of Black motherhood at the time. 'Something startling and significant has been happening in the kitchen,' it said. 'Just ask Junior, who's been getting his bread and peanut butter sandwiches regularly after school … Or ask Pop, who now comes home to a hot supper of pork chops and greens instead of eating a lukewarm blue plate dinner at Nick's Cafe.' Reading it, you could have believed that the magazine dream had really happened – that now more men were in white-collar jobs, women could leave white people's kitchens and enjoy their own. Homemaking would be a kind of closed-system emotional thermodynamics where no creative energy was lost to the world outside. The story ran under the headline 'Goodbye Mammy, Hello Mom'. Maybe it could be true sometimes. Or maybe not. In New York in the late forties, six out of ten working Black women were still working domestic jobs in other people's homes.

Freda DeKnight died in 1963, and the *Ebony* recipe column changed hands. It was the middle of the Civil Rights movement and a time when ideas about gender and the home were changing. In the sixties and into the seventies, women's liberation and second wave feminism asked if the home was all it was cracked out to be. A perfect cocoon – it can be a safe haven, or it can be a prison. What if being a full-time homemaker didn't make you happy? What if *all* homemaking had been compromised by its roots in a system where women were just expected to do it, no matter what? It wasn't that the high-skill hustle of homemaking was bad, just that it tended to preclude some women from ever doing anything else. And then, there were the people who never got the chance to be shut in – people who either always had to juggle both work *and* keeping a home, or people who never had the pleasure of their own home in the first place. No matter where you stood, the knots that had always run through homemaking were tightening.

Feminist cookbooks worked through these contradictions. *Turning the Tables*, a British cookbook published in the late eighties, featured a few dozen contributors, each with a recipe and reflections from their lives. These are real-life recipes, which is to say recipes that you can tell have actually been cooked, more than once, and not just to test them for the book. Rosamund Grant talks about running a co-operative restaurant. The Chinese Lesbian Group has a recipe for steamed fish with ginger and spring onions. Some people write about their grandmothers' recipes, others about making packed lunches for the night shift. 'This particular time in my life is one of rushed meals,' Sona Osman writes, in the preamble to her rush-rush curry. 'There is a part of me that associates the making of recipes with a middle-class type of book,' she goes on. 'But that is not how I want to write this.'

'We pick our way among our ambivalences.' This is the strength of the book. '[The cooks'] reflections are not homilies for successful femininity,' Dena Attar writes in the introduction. 'Many of them explore the underbelly of family life.' And so they juggle the delicate interconnections of home and childcare, the necessity of work, body politics, questions about taste, race, migration and sex. Cooking is all these things, and it is also a hand-me-down recipe for cornbread. I like the tenderness of this book. You can't separate cooking from gender and home life, but you can complexify its texts.

Turning the Tables built on a couple of decades of work by Black and feminist writers to figure out some other way that cookbooks and cooks could be. 'White folks act like they invented food and like there is some weird mystique surrounding it – something that only Julia and Jim can get to,' Vertamae Smart-Grosvenor wrote in *Vibration Cooking*, first published in 1970. 'There is no mystique. Food is food.' No mystique, maybe, but there are vibrations – undulations and reverberations, through time, between people, tremors along bigger ideological faults. There's redneck ragout and something called 'Nat Turner apple pork thing', for which you aggressively brown pork chops then finish them in a pan with onions and apple. In between, there are letters and observations and recollections from her travels. There's friction – she resists her cooking getting flattened by labels like 'soul food', or by white food media. There are moments when old ideas about gender come to the surface. 'Cooking for a man is a very feminine thing,' she writes, 'and I can't understand how a woman can feed her man TV dinners.' There is also great warmth in her writing, a depth that can only come from loving cooking and what it represents. To really love something is to allow it the space to be complicated – this is as true for cooking as it is for people.

Of course the problem with ambivalence is that it doesn't sell. At least, it doesn't sell ad space. And it doesn't sell crystalware. And if it doesn't do these things, then who's going to publish it? Food media is about consumption. It is, as Nora Ephron put it, 'the new porn'. Once the politics of home cooking became too difficult to be marketable, what do you do? You take the home out of it. You carefully remove the offending contexts and implications, leaving the food free to be only that – food. *Gourmet* started out in 1941 but came into its own in the seventies and eighties when it got bigger and more beautiful and pointlessly luxe. It benefited from the roll-out of full-colour photography, which meant you could see in perfect detail the liver mousseline canapés that you were never going to make. It was all about menus: How about kir with some filled gougères, and jambon persillé, green pepper and potato salad and blueberry streusel? How about canard à l'orange en gelée followed by peach coupes? This was categorically not a homemaking magazine. When it started, it wasn't even written with women in mind.

Around the same time as *Gourmet* hit its stride, *Bon Appétit* went from being a free Chicago periodical to *the* magazine for a new generation of kitchen hobbyists. The circulation of these magazines went up, and the relative popularity of more homemaker-ish magazines like *Good Housekeeping* decreased. Most of the readers were women, but the emphasis had shifted on to food lore, ingredient know-how, travel, hardcore prep skills and cultural deep dives. This level of obsession about food used to belong to committed gourmands, a subculture composed mainly of Liebling enthusiasts, but the magazines – and now the internet – made it mainstream. It marked a huge shift – and one that has shaped the bulk of food culture through until now – away from homemaking kitchen content and towards a way of thinking about food that connected it more directly to either consumption-centric lifestyle content, or capital-C culture. In any case, domestic science and home economy are definitively out. Cooking, if you could even call it that, has nothing to do with domestic work any more. Cooking is about learning, travel, self-improvement, hobbyism, entertaining and impressing people – pretty much everything except feeding the household or yourself.

Since magazine publishing crashed out, it's social media where all of this unfolds, and it's not difficult to find cooking content that caters to your personal needs. You can log on to Pinterest: an ambient, zero-pressure, infinite scrapbook, where the only thing you need to do is look. You can go to the photo and video apps – Instagram and TikTok. Here, there are thousands, millions, of people who will happily show you the right way to cook. Everyone has a personal brand and an aesthetic that's been delicately curated to maximise algorithmic lift. We have influencers, as well as the big-name magazines with legacy standing. *Gourmet* is dead. What's consistent, though, is that we're as ambivalent about homemaking as ever. There are two groups in the food media Venn diagram, and the overlap is the thinnest wisp. One side – the full-ceremony tradwives, and the counterculture of pointedly down-to-earth mommy bloggers, and the homesteaders, and the delightfully practical blogs about how to use up leftovers or feed two people for seven days for £10. On the other side – the ostensibly serious food media, from restaurant critics through to the esoterica of somewhere like Serious Eats. These things do not need to be separate, but they are. I was minding my business the other day, looking for a cookie recipe, when I realised that of the hundred or so cookbooks on my shelves, I could only think of three that actually talked about food in the context of the home. On both sides, we're having trouble letting the ambivalence in.

Recently, because of the political climate and the backslide when it comes to gender and, well, everything, things have started getting spicy in my usually relaxing social media grazing spots. If you've been online at all, you will have noticed an uptick in ambient regressive energy. We're seeing a hardline tradwife revival – not just aesthetic tradwives, but people who weren't alive on the other side of the millennium, and so don't remember the real fifties, or even the real eighties, or even *Nuts*. Before you know it, you're watching reel after reel from a former opera singer turned Mormon influencer farm mom, who by the way might be an anti-vaxxer. The emotional anaesthesia I used to get from lifestyle content is beginning to wear off.

There was a rumour a while back that Nara and Lucky Blue Smith were Trump supporters. Some people were surprised by this, but I took it the same as when allegations came out that Marilyn Manson was a bad guy. The rumours might not be true, but it hardly matters. The Smiths are avatars for something bigger than themselves. American politics are shifting, and the home is coming into focus – again, after all these years – as the battleground on which these ideologies are going to be fought. Reproductive rights, race, gender, queerness, so many rights brought into question in the name of safeguarding the nuclear, neo-1950s home. The pitch-perfect fashion choices of Nara Smith are really beside the point.

There are still corners of the internet where I can tune into a weirdly off-beat, but non-toxic variety of homespun trash. The trick is to let it wash over you, watching it like a Windows XP screensaver, or in the way you'd flick through the photos in a dentist lobby magazine. Don't try to make Cheerios from scratch. Don't fuck around with keto pancakes. You will regret that Shaker kitchen. Listen to me. This is theatre: the silver coupes, the upwardly mobile dessert ideas, the innumerable ways with smoked salmon, the homemade Takis.

This is what the internet does: it confounds things with so much earnest misunderstanding, and then subsequent perversions from the world of memes, until you find yourself looking at a twenty-something-year-old mother of three, making hotdogs from scratch – literally, from ground meat through to the dog-in-a-bun – after a ten-hour flight and in a deep red, heart-front peplum dress, and wonder if she's for real.

There has to be a better way. It will almost certainly be a more complicated way – where the cooking and culture and craft roll into one. Not a fantasy. Not a loveless place where the kitchen is a lab. Not a prison. Not an anthropology lesson. Not an RPG. An ambivalent kitchen, where food can hold multiple meanings at once. This isn't making cooking harder – it's respecting how difficult it already is.

Over the last couple of years, mainly because all this writing has totally thrown my imagination out of joint, I have lost almost all curiosity about cooking. I used to be a hobbyist, one of the pro-amateurs who wanted to understand the technique and deep historical pathways of the things I cooked, and make them with no regard for anything except the food itself. That's gone, at least for now. It's often cereal for meals – a rotating selection of Shreddies and porridge and granola. I used to make the granola myself, though in recent months even that's stopped and I just mainline Nara Smith content on the internet. She's working through something. So am I. But cooking does get done. Usually, it starts because my partner wants something and I want to make him happy, even when I can't be bothered to feed myself. Chicken alfredo. Spinach rice. Yorkshire pudding. This is our home and we work together on feeding it. 'I'm talking about being able to turn the daily ritual of cooking for your family into a beautiful everyday happening.' That's how Vertamae Smart-Grosvenor put it. 'Now, that's something else again.'

How not to use a cookbook

Or, the power and limits of writing about food

Recently, I went to the biggest bookshop in the country and caught cookbook fatigue. The cookbook section of the Waterstones store on Piccadilly is, for those in the know, the centre of the British cookbook world. It stretches uninterrupted, across shelves and groaning tables, snaking around corners, into and out of nooks. Baking, drinks, European, national and regional cuisines, food writing, vegetarian, diets. Everything a person could ever need is here: cookbooks of Instagram-derived recipes with cute covers that could have been designed by Monki; a sea of books by the TV Food Guys – already the biggest over-polluters of the cookbook world during the millennium so far; Phaidon books so heavy that their gravity course-corrects me as I try to walk past. Among them are classics, too: Julia Child, Madhur Jaffrey, Ken Hom.

Many of these are good. Some are even outstanding – the kind of books that you keep as heirlooms or cook from until they're so beaten up that they're barely usable any more. There are cookbooks here that have been written with palpable love and care. There are cookbooks here which have a legitimate claim to having changed our food culture. But I'm in the middle of one of the biggest collections of contemporary food writing in the English language, and I'm fried.

The problem is this: standing surrounded by cookbooks, I can't figure out what all this is *for*. When I step outside, the power of their pages evaporates. I'm tempted by the McDonald's on Shaftesbury Avenue or a ready meal from M&S. If I go home and cook, it will be from a recipe that I search for online. It will never occur to me to open one of the many cookbooks I have on my shelves. Cookbooks have no jurisdiction over the actual food I eat most of the time. The real muscle lies with business, advertising, real estate, social media, industrial product development, the neural link that I now have – and wish I could break – with Google. Meanwhile, Edna Lewis is collecting dust.

The historian Diane Purkiss talks about this – the gap between the stories cookbooks tell and the real food we eat. 'Cookbooks are not the best guide to food history,' she writes in *English Food*. Restaurant menus tell us more because, for the most part, chefs only keep a dish on the menu if it sells. But a recipe can be preserved in a cookbook – even recycled across multiple cookbooks, plagiarised, rehashed and yassified over the generations – and never once be cooked. 'Food in cookbooks is more often a form of what might be than a record of what is.'

In most places, for most of human history, people have learned to cook by talking and showing, and by cooking together in the slow, sometimes frictionful way that works a dish into your memory. Nobody needed a cookbook, so when they were written, it was to create something else more nebulous, and more interesting, than dinner. Cookbooks control the narrative. In the temperature-controlled catacombs of the British Library, I saw one of the versions of the *Forme of Cury* – a manuscript originally written in the fourteenth century by the cooks of King Richard II. The version I saw was a whisper of pages with semi-gothic letters packed tight as Lego bricks. 'First it teacheth a man for to make common pottages and common meats for the household,' it goes, and then there's a recipe for rabbits stewed in a sweet and sour sauce with red wine vinegar, cinnamon and currants. Ultra deep-fill, castle-shaped pies with ramparts and towers and multiple pastry compartments of pork with saffron, almond cream, custard, and fig mincemeat.

This doesn't represent the food of the people. It probably doesn't even accurately reflect the food of the royal court. Even when cookbooks are records of cooking that's already been done, they're only ever interpretations of a truth. In the case of the medieval manuscripts, they tell us about power – how it would look, how it might taste, the recipes that somebody thought reflected well upon the king – or his chef.

Nothing has really changed. In the UK last year, around 700 new cookbooks were published. A decade ago, the figures were even higher – about a thousand cookbooks a year. You wouldn't necessarily guess it, judging by what and how we cook. But there are other ways to read a cookbook – and the cookbook industry. The recipes in the book are just one part of a whole. There is also the shape and tenor of the instructions, the way that photos are used, the introductions and the image captions, the catty foot-note about a recipe that was misquoted somewhere else. There's the paper that they're printed on, the 'As Seen On TV' on the cover, the binding that's designed to stay open on a recipe – and to which no reader has given a single moment's thought. Beyond the cookbook itself, there's how publishing houses are set up and who in those institutions is actually the gatekeeper of the culture, deciding where the commissions get made. There's the way that cookbooks acquiesce, or stand up, to the stranglehold of the super-markets. And there's the frenemy relationship between the restaurant business and the cookbook industry – two mutually parasitic parts of our food cultural world.

The cookbook industry. I want to stress this, because it *is* an industry, and an economy, a market and a matrix of power. This hit me in Waterstones when I was surrounded by those thousands of cookbooks with evocative and some-times emotional stories inside – all of them products to be sold. This materiality is the most interesting thing about them. Especially in a world where you can find any recipe online, for free, any time. The substance of cookbooks is what sets them apart. This is what we pay for. Maybe it sounds romanceless, but I find it refreshing to look at the books this way, not just as culinary bibles, but as objects – and specifically products – in their own right. As records of cooking culture, they're unreliable. But as accidental witnesses to the bigger forces that shape our world, they're invaluable. Between the lines, you find the stories that the recipes leave out. Cookbooks can tell us something about our food culture. They can even shape our diets, some-times. Just not, perhaps, in the ways we might expect.

A Book of Mediterranean Food –
Elizabeth David (1950)

Gregorian history pivots at Anno Domini. British food history, according to British food writers, started in June 1950, or 0 AED, the year that Elizabeth David published *A Book of Mediterranean Food*. When she wrote the book, Elizabeth David was living in a cold London attic flat. A couple of years before, she'd been in the Mediterranean, travelling from the Greek islands to Corsica, Athens and Provence. She lived in Egypt. And now she was back, and even though the war was over, rationing was still going and there was fuck all good to eat. And so she started to write.

She remembered the scent of string-tied bunches of wild marjoram and tiger-striped fish and the way the air whistled through sheep's lungs when you fried them in olive oil. She remembered about market stalls piled up with plump and bruisable figs and 'those long needle fish whose bones so mysteriously turn out to be green'. When she couldn't remember any more, she sank into books about the cooking of Italy and France and filled in the gaps with words. Eventually she'd written a slim, esoteric volume, made mainly from her memories and patched together with scholarship and reading and quotes. She called it *A Book of Mediterranean Food*.

When food writers tell the story of British food – how we went from wartime cookery to being enlightened and worldly and culinarily well-travelled – this diminutive cookbook is usually where they start. Through Elizabeth David, British cooks discovered the tastes of the Mediterranean and then the country cooking of France and Italy. Shops started stocking olive oil. People got word about paella. To cut a long story short, she set off a culinary glow-up that led to everything from the sun-dried tomato supremacy of the nineties to being able to get DOP. Parmesan from a Tesco Express. 'A food writer credited with almost single-handedly changing the cooking in her native England' – that's how her obituary in *The New York Times* described Elizabeth David, when she died in 1992.

Food writers love telling the Elizabeth David story, mainly because it seems to confirm something that we desperately need to believe – that anything we do makes the slightest bit of difference to how other people eat. But this isn't always how things work. In fact, it's rarely how things work. Whenever I think about Elizabeth David, I think about a quote by Mimi Sheraton, the late *New York Times* restaurant critic, who once said that of all the revolutionary changes to food in the post-war years 'not one of these stories began with a food writer'. It was pressure groups on the one side and money on the other side. 'Where are they, these food writers?' she wrote. 'They're off wondering about the boeuf en daube and whether the quiche was authentic.'

Elizabeth David *does* have a recipe for boeuf en daube, by the way, on page eighty-five of my copy of *A Book of Mediterranean Food*. But as Diane Purkiss has pointed out, Virginia Woolf was writing about middle-class families cooking boeuf en daube in 1927. And you could get olive oil by the pint or the litre in late Victorian times, in wholefoods stores where you could also buy Egyptian lentils and Persian dates.

If 1950 was a pivot year, it was for other reasons.

Sainsbury's opened its first self-service store. That same year, the number of British people holidaying abroad hit one million for the first time. Over the next decade, changes in aviation law made flights cheaper and more accessible; people went on package holidays, and took the newly routed commercial flights to places like Valencia. By the end of the Second World War, there were ten times as many Turkish-run cafes in London as there were at the beginning. During the 1960s, because of conflict in Cyprus, thousands of Turkish Cypriots came to the UK too. Native Brits started hearing about feta or halloumi, or went to a local taverna, or ate at a Turkish grill house. Around this time, many Italian people moved to the UK, settling mainly around the south-east. The first Spaghetti House opened in 1955 with the slogan 'spaghetti, but not on toast', with a statement menu, entirely in Italian, that included an antipasto of little sardines and saltimbocca as a main. On it, you can also see the DNA that lives on in every red-checked-tablecloth Italian trattoria in a mid-sized British town – prawn cocktail, meatballs, lasagne, bolognese, escalope, which have so successfully entered the British gastronomic gene pool that they register as comfort food.

In 1973, Britain entered the European Common Market and things like green beans and feta got cheaper and easier to find. When the exchange rate was favourable, people started buying apartments on the Spanish coast. It was like this, really, that we got to the cultural saturation of Mediterranean foods in the eighties – not one origin event but thousands: migrant workers, lines of legislation, trade rules, holiday rental landlordism, tax breaks, employment drives, sun-seekers and subsidies. In that same year, Delia Smith wrote that Elizabeth David had 'influenced eating in Britain more than any other single person' – that she, and her friends, were always cooking from Elizabeth David's books for dinner parties and functions. But that's exactly it: dinner parties, functions, a food writer in a crowd of food writers. Elizabeth David was highly regarded among the people who decide who is highly regarded, which is to say writers, critics, chefs, the dinner party class, an extended ecosystem of tastemakers for whom cooking is a discipline you practise, not something you do.

But this is its own kind of legacy, and maybe it's enough. *A Book of Mediterranean Food* wasn't supposed to track or influence the way that British people ate. It was published four years before the end of rationing. You couldn't make the recipes if you tried. For piments farçis de cailles, you were meant to bone quails, stuff them with foie gras, roll them in cooked rice, stuff the bird into a red pepper, put the red peppers into a dish with butter, tomato sauce and stock, then braise it. There are no quantities, and no explanation about where the dish is from, what it tastes like or how you'd serve it. David knew even while she was writing that these recipes were more like thought experiments than actual texts to live by. This wasn't a problem – the fact they were impossible is exactly why she did it. 'Even if people could not very often make the dishes,' she wrote later, 'it was stimulating to think about them.'

There are few loves as great as that of a person for the cookbooks they never actually use. This is the magic of *A Book of Mediterranean Food*. I don't know if you can really say that Elizabeth David transformed British cooking. But she *did* transform British cookbooks, introducing a generation of cooks to the idea that a cookbook can, and even should, be a work of fantasy. In the era of mass-market cookbooks published by oven manufacturers, and recipes from British Gas, and extremely useful budget cooking pamphlets hanging over from the wartime years, this idea must have been exhilarating. She reimagined cooking literature as exactly that – literature, which you could interweave with quotes from classic novels, and vivid descriptions of places far away. If cooking could share the page with serious, critically legitimate, worldly forms of culture, then maybe cooking was culture, too.

Indian Cooking – Savitri Chowdhary (1954)

A few years after *A Book of Mediterranean Food*, the publisher André Deutsch asked Elizabeth David to edit a series of cookbooks, figuring that when food supplies got back to normal after the war, the middle classes would probably want to recomplicate cooking on their own terms. Elizabeth David set to work commissioning a set of books themed loosely around ingredients or national cuisines. There was a sweet book about cooking with berries, another about Hungarian cooking. Most were smart but forgettable. And then in 1954, the year that rationing ended, they published *Indian Cooking* by Savitri Chowdhary.

The recipes in *Indian Cooking* reflect the everyday complexity of mainly Punjabi home food: semolina halwa and pan-fried gobi, lentil cakes and a medley of pulaos. There are dishes that speak to the melding of Anglo-Indian tastes – kedgeree, dishes soured with tomatoes instead of amchur or tamarind. There is homestyle dahi ki kadhi, made with yoghurt and thickened with besan. Each of these recipes takes a quick but competent racing line – no waffle, no photos, no fuss. Chowdhary wasn't a career food writer but a home cook and housewife, living in Essex. This was her strength. Instead of giving people what she thought they wanted to hear, she started with what was worth knowing.

Indian Cooking was one of a vanishing number of Indian cookbooks written in English at the time. In the 1930s, Veeraswamy's – one of the first Indian restaurants in the UK – produced a cookbook; by the sixties, there was *Mrs Balbir Singh's Indian Cookery* and *Cooking the Indian Way* by Attia Hosain and Sita Pasricha. After the war, Partition had happened, India gained independence, tens of thousands of people came to the UK from India, Pakistan and Bangladesh, and almost nothing else was published about South Asian food in the UK until Madhur Jaffrey's *An Invitation to Indian Cookery* in the seventies. It defies belief, but that's how things go. There's cooking we do, and then the recipes we publish – these things are less connected than we like to think. This gap is partly the work of the publishers and editors who decide which parts of our cooking culture are worth setting down in print.

So much of the story of British cookbooks can be told through the ambitions of its editors. After the André Deutsch series, the Penguin cookery list took over in the writerly, scholarly cookbook niche. Its editor was Jill Norman, who was handed the job of building up a cookery list in the sixties – and not as an honour, by the way, but by men who felt the work was beneath them. Norman bought rights to Elizabeth David, Jane Grigson, Kenneth Lo and more, and published them as small paperbacks, barely illustrated and inexpensive. She was, behind the scenes, one of the most powerful architects of British foodie culture. If editors can be gatekeepers, maybe they can be wayfinders too.

In the end, *Indian Cooking* was one of Elizabeth David's pet commissions. But there's praxis, and then there's just being able to read the market. David was hardly a champion of South Asian cooking or writers – she'd previously described Indian food as 'perfectly frightful' and said that chilli left her unable to taste for weeks. It was a case of right place, right time – a publisher and an editor, meeting at a dinner party in an era of middle-class culinary Columbus-ing and asking themselves under what conditions Indian cooking might sell. In Savitri Chowdhary, they found their talent. Introducing her book, Chowdhary kept things tight – just a few sentences in necessary self-defence. 'I think many people here believe that Indian food is always "hot",' she wrote, presumably in the vague direction of Elizabeth David. 'This is not true.'

Belling Cookery Book (1958)

I never like the answer when I ask my grandmother where she got a recipe. I'm always hoping for something better than: 'I got it from a tin of condensed milk in 1955.' A home economics class in the rationing years. An eighties WeightWatchers card. The back of a cereal box. Or, in the case of her cottage pie – which, if I recall correctly, you make with onion, minced beef, a stock cube and a tin of mushroom soup – 'In my Belling cookbook. It came with the oven.' She's been making it the same way since 1962. I recently bought the 1958 edition of the *Belling Cookery Book* – a baby-blue book, very much slimmer than a Screwfix catalogue and with about as many things that I want to eat. It does not have the cottage pie recipe in.

When we think about our food heritage, we usually pass over books like these. They don't seem to tell a story – or at least, not with their words. The recipes in the Belling cookbook, like so many appliance cookbooks, are bare bones. The preamble is technical: oven temperatures, glossary, grill plate settings. There's no plush sensory descriptions, no world to escape into. Most of the time there's not even an author – these books are ghostwritten by home economists.

And yet this was the way that recipes came into so many people's lives – kind of by accident, on the back of some purchase or other. What happens in cookbook culture is often just the aftershock of whatever is happening in manufacturing, the economy or tech. The Belling oven cookbook told cooks how to use new electric hobs and ovens, lots of them for the very first time. Early career, pre-TV Mary Berry wrote Aga cookbooks. Fanny Cradock was commissioned by the Gas Council to soft-sell gas cooking. You can put most of the cooking literature of the post-war years into two strands: unnecessarily intellectualised little books about European food; and free pamphlets from Kenwood or similar, with recipes for beef rolls. Now, we're living in the age of the air fryer cookbook – they accounted for over half of the top ten best-selling cookbooks last year – which begs the question: When my grandchildren ask me for my recipe for something or other in fifty years' time, am I really going to have to tell them it's from *Pinch of Nom Air Fryer: Quick and Slimming Meals*?

Sainsbury's *Cooking with Herbs and Spices* – Josceline Dimbleby (1979)

'We are living through an exciting moment in the history of food in England,' Josceline Dimbleby wrote, in the introduction to her Sainsbury's cookbook. We used to know how to season our food, she explained – the root-to-stamen school of medieval flavourings meant ginger powder, chervil leaves, peppercorns, rose petals and saffron filaments. And then the Victorians dropped the thread, and French cooking came in vogue, and two world wars happened. But now – in the late seventies – 'after many bland, unadventurous years,' she wrote, 'herbs and spices are creeping back into English kitchens.' There are recipes for lamb's liver with paprika and cumin, spiced eggs with cucumber, and Marrakech meatballs.

Cooking with Herbs and Spices doesn't have ground-breaking recipes, but it is a culture-shifting book. It was one of the first Sainsbury's cookbooks, commissioned when supermarkets were ascendant and British tastes were opening out. You could buy it in the store, and it told you what to do with the possibly novel ingredients that you'd find just a few swings of the trolley away. Over the next fifteen years, Sainsbury's commissioned a couple of dozen cookbooks covering everything from Chinese cookery to cooking for one and regional French cuisine. The authors included Jane Grigson and Ken Hom. Marks & Spencer published cookbooks too, then Tesco. You saw the spice range expand, and packets of wok-ready noodles rise through the shelf hierarchies to eye level. The recipe dreamers and the retail tacticians, the heart and the head.

Serious cookbook authors have long been troubled by a loveless truth: that the reason why people eat what they eat is, more often than not, because that's what the supermarkets sell. You can direct people towards micro-regional Sicilian food all you want, but if the fantasy snags against what you can actually buy in Tesco, it unravels. Food writers try to write around the problem. Elizabeth David described the tactile pleasures of Greek markets the same year that Britain got its first self-service Sainsbury's. Action, reaction; mass culture, counterculture – this is how food writing goes.

The truth is, cookbooks are more powerful when they work with the supermarkets – when we admit that even dreamy, ambitious books are products, just like ingredients as products, and that these products share a commercial ecosystem. When I was writing cookbooks, I remember how much energy was spent trying to make the cookbook the right look, feel, size and format for supermarkets to stock it – this is where the serious sales happened. Delia Smith's publishers warned supermarkets which ingredients they could expect to sell out of when her recipes dropped. Cookbook fanciers will know Claudia Roden for her books about Jewish and Middle Eastern cookery (there's more on her cookbooks later in this list), but as *the* Middle Eastern food expert of the eighties and nineties, Roden was also asked to consult for supermarkets. This was the spinal tap: influencing a product line here, introducing an ingredient there, curating the contents not of a book – which will only ever be read by Food People, anyway – but of supermarket shelves.

Delia Smith's Complete Cookery Course – Delia Smith (1982)

The food your ego wants to make is probably not the food your guests want to eat. All good cooks know this – it's the sense-check that stops us serving canapés and things en croute – but food writers, who have to believe they know best, have trouble accepting it. Cookbook authors try to inspire by edifying, by changing tastes and minds, but lose sight of the fact that most people just want to cook incrementally better, clearer, more reliable versions of the recipes they already know. We want cookbooks with foolproof instructions. We want dust jackets impervious to even the most spiteful turmeric stain. We want to know how long to boil an egg – again, and again, because the answer never sticks.

The success of *Delia Smith's Complete Cookery Course* omnibus is it gave neophobic cooks the things they liked, all in one place, and with absolutely no room for misinterpretation. When you make the English salad sauce, you boil the eggs for 'exactly nine minutes'. You simmer gently. You cover and uncover pans when Delia says so. Ingredients are calibrated down to the quarter-teaspoon.

Delia speaks to risk-avoidant British cooks on a soul level. We avoid surprises at all costs, even if they might be good ones. And so a cookbook of reliably average recipes will fare better, among home cooks here, than one of potentially – but not provably – delightful ones. The only books that have spent more weeks in the bestseller charts in the last fifty years are *Men Are from Mars, Women Are from Venus* and *A Brief History of Time*. The cosmos, the volatile astrophysics of heterosexual gender relations, and then Delia – down to earth, and here to remind you that a soft-boiled egg takes a minute at a simmer, then another six minutes off the heat, in the placid burning water in the tightly-lidded pan.

With hindsight, *Complete Cookery Course* was a blueprint – the first real success story of BBC cookery books. The book was self-contained, with everything a cook at that time could realistically need, but it was rooted in the ten-part BBC series that Delia had presented in the late seventies. For a while, the BBC avoided selling its own cookbooks or promoting those of its stars, because of the commercial conflict. Eventually it figured out a compromise: the world-building TV show, through which you get the vibe of the food, and then the cookbook – published by the slightly separate, commercial arm of the BBC. The two are parts of a whole. '[TV] is a medium of emotion and general impression, but not a medium of detail,' as TV exec Peter Bazalgette put it. 'The programmes axiomatically give rise to the need for recipes.'

Delia's set-up was straight – much the same as a department store appliance demo. But producers learned how to lean into the strengths of the medium, evoking and enticing, rather than teaching. The same year as the omnibus edition of Delia's book came out, there was Madhur Jaffrey's *Indian Cookery* – the series and the accompanying BBC book. A couple of years later, it was Ken Hom. By the nineties, BBC Worldwide was the most powerful cookery publisher in the country. Antonio Carluccio, *Ready Steady Cook*, Rick Stein, Hairy Bikers, *Bake Off*. The magic is in the shows, where the story lives – and the cookbooks make bank.

The Book of Jewish Food – Claudia Roden (1996)

Before she wrote *The Book of Jewish Food*, Claudia Roden wasn't convinced that there was such a thing. No cookbook had meaningfully tackled Jewish food in its entirety before. Some covered the cooking of the Levant, with side notes on the dishes of Jewish kitchens. Others traced the Sephardic Jewish cooking of Spain and North Africa, following a community along specific migratory routes. Some cookbooks thought they spoke about Jewish cooking as a whole, but even then they were really talking about Ashkenazi Jewish cooking – a beginner's lexicon of matzo, apple cakes and chicken soups. Is there Jewish food, really? Or are there only Jewish cooks?

It took Roden nearly fifteen years to arrive at an answer. She tested recipes from every corner of the Jewish world: pumpkin flan from Veneto, walnut and orange Passover cake from Istanbul, a Baghdadi Passover dish of meatballs with garlic and minty sweet and sour sauce, Syrian kibbeh, Hungarian walnut and poppyseed kugel. She wrote about the exacting miniatures of her maternal grandmother's repertoire – pies called pasteliko or bourekita, diminutive but perfectly formed, with mashed aubergine or spinach inside. She invited friends round, who shared their own families' recipes, and others picked up in exile, on work trips, on holiday and at restaurants. As much as it's a Jewish cookbook, this is also a London cookbook: here, in a garden-suburb cul-de-sac, Roden had access to the combined knowledge of representatives from just about every diasporic Jewish group. It is the single most important cookbook ever written on Jewish food. 'Every cuisine tells a story,' Roden wrote. 'Jewish food tells the story of an uprooted, migrating people and their vanished worlds.' You could say Jewish food – as a coherent entity, as a totality – didn't really exist until Claudia Roden wrote it into life.

Cookbooks come alive in moments like this: in exile, in migration, in moments of culture warp. Some of the best cookbooks ever written have been written from just on the cusp of a time, when knowledge is about to slip out of memory, or in a new place, where the chain of transmission of normal, inherited knowledge has been stretched dangerously thin. In the thirteenth and fourteenth century, Muslim scholars wrote recipes about the cooking of Andalucia, collecting their stories in delightful and sometimes passive-aggressive manuscripts. Nobody needed the recipe for sweet-sour beef and chickpea stew. But there are other reasons for writing these things down: this was a time when the Muslims of the Iberian peninsula were being driven out by Christian armies. And so as a scholar, displaced in Tunis, you might want to note down some of the core principles of the food you grew up with – food which, as people are uprooted, could get lost along the way.

So you write down your recipes that use coriander instead of the Christian-coded parsley. You write your beef stew recipe, as one thirteenth-century writer did, and you make a point of mentioning that it's best made with a particular variety of plums. You could only import them 'from the land of the Christians', he wrote. 'May Allah destroy it.'

Some recipes create instant shockwaves – the sheet-pan drop cookie technique, the viral tomato feta pasta – and are forgotten just as quick. *The Book of Jewish Food* isn't like this. Over the last twenty-five years it has diffused slowly through the culture and its gravity is now inescapable – the ur-text for all subsequent work on Jewishness and food, not just a book of Jewish food, but *the* book. Read any cookbook about Jewish cooking, go into a new-wave deli, cook from an Ottolenghi recipe, open a magazine about food culture and you'll feel the influence of Roden's masterwork. Its stories are retold by countless food writers. Its references and recipes are rehashed. Roden has got to be one of the most cited – and plagiarised – food writers of the past century. This is the measure of her power.

Mary Berry's Baking Bible – Mary Berry (2009)

There is nothing particularly interesting about the recipes in *Mary Berry's Baking Bible*, and yet in a roundabout way this book has had a greater impact on British baking than the previous fifty years of cooking literature combined. More than Elizabeth David's Talmudic *English Bread and Yeast Cookery*, or Andrew Whitley's cult favourite *Bread Matters. Baking Bible* was published the year before the first season of the *Great British Bake Off* aired on the BBC: it set the tone for the show, it cast the judge, it provided some of the recipes. It was the first unofficial *Bake Off* book.

Bake Off has been, to the publishing industry, what a long, hot summer is to Walls. Each series presents twelve potentially lucrative nerds and screen-tests them in front of a few million viewers. There's time to drill down into your niche: the baking science one, the gluten-free one, the experimental one. When I went on the show, we were given the contact details of literary agents before the first episode had even aired and given the licence to the *Bake Off* roundel for the front of our inevitable cookbook, like a royal seal. By 2016, over four million official or unofficial *Bake Off* cookbooks had been sold. By now, about a hundred such books have been published. In the *Great British Bake Off* tent, the Battenbergs are a front for the printing press out back.

I did write a baking book in the end. I took this seriously, and justified being a twenty-one-year-old in the already overwritten world of baking books by coming up with 'new' recipes, like lemony cupcakes with chunks of marzipan, and an opera gateau with blackcurrant jam and coffee liqueur. Nothing hung on these recipes being definitive or even good. A cookbook like this is just the thinking cook's souvenir T-shirt. Not that I realised this at the time. I thought I was going to set down a new canon of modern baking with my passionfruit curd Swiss roll and my refusal to touch a piping bag. A new way of doing things, I thought, while I copied the sensibility of Dan Lepard's *Short and Sweet* almost note for note.

It reveals something that serious cookbook fanciers don't

like to admit about their recipes, but must: that cookbooks – even the most high-minded ones – are ancillary to
screens. It used to be TV chefs like Keith Floyd or Delia.
Then it was the many cookbooks of the *MasterChef* and
Bake Off factories. More recently, printed recipes follow
on from Facebook pages, TikTok videos, YouTube channels and blogs. In 2022, Jamie Oliver hosted *The Great
Cookbook Challenge* – a hybrid cooking slash reality competition show format in which contestants competed for a
Penguin cookbook deal. It was axed after the first season,
the producers having had the audacity to say the quiet
part loud.

Plenty – Yotam Ottolenghi, photography by Jonathan Lovekin (2010)

A recipe writer is lucky if they create just one recipe that
people actually make – a recipe that alters, in some tangible
way, the course of food culture. Yotam Ottolenghi, with
his collaborators and test kitchen, has written at least four
cookbooks that you could credibly accuse of doing just
this. The debut, *Ottolenghi*, was co-authored with Sami
Tamimi and became one of the most successful restaurant
spin-off cookbooks ever published in Britain. *Jerusalem* –
another Tamimi project – complicated the stories of the
city where the authors both grew up and introduced thousands of British cooks to a Mediterranean beyond the sliver
of Provence and Italy on to which Elizabeth David had
opened the door. *Simple*, co-authored with Tara Wigley and
Esme Howarth, has sold almost half a million copies in the

UK and secured the fortunes of rose harissa for the next decade. But it's *Plenty* – the second Ottolenghi cookbook, published in 2010 – which has done the most to change how middle-class British people fuss over their food.

Like Jane Grigson's *Good Things*, *Plenty* is an edited collection of newspaper columns – in this case from Yotam Ottolenghi's *Guardian* column, 'The New Vegetarian'. The 'new' really meant something – it *was* new, at the time, to write vegetarian recipes not as a vegetarian, not as praxis, not as a kitchen gardener, but starting from the happy, contagious belief that these flavours were just exciting. A 'mixed grill' made with kohlrabi and courgettes and turned with parsley oil. Spiced red lentils with cucumber yoghurt. Soba noodles with aubergine and mango. If these kinds of recipe sound nice, if normal, now, it's because *Plenty* has done its job – it has, over the intervening fifteen years of prolific recipe content creation, course-corrected the entire culture.

'We never replicate a recipe,' Yotam Ottolenghi said in a *New Yorker* interview back in 2012, a couple of years after *Plenty* came out. 'We replicate the *idea* of a dish.' He was talking about the iterative power of Jewish food as its cooks move from place to place, but this one point – *the idea of a dish* – has since become not just the bedrock of the Ottolenghi philosophy, but the foundation of a modern recipe culture. I talked about this in the first chapter of this book, but it's hard to overstate just how seismic this shift of mindset has been. From named dishes to permutations of ingredients, from a cuisine to individual constructions, from time-honoured flavour accords to pick-and-mix blends drawn from a global pantry. It is everywhere, it is Mob, it is za'atar in Waitrose, it's the many scions of the Ottolenghi Test Kitchen, it's a way of looking at recipes – breaking them down, building them up. When you cook this way, you find that there are as many recipes to be made (and sold) as stars in the expanding sky. 'I'll start with something as simple and unassuming as rice,' Ottolenghi wrote, opening the cookbook that changed it all. 'I immediately go dizzy with the countless possibilities.'

The Roasting Tin – Rukmini Iyer, photography by David Loftus (2017)

Cookbooks belong to one of three categories. First are the self-improvement books – diet books, even if they don't call themselves that – that promise to transform your body or your wellbeing. These run the gamut from old-fashioned calorie counters to protein-packing regimes. The second group are the 'problem solvers', designed to make cooking as frictionless as possible or at least get it over and done with quickly. Thirty-minute, five-ingredient, one-pot recipes made in an instant pot or an air fryer – anything that promises a hack. The third genre is the dream cookbook. This includes anything from Martha Stewart's fever dream Christmas books to *A Book of Mediterranean Food*. Here there's less of the food, and more of the context.

Of the three categories, the optimising and problem-solving cookbooks are by far the most popular. It has always been like this. In the sixties it was Peg Bracken's *The I Hate to Cook Book*. By the nineties it was *The Cosmopolitan After-Work Cookbook*. But there's an intensity now in this kind of publishing, as if we can never cook – or write – fast enough to keep up with our appetites. Look through the bestseller charts and you see that of the thousands of cookbooks published in the UK in 2023, the top twenty contained just one cookbook that wasn't about diets, air fryers or cooking as quickly as you possibly can. These are the optimising, problem-busting, keyboard-mash modern cookbooks, forced to compete with an online recipe universe that will always beat it in practical terms. As how we find and buy books has changed, so have the books themselves, skewing towards SEO micro-calibrated concepts, their titles and covers optimised for the internet instead of the browsable bookstore shelf. These are cookbooks for the Amazon age. *Pinch of Nom. How to Make Anything in an Air Fryer. Bored of Lunch.* Mob. *The Ultimate Air Fryer Cookbook.* Thug Kitchen. *Complete Air Fryer Cookbook.* Bosh. Jamie's *5 Ingredients.* Jamie's *One.* Jamie's *Easy Air Fryer.* Jamie's *15-Minute Meals.* If you're a cookbook nerd, you won't want to believe this. Everything is hacked and reduced to prime factors. This is what you'd get if you handed over the creative, tactile process of cooking to a management consultancy firm. It is what you get when cooking, like so much of our harried lives, becomes a job to be optimised.

There are more humane ways of doing things. I met Rukmini Iyer when she was working as the food stylist on my first cookbook, when I was fresh out of *Bake Off* and she was a *MasterChef* graduate. My cookbook didn't do much in culture-shaping terms, but Rukmini has arguably had more of an impact on day-to-day British mealtimes than any other writer in the last decade. Her idea was simple: dinner, but cooked in a single roasting tin. It was the cookbook industry marketer's dream, riffable along every conceivable theme, from vegetarian cooking to speed cooking. (*The Quick Roasting Tin* crossover book has, predictably, been the best seller in the series.) Under the stewardship of cooking authorities like Harold McGee or J. Kenji López-Alt, we've been conditioned to fear and revere cooking science, but Rukmini's coup was to realise that you could avoid this worry, for the most part, if you simply shut the oven door. You can even make risotto this way. 1.75 million copies sold and counting, and the exhilarating moral of the story is just – 'Do Less'.

People have been cooking one-pot dinners for as long as they've had to bear the cross of washing up, but this was cute and intentional, styled out like a pair of immaculate, pre-distressed, jeans. The aesthetics are integral – and this, just as much as the methodological home run, made the *Roasting Tin* books what they are. Stew, lurking in the twilight of a deep crockpot, is an undifferentiated muddle, trusty but unchic. But in a broad, flat roasting tin everything pops: pasta dishes can be presented with expressionistic flair, tomatoes take a char, halloumi crisps and its vertices deepen through shades of copper and taupe. David Loftus, one of the most prolific photographers in modern British food, created a world of tightly schematised visual overload: flat-lay shots where the tins become the picture plane, artfully styled, laid against bright colour backdrops. There's no outside world here, no context, no light and shade, no fuss – just a single perspective point, all eyes on the roasting tin.

Dishoom – Shamil Thakrar, Kavi Thakrar and Naved Nasir (2019)

It is getting increasingly difficult to escape Dishoom. In 2010, the first Dishoom restaurant opened in Covent Garden, serving food influenced by the Parsi cafes of Mumbai. In the years since, it has expanded laterally in the ways you might expect: more branches across the city, then in other British cities, and – rumour has it – potentially overseas. People come out in numbers for Dishoom. You see them queueing halfway down the street for the lamb chops. But in the last few years it has also started to break into homes. It comes in various guises: Dishoom chutney sets, Dishoom IPA, Dishoom prints, Dishoom body wash, and the pandemic-era Dishoom bacon naan roll kit. In 2019, co-founders Kavi Thakrar and Shamil Thakrar, and chef director Naved Nasir, wrote the *Dishoom* cookbook.

Restaurant cookbooks have been around for a long time. In 1936, S. K. Cheng of London's Shanghai Restaurant wrote the *Chinese Cookery Book*. The 1970s saw an uptick, the *Cranks* cookbook brought the particular beige of a vegetarian restaurant in central London to the suburbs, while in the United States, there was the *Moosewood Cookbook* and titles from Chez Panisse. During the nineties, there was *The River Cafe Cook Book*, and the Ottolenghi era started in 2008, with their self-titled debut based around the food served in the delis. These books vary. Some are more about the chef, while others foreground the restaurant. Some are only loosely inspired by the restaurant dishes, while others follow the menu almost to the letter.

It can feel like a binary – maybe even *the* binary upon

which British food culture is built: dining out versus home cooking. But restaurants and cookbooks are symbiotic, and the two feed inexorably and circularly into each other's hype. The *Dishoom* cookbook has all the greatest hits, from the gunpowder potatoes to the house black dal. I've seen these dishes hundreds of times online – photos from the home cooks dovetailing with Instagram stories from Americans on nights out at the restaurants. What emerges is not just Dishoom the restaurant and *Dishoom* the cookbook, but Dishoom the cohesive, omnipresent, multi-ruthlessly effective brand. The cookbook has sold about 300,000 copies in the UK and is still going strong. It's arguably the most successful restaurant cookbook of the last twenty years.

The impact of the *Dishoom* cookbook is even more impressive when you look at the state of the cookbook charts. Of the hundred bestselling cookbooks of 2024 in the UK, *Dishoom* was the only one to specialise in a non-Western cuisine. There were diet books and baking books and pan-Mediterranean books, plus a couple – Rukmini Iyer's *The Roasting Tin Around the World* and some Ottolenghi ones – that used global ingredients in a non-specific, fusiony kind of way. But only *Dishoom* represented a specific cuisine from outside of Europe and North America. We pride ourselves in the UK on the breadth of our palates, but if the average British person is eating other cuisines, they're not cooking them at home.

But Dishoom gets around that predictable white British mental block about cooking South Asian food. People have been there, they have tried it, they know how these flavours knit together. Maybe now, in the Dishoom age, British people will finally learn not just how to eat spice, but how to use it. Or perhaps the *Dishoom* cookbook will sit there, beautiful and unbothered – a forever souvenir from a great meal out you once had.

'Cook remaining 100 lobsters'

Or, the modern cook's guide to entertaining

I was thirteen when *Come Dine with Me* first aired. I remember it being there in the sub-primetime miasma and I'd end up watching it after school. The premise was so simple, so obvious, that it's amazing that it hadn't been done before. In this show, which has now been on British television for twenty years, contestants take it in turns to throw a dinner party at their home. This is usually a painful thing to watch because very few of the contestants can cook, but also – and I guess this is for the cameras' sake – the dining rooms are lit like interrogation rooms. Everyone scores the parties out of ten in the taxi home, and then after all is done a winner is announced. It's an elegant format, competitive dinner partying, because this is ultimately just what dinner partying is, cameras or not.

This was during the late Cretaceous period for terrestrial TV – the lively few years before streaming came along and changed it all. Nobody searched for the good stuff, you just channel-hopped until you landed on the least bad thing that's on. This suited *Come Dine with Me*.

If you were born before the millennium in Britain, you know the beats, you've seen the second-gen memes, you know the note-perfect schadenfreude of watching a person serve disastrous soufflé to a group of people who've only met each other twice and already hate each other with a passion worthy of the Greeks.

Looking back now I wonder whether thirteen was too young for this. You only need to look at what happened next. By age fourteen, I was getting into baking from my mum's copy of *How to Be a Domestic Goddess*. By fifteen I was drinking. By sixteen I'd fallen into a crowd who were running their own *Come Dine with Me* ring. Who knows what any of us cooked. All I know is that I wrote about a dozen versions of my menu before I got things straight. I vaguely recall that the highlight was Hayley's Christmas dinner, where the food ran the whole length of the table and for which her parents did nearly all the prep. I considered this cheating at the time, but it was for the best.

There are things a person can learn from *Come Dine with Me*. Firstly, not to mess with chocolate fondant. It reminds you that you are a host, not a chef, and you can't spend the night in the kitchen – not least because every minute you're away from the table is a minute your guests can spend talking about you. But we were thirteen and all this was lost on us. We thought the contestants were ridiculous and we could do it better; we didn't realise yet that the dinner party itself was the butt of the joke.

Every generation puts their own spin on entertaining. 'In America since the repeal of the Prohibition Amendment,' James Beard wrote in *Hors d'Oeuvre and Canapés*, 'there

has developed a new and, at times, delightful form of hospitality – the cocktail party.' This called for a new menu of
snacky but impressive pre-made buffet fare and finger food.
In the mid-thirties, Beard opened a hyper-specialised cocktail party shop selling sandwiches where there was sliced
meat in place of the bread, and cucumber slices topped
with who knows what, and pâté-stuffed artichoke hearts.
They sold baked hams and, for buffet set-ups, pre-made
vats of vichyssoise. It was all so unnecessary and so magical.
It makes sense that one of his business partners, Bill Rhode,
ended up being one of the first editors of *Gourmet*.

The shop didn't last, but in 1940 Beard wrote the hors
d'oeuvre book. 'The appetizer has become streamlined,' he
wrote, 'along with our trains and automobiles and living.'
Apparently this meant out-there fruit curry, salpicon of
celery and puff pastry allumettes. These days most people
would die before they hosted a party for which the primary instrument is a piping bag, but it felt modern at the
time and you have to remember that outrageousness is
subjective. In other times, people threw banquets, formal
Victorian dinners with quantum etiquette, or luxury picnics. Every one of these, from the menu down to the
geometry of the napkins, is the ultimate in small-time
ambition – silverback stuff, but through the medium of
River Cafe 'Chocolate Nemesis Cake'. ('I don't know why
everyone finds it so difficult,' they would say.) They're a
fairground mirror for the bigger neuroses of the time.

Dinner parties as we know them peaked in the seventies
and eighties. As far as I can tell, this period was bookended
by two things: women's lib, and the invention of Viennetta.
Who wants to be a good housewife if you can be a great

host? The ur-text for aspiring hosts was *Gourmet*, where each month about 500,000 readers could dream about, but almost certainly not cook, the centrefold menus – for, say, a summer luncheon of chicken in tarragon jelly or a cocktail party menu including endive barquettes piped with Roquefort cream. Everything about these spreads was deliciously contrived, and the full-page photos showed mathematically precise place settings. Nothing was ironic. Of course you'd serve toasts à la suisse with a bottle of Scharzhofberger '71. What a fantasy – a life where this stuff was just kind of a given.

In the eighties, dinner parties reached their delusional zenith. Rich people were richer and had to invent increasingly stupid ways to spend their money. Chefs had the latitude to define themselves as creatives. A cult of creativity brought dishes into conversation with each other: now things didn't keep to themselves on their own menu in their own restaurant; more than ever, they were cross-referenced with this dish across town, or this other chef's take on the same premise. Home cooks must have absorbed this energy, because before you knew it cooks had thrown out cocktail parties and were turning their own homes into restaurants, with sit-down multi-course dinners and high-concept plating. Martha Stewart had manifested – as befits the decade, she was an investment banker before she was an entertaining guru – and it all got out of hand.

By the tail end of the dinner party golden age, people were tired. You started to see freezer food appear, lifting the burden of ornamentation that home cooks had taken on. There were things like hand-finished chocolate orange gateau, cloaked with chocolate shavings and topped with rosettes of something similar to cream. You didn't have to belong to the *Gourmet* elite any more to know the grammar of raspberry vinegar and cheese fondue. And then Viennetta was invented in the eighties, and that was that. It was all too easy, and once it was too easy you had to find something else difficult to do.

Nobody admits to throwing dinner parties any more. They were done even by the time *Come Dine with Me* started. I put the omertà some time around the turn of the millennium, after the general nineties shift towards more low-key food styling. You had natural erotics – things like zoomed-in photos of roasted, collapsing figs in juice. You know the deal. In the early era of Jamie Oliver, his shows were mainly about him having people over to eat – just a bunch of guys in a set designed to look like a bachelor pad. *Having people over.* This was the way you put it. Even Nigella has renounced dinner parties. Instead, she has ten to twelve people over for a casual, home-style meal, in the garden under a canopy of fairy lights and with a table setting colour scheme of pink and pale jade green.

This has led to widespread confusion and I think it's important we clear things up. For the last twenty years, middle-class hosts who would never dream of throwing a Martha Stewart-style dinner party – and who will not fail to tell you this – have been worshipping at the Ottolenghi altar of contrived carelessness. Nothing is placed, even a herb: things are strewn and scattered; things are designed to come to the table in the dish they were cooked in, 'family-style', which has had the effect of sending the sales of gorgeous, colourful, show-piece cast-iron cookware through the roof. Nora Ephron stopped buying *Gourmet* magazine in 1972: 'One night at a dinner party, a man I know looked up from his chocolate mousse and said, "Is this Julia's?" and I knew it was time to get off.' I've had similar experiences with Ottolenghi, except now it's not a dinner party, it's just dinner, or having people over, or dining in, or throwing something together, or whatever thing you want to call it that skirts around the facts.

Anyway, there are a few ways to tell whether you're at a dinner party. If there are nibbles, it is a dinner party. Nobody will call them hors d'oeuvre, but that's exactly what they are. Other aliases include crudités, snacks, dips, picky bits and appetisers. Running the numbers on dinner parties can be difficult, but as a rule the following is true: a dinner party has a minimum of five people (this throws off the balance, which allows awkwardness, which is what sets this apart from a normal dinner); at least three of the diners cannot be family or flatmates; and ideally at least two people must be strangers to one another. You will get the hang of all this. If the table is already set when you arrive, it is a dinner party. Most importantly: if anything – even the position of a table lamp – has been done to alter the lighting of the room from its usual state, it is a dinner party.

I've been guilty of this. My *Come Dine with Me* era stopped in my late teens, and I disowned any cooking that seemed like trying too hard. Style over substance, I would say about the Magnolia Bakery-era bouffant-buttercream cupcakes that I actually secretly liked. And then I entered *Bake Off*, and despite everything that show stands for, I made a point of not doing anything that could be understood to look beautiful. I leaned towards the crustier side of baking – kamut flour instead of rose sugarcraft, traditional wreaths instead of novelty shapes – and even when the judges mandated making something extraordinary, I thought it would be better to subvert it. This is how I came to make a foot-tall biscuit tower, but in the shape of a dropped ice cream cone.

The trouble is this: when you're cooking for yourself, the question you probably start with is – how much effort am I willing to make today? When you're cooking for other people, the question is how much effort do I want to look like I'm making? This is where things start to go wrong. I never wanted to look keen, but by the time you're on *Bake Off* – or throwing a low-stress dinner for which you've had to hire a chafing dish – the jig is up. Think of it as a quadrant chart, running from low-effort to high-effort cooking across one axis, and *looks like* low effort to looks like high effort up the other. Something like *Gourmet* is high-effort food, made to look as taxing as possible, leaving guests in no doubt about how much you resent them for eating it. Cocktail parties at their most popular were low effort – housewives were helped by a gamut of processed convenience foods – but designed to look fancy. Low-effort, low-aesthetic food is just having people around for a pizza – what most of us really want. But now the way to do things is making a lot of effort, while making things look carefree.

Nobody is doing this better than Alison Roman, a former *Bon Appétit* recipe developer who became a celebrity in her own right in the late 2010s. Her books have become manuals for every thirty-something with an Ikea dining table big enough to receive guests. *Dining In*, *Nothing Fancy* and *Sweet Enough* – her approach skews louche but also candlelit and garlic-forward and sexy. It is sprezzatura in action. It is exactly the right number of buttons left undone on a crisp white shirt. The recipes *are* less involved than the old, piping-bag-centric menus of the seventies, but this isn't to say they're totally honest. The effort has only been moved: instead of putting hours into presentation and calligraphy lessons just to write a place card, all the effort goes into sourcing the best produce and calibrating the exact level of char that will make something look like you left it in the oven for a minute too long, while you were busy lighting a Diptyque candle for the table. It's the behind-the-scenes effort of top-and-tailing gooseberries or going to the different shops to find the ideal pasta shape.

I had a change of heart a while back. I don't know exactly what brought it on, except that one moment I was cooking fifteen-minute pasta dishes for my dinner – which I would take in bed, and with Netflix on – and the next moment I was planning a croquembouche for my first time hosting a dinner party since the DIY *Come Dine with Me* years. I ended up baking over 100 choux buns, each the size of a ping-pong ball, in five batches. I had to use a calculator and revisit my secondary school maths to figure out the incline of the conical tower, and how many puffs I'd need for each tier. I filled half the choux with chocolate hazelnut cream, and the other half with vanilla custard, and fortified the structure with almost a kilo of hard caramel. Everyone loved it as far as I can tell, although you have to wonder whether it would've been so impressive back in the croquembouche era, when young urbanites were, presumably, faced with a few of these every month.

After the party, when I was packing away the eighty-odd leftover choux buns, I felt great. This is the thing that everyone understands about entertaining but nobody is supposed to say: that it is about the host, no matter what they tell you, and this is fine. This is my dinner party. The problem, in this earnest not-dinner-party era, is that we're so scared of seeming fake that we want even the most special food to seem like it's what we eat everyday. 'This isn't how people cook,' you might think when you see a *Bon Appétit* Thanksgiving mega-feature or a Martha Stewart menu for a fifty-person pie party, but you would be wrong. Real cooking is *exactly* like this – making the same five dishes on rotation for 363 days of the year, and then getting wildly above your station for the remaining two.

I have been thinking a lot about this, and I think it's time to seek counsel from Martha Stewart. If you have not seen her eighties debut cookbook, *Entertaining*, you need to find a second-hand copy. 'When I lived in a six-room apartment on Riverside Drive,' she begins, 'I used to have sit-down dinners of eighteen as a monthly matter of course.' And you are in. Who can find the strength in their heart to find a dozen extra glasses, let alone wash them up afterwards, just so you can serve sautéed mushrooms under a cloche? Who is making eight dozen pierogi as just one part of a multicourse Easter meal that includes madeleines baked in the shape of bunnies and dipped in chocolate? Who is dressing a serving table with asparagus ferns? It's despicable. It's also fantastic. What Martha has been trying to teach us all for over four decades, even though nobody seems to be listening, is that entertaining is *not* cooking.

Entertaining is to real cooking what drag is to the sweat-shirt you wear to the gym.

It is hard to unsee what you will see in Martha's book. I love sentences like 'you might borrow or rent a silver samovar' or – my favourite – 'cook remaining 100 lobsters'. I'm afraid we'll lose this in the AI age, because what intelligence outside of the dankest, most brilliant corners of a truly human mind could come up with 'Summer Omelette Brunch Outdoors for Sixty'? Lesser cooks try to simplify entertaining, but Martha sees your tired old formats – the cocktail hour, the dinner party – and raises you a dozen new ones, from the omelette brunch to a country pie party for fifty. The soirée dansante menu is a dessert party for forty people, featuring oeufs à la neige, kiwi tartlets, meringue kisses, Robert heart, almond torte and a handful of other desserts of your choosing. You invite people over late in the night, get them drunk and then open the doors to a second room where the lights are dim and tables croak under the weight of desserts, cakes, fruit, coffee, and cream. White damask cloth. A tiny crystal bell. Crème caramel garnished with candied orange peel. You can read this stuff like poetry.

Martha learned to entertain from her mother, she says, who seemed to be able to put together something special even at late notice. This instilled in her a love of caring for people through food, making them feel at home. James Beard said the same thing – a memory of a mother who somehow made everything feel so magical, no matter whether she was serving cold roast meats or making a feast on an old wood range. Both took these memories and made it their mission to delight people – before they went mad with the power. It's about allowing your guests the illusion – just like parents allow us – that beautiful things don't have to hurt. That's the real gift.

Everybody seems to have their own rules for entertaining, and they rarely agree except on principles so vague as to be useless, like 'don't overcomplicate things'. James Beard's hors d'oeuvre book starts with eleven pages of dos and don'ts. Here are a few things that I will add to the noise, because I want you to experience the rush I got when I presented that croquembouche to a candlelit table of friends. Everybody was delighted, and I was delighted, too – not because people were pleased, but because *I* was the one who had pleased them, and it really did feel good.

- Firstly, delusional thinking transcends class. You do not have to be in the striving middle class to entertain. The beginning of any dinner party is making an unrealistic budget that you'll definitely overshoot. You can do this at any price point.
- There must always be too much food. This isn't right but it's true.
- For those who want to slip around the dinner party injunction, a few Martha-inspired suggestions, while you're here: pie parties, chicken wing and beer parties, build-your-own ice cream sundae parties, Iceland party foods parties, dumpling-making parties.
- Adjust the lighting. Nobody wants to eat under The Big Light. And besides, how else will people know it's a dinner party? Candles are cute, and fairy lights are even better.

- Everybody will be happy to see you bring out a tray of hot sausage rolls, and even happier if you haven't made them yourself.
- Better to turn to novels and films for inspiration than to cookbooks. Cooks get caught up in practicalities, but novelists live in a dreamier state, and this is exactly how you want your guests to feel. It's this contempt for practicality that makes Martha so mesmerising. She cites D. H. Lawrence as an influence – the magic of the picnics in *Women in Love*, with that 'large broad-faced cut ham, eggs and cresses and red beetroot, and medlars and apple tart and tea'. To this end, I can also vouch for Brian Jacques' *Redwall* books.
- Dress up.
- Entertaining is an invented and avoidable problem. Nobody is making you do this. If you're not enjoying it, almost nobody else will, and you hate the one person who does.
- The easiest way to get visual contrast is simply to cook things very slightly too high, and for very slightly less time than you think. (With the help of a meat thermometer, please.) This way the outsides get crisp and conditions are met for chiaroscuro skins and deep tan crusts, and saves you the trouble of scattered herbs.
- You can't do 'natural cornucopia' without money. I'm sorry. Platters of strawberries and fresh whipped cream are romantic when the Instagram girls do them, but if you're working with Teflon strawberries and Elmlea, an ice cream sundae is a smarter way to go.
- Nora Ephron wrote about the rule of four. Often dinners are organised around a trinity – meat, starch and

veg. But you should add a fourth thing, she said, something fun, something to unbalance the composition. This makes things interesting. 'A shallow dish filled with tiny baked apples,' she suggests. 'Peaches with cayenne pepper.' Later, she went on to concede that better than the rule of four is the rule of five, or even six. She is right. These unnecessary additions should be weird. A jellied tureen. Clam bake for thirty. A simple croquembouche. Of utmost importance: this thing, whatever it is, contributes nothing to the menu as a whole.

- Get into a Martha state of mind. 'A youthful belief,' as she puts it, 'in the value of treats.'

Impulse buy

impulse buy

Supermarket fugue

Or, an experiential history of four superstores

In 1930, Michael J. Cullen – a man with a messianic belief in high-volume retail – wrote a six-page letter to the vice-president of Kroger, the American grocery store chain. As a store manager, he was frustrated by the inefficiencies, overheads and high prices of the small stores. His letter laid out a plan: self-service would replace costly and labour-intensive counter service. Car parking would expand the stores' catchment area. He proposed 'monstrous' shops with economies of scale and slim profit margins. Some of these elements existed piecemeal across other grocery chains, but they'd never been brought together under one roof. 'Nobody in the world ever did this before,' he wrote. 'Nobody ever flew the Atlantic either, until Lindbergh did it.'

Together, these changes would add up to what we'd recognise now as a modern supermarket. It would be big and intense and free-flowing and, most importantly, somehow fun. It would gamify what for most people had been a chore. 'Weekdays would be Saturdays, rainy days would

189

be sunny days,' Cullen wrote. 'It would be a riot. I would have to call out the police.' He wrapped up by asking for $15,000 investment in the project. He got no reply so he did it himself, buying a vacant garage in Queens, New York, and turning it into a madcap temple to the American bargain.

The first branch of King Kullen opened its doors on 4 August 1930. Cullen took out ads for 'The World's Most Daring Price Wrecker – KING KULLEN'. People travelled 100 miles to try it out. It was built for the needs of the suburb – large, sedate and amenable to cars. A photo of the Rockville Center King Kullen from 1940 shows a long, low building – around 6,000 square feet of floor space – with dedicated parking in the front of the store. 'How does he do it?' one huge sign read. Today, deep into the age of the supermarket, this would come off rhetorical. Well, he does it by doing things the way that things are done. But back then the question still meant something. How could you have a store this big, and this cheap? What kind of economies could sustain a place like this? Cullen grew the business from one warehouse to a chain of thirty stores.

The Smithsonian Institution has a definition of super-markets: low prices, high volumes, subdivisions, being part of a chain – pretty much everything Cullen suggested. We know a supermarket when we see it. You distinguish it by its size, or metres of shelf space, footfall, parking, turnover, the number of products, conveyor belts, its ambition, whether or not it's possible to navigate a trolley through its aisles, whether it even has trolleys, whether it even has aisles.

At the centre of all this is self-service. Until the early twentieth century, shops ran on counter service: you asked a sales clerk for whatever you needed, and they picked it from behind the counter, then wrapped and bagged it. It was a sociable way to shop. It was also long-winded – you can see why homemaking was a full-time job. Today, sales-people are pretty much gone and the packaging sells the products. Walk down any supermarket aisle and thousands of impeccably marketed foods will scream at you with all-caps promises and bright colours and logos so burned into your psyche that you could recognise them at 100 paces.

I love supermarket fugue states – staring, touching things, picking food up, putting it down, meandering without really remembering why I came here in the first place. I pick up and put down a pack of Haribo Goldbears and a two-litre bottle of cherryade. I'll wonder whether today's the day that I'm finally going to buy a gala pie, but I never do. I'll get a marked-down loaf of bread that will definitely grow mould before I can eat it. I'll walk around this store – this one node in a global consumption economy that has completely reconfigured what and how we want – but I won't see it. All I will see are tens of thousands of products, from every continent, packaged any time between five years ago and yesterday. I'll start feeling the effect of the edible I took before I went out, and the possibilities will wash over me. On 12 December 2022, on X (formerly Twitter), @boywaif tweeted: 'I had a french professor who once said if you just did something like going to the supermarket and experienced it fully without the goggles of habit and catégories you would go crazy with pure sense and joy.' For better or worse, I know exactly what they mean.

Supermarkets are designed to work on these easily

hackable circuits of the human brain. What if you cut the distance between wanting and buying to the narrowest synaptic jump, so that anything feels possible? The academic Rachel Bowlby describes the feeling as an 'endless perhaps'. By 1955, almost half of all groceries sold in the United States were sold through supermarkets. 'They continue to dazzle the ladies,' explained a feature in *Life* magazine that year. 'To the woman of today, the grocery store is not a challenge but an inviting place to spend an hour.'

It's not even been a hundred years since King Kullen, and look at us. Supermarkets have replaced cathedrals. This is where we perform our secular modern rituals – the slow procession around the stations of the shop, up and down the rows of shelves and outside of real-world time. Instead of the altar, everything defers in the direction of the tills. The awe axis in a cathedral is vertical; in the supermarket it's horizontal, just a feeling of complete overwhelm and confused gratitude at the way the aisles roll out. The first large American grocery stores had a few hundred items. Today, a supermarket will have anywhere between 15,000 and 60,000 product lines in stock. We've come to accept this as totally normal. Supermarkets are perhaps the most powerful force in modern food culture. It's hard now to imagine they ever needed a hard sell.

Every supermarket is an American supermarket, no matter where it is. There's the square footage, which wouldn't usually work in compact European cities but which we've made room for in out-of-town retail parks and other non-places. A truly huge supermarket will have a devil's cornucopia vibe, like everything evil or extraneous to nutrition is here, and it's Buy One Get One Free. There are recognisable brands. And so much wonderful junk. Every purchase feels kind of like democracy, like casting a vote for choice itself. And it feels good. It even can feel like freedom. Even if you know about the evils of industrial agriculture, or capitalism, or any of the other architectures of modern retail, a supermarket can still get you. It gets you *here* – here being the vestigial hunter-gatherer in the deep circuits of your brain. Who can argue with dozens of breakfast cereals and yards of shelving just for crisps? The only thing better than three things you don't really need is four. All this is to say that supermarkets are the most successful advert for American culture since Hollywood.

For a few decades after that first King Kullen, supermarkets stayed busy lowering prices, advertising harder, getting stacked, doing what supermarkets do. But it wasn't until the Cold War that they became what they are today – something more than a store, or even a very big store, but a symbol of an entire way of life. In 1953, there was a small article in *The New York Times*. 'Food has proved to be the most effective weapon in the Cold War,' it said, on the topic of sending American food surpluses to Europe to embarrass the USSR. During the Cold War big battles were fought out in small print and subtext. And so you'd set up some psy-ops or start a space race or send some passive-aggressive food supplies. The egos involved – capitalist United States, communist USSR – were huge. It was a WWE storyline, WWE characters, but played according to the rules of chess. Food was as good a pawn as any.

And so this is how on 10 September 1957, a 10,000-square-foot facsimile of an American supermarket opened in socialist Yugoslavia. The year before, the US exhibition in the Zagreb International Trade Fair had been a pumpkin-shaped 'American home' in a disused fairground. But now it was a vast pavilion, with a laundromat, farm machinery, a showroom of home appliances and – the jewel in the crown – the kind of average American supermarket serving countless average American towns. It was the largest over-seas exhibit the United States had ever put on. Countries built pavilions at these fairs for the same reasons people sent their daughters to debutante balls – status, power, feuds, petty politics, alliances and the pageantry of wealth. At the time, Yugoslavia was a socialist state with a record of anti-Soviet resistance, just close enough to Moscow to serve as a proxy target for American propaganda but just independent enough to be swayed.

The pavilion was an imposing, glass-fronted building with the profile of an open book. Inside was a partial replica of an American superstore. There were freezers of fish fingers and frozen peas. You got to see the diversity of American produce: Kellogg's Corn Flakes, GrapeNuts Flakes, All-Bran, Sugar Snacks, Cheerios, Peps and Rice Krispies. There were candy dispensers for kids and fridges of shrink-wrapped meat for grown-ups. There was Californian lettuce in the salad section, and fresh tomatoes to be shipped from New Jersey every five days. Outside in the parking lot, there were ranks of American classic cars. To go into the store, you had to pass under a huge sign in bold, black capitals: SUPERMARKET USA. The Yugoslavian president, Marshal Tito, opened the exhibition. 'Just the thing for Yugoslavia,' he is supposed to have said, although that's exactly what American newspapers would say.

'Too much tradition in food has hurt the European' – this was in *The New York Times* article – but maybe if they just tried American distribution systems, American mass production and American modern merchandising methods, maybe they'd see what they've been missing. The idea was to move the balance of power. The centre of the food web wasn't the producers any more, or even the people eating. It was the middlemen – a vast, shimmering, multi-billion-dollar matrix of shops, trucks, distribution centres, packagers, marketers, ad men and supermarkets.

You couldn't actually buy the stuff in the store, but the exhibitors knew what's obvious to us now, which is that there's power in even the idea of a supermarket, regardless of what it sells. In 1959, Anastas Mikoyan, deputy premier of the Soviet government, went to a Giant Food supermarket in White Oak, Maryland. He bought Pepper Delight pickles, shredded coconut, coleslaw, aubergine and bottled lemon juice. Nine months after Mikoyan's big day out, Nikita Khrushchev went to a grocery store outside San Francisco. Then there was Boris Yeltsin's 1989 visit to a Randall's grocery store in Clear Lake, Houston, which was credited as the beginning of the end of communism. Nearly every major power shift of the entire Cold War happened either in space, or in a supermarket.

I guess it seemed obvious at the time that this really was just the best way to do things – that it's better to have choice than not have it; that there is nothing more important than having your cravings flawlessly and immediately met. 'Freedom of choice and expression' – that's how planners put it in secret memos for the American National Exhibition in Sokolniki, north of Moscow, in 1959, because the basic premise of American commerce is that these things are the same. If a supermarket works, then maybe capitalism works, and democracy works, and consumerism works. Before the supermarket can sell the food, you have to sell the supermarket. And so that is what they did.

Nobody had to stage a Supermarket USA in Britain. Things just kind of happened the same depressing way that most change does: you cut corners because you have to, and then you keep cutting even when you don't need to any more, because now you know how cheap it is, how easy, and there's no going back. It started after the Second World War. The workforce was thin and the more that customers helped themselves, the fewer workers you needed. This seemed like good maths. And so, Sainsbury's execs were given diplomatic passports to travel to the United States and see how superstores worked. The Ministry of Food – the wartime arm of government responsible for rationing – granted self-service licences so that existing grocery shops could convert. Slowly, people started coming around. Britain is a nation of shopkeepers, but shopkeepers don't run supermarkets. Numbers run supermarkets, and spreadsheets and computing systems and trade quotas and exchange rates. Customers run supermarkets. Systems run supermarkets.

In 1948, Co-op, Marks & Spencer and Tesco all opened self-service branches. Sainsbury's opened a self-service store in Croydon in 1950. People needed some coaxing at the start. Stores put up signs telling people to go in here and exit there and that, yes, you could help yourself to the things on the shelves. Sainsbury's published a guide on how to use a self-service store. It starts at the door. 'As you go in you are given a wire basket to hold the goods you choose.' There's a photograph of a new conveyor belt in Hemel Hempstead and a deli counter in Aveley. Women look into the fridges. A child puts an apple in a basket. 'You pay as you go out,' the book clarifies.

The second level-up – from self-service shop to super-market – was slower. You can't build a state-of-the-art supermarket from parts of an analogue store: it has to be made with supermarket rules in mind, with space to push trolleys down the aisles, with extra shelves to fill with extra products just for fun. The first Tesco supermarket opened in 1958. Sainsbury's came into their own in the New Towns built after the war. Croydon, Harlow, Chigwell – all these stores were built to serve newbuild housing estates. People need groceries. And so, some of the biggest civic development projects in British history came with a new branch of Sainsbury's. Within twenty years of the first self-service stores, full-scale American-ish supermarkets were the default way to shop.

When supermarkets spread, packaging had to adapt. In a self-service shop, packaging has to work twice as hard. It protects, like always, but now it also has to sell. But what was it selling? In the thirties, a Sainsbury's egg carton just said 'J. Sainsbury' and 'Freshness Guaranteed'. But in 1950 – the same year Sainsbury's opened its first self-service shop – it started using a new design. It was a four-egg carton made from interlocking slips of card. Its sides were yolk yellow, with '4 EGGS' overlaid in vermilion Albertus typeface. Behind the words, there were two off-white ovals – no outlines, just egg-shaped negative space.

There was no continuity with the previous eighty years of nation-of-shopkeepers Sainsbury's. It was modern and weird and had a Bauhaus-lite kind of vibe. It '[brought] order from the chaos,' the designer, Peter Beaumont, said.

The egg box was Beaumont's first project when he started as Sainsbury's design consultant. He went on to work for Sainsbury's for another fourteen years. During this time he nailed down a few design principles that would become Sainsbury's signatures. That Albertus font, for example. Or the slide towards geometrical, saturated colour designs. Selling the food was straightforward enough – keep it simple, remind people what it is and tell them that it's good. But how do you sell Sainsbury's? That was Beaumont's job. He standardised typefaces and streamlined the designs. Punchy labelling replaced lengthy assurances of quality or provenance. By 1960, there were 1,000 Sainsbury's own-label products, all unified through a common visual language.

Sainsbury's opened an in-house design studio, headed by Peter Dixon, and began a twenty-year stretch of producing some of the most iconic British design work since Frank Pick's London Underground. A packet of trifle sponge cakes has ultra-bold white text on contrasting bands of red-orange and magenta. The wide, uneven planes of colour are as close as you'll come to an own-label Rothko. A set of jam labels looks like Pantone colour swatches. There was a design for a Christmas pudding package that could've been designed by the Russian constructivist school: in squat, sans serif and fully capitalised lettering, the words SAINSBURY'S and CHRISTMAS PUDDING are stamped in the middle of the circular design. The colour scheme is pared back, almost monochromatic, with white and near-black rectan-gular-ish forms orbiting against a field of red.

Or how about Bill Wilson's 1970 cornflakes box? Beneath the 'corn flakes' – which is huge, in slim, angular lettering – are thirty-five golden circles arranged into a neat grid pattern. It's almost totally abstract, more like Agnes Martin's 1959 work *Buds* than any cereal box. Who cares if you can't see the cornflakes or if they're not really this shade of saffron. You know what cornflakes look like. The packaging didn't just serve the product, it served the shop. Every bottle, box and tin had to be a physical expression of the idea and identity of Sainsbury's.

Because here is the thing: once you've sold people on the idea of a supermarket, you have to sell people *your* super-market. Through the mid-century, the chains increased their reach – Sainsbury's, Tesco and Waitrose stores spread outside London, Marks & Spencer and Asda came down from Yorkshire. Instead of thousands of small stores run by either independent shopkeepers or regional chains, there were a few supermarket empires – ambitious stores, all of them a one-stop shop, all their territories overlaid. Maybe it was enough, at the start, just to be a supermarket. But now they needed an identity beyond the slick, sanitised plenty of a template store. Sainsbury's aesthetic of choice was modern, cosmopolitan, efficient but quietly aspirational. 'Our design will have failed,' as Alan Sainsbury put it, 'if our customers have to read the name over our entrance to know the shop they are entering.'

Sainsbury's was our supermarket when I was a kid. We went there every week until an Aldi opened next to the sewage works and my parents defected to there because, although it was uglier, it was also cheaper, and that was enough at the time to buy their loyalty. I get sentimental about it even though I shouldn't, and even when I'm looking at designs from well before my time. There's a Sainsbury Archive where you can see some of this packaging – ephemera that was never supposed to outlive the food it contained, but that now has relic status and is beautiful enough to radicalise even a loyal Waitrose person. They made a set of prompt cards for people with dementia, with photos of Sainsbury's packaging from different eras, knowing that these objects wear on you – that they get as deep into your emotional root system as the opening bars of a favourite song.

I don't need to tell you that the design has gone downhill, but it doesn't matter. British supermarkets have been around for seventy-five years and it's hard to imagine a world without them now. Everyone has 'their' supermarket, even if they don't go there all that much. For example, I'm a non-practising Sainsbury's person, but there are also Tesco people, Waitrose people, Lidl, Aldi, Asda, Morrisons and M&S people. (There are no Co-op people – a Co-op is a situationship, not a love match.) Despite sharing 99 per cent of their DNA, each of these chains has its own identity. They give you the feeling of shopping somewhere more human and idiosyncratic than they actually are. This is how you can go to the Tesco megastore under the flyover in Pitsea, say, and know that you're feeding a huge and homogenising and seemingly malign food system giant, and feel like you've somehow come home.

*

A couple of years ago, I went to a big Erewhon grocery store in Los Angeles. It's hard to describe this experience. Only flashes come back to me: an $18 smoothie, keto doughnuts, a cordyceps aisle, having an argument with my partner who realised this wasn't fun any more five minutes before I did, Sex Magic Elixir Powder, somebody carrying their cat in a baby sling, cacao. I remember the general feeling of it: a kind of radiant, manic experience, in which I bought three small, expensive items – not even good – and knew immediately that I would have to write about it otherwise I would have wasted $40.

If you have spent any time at all in the internet meme-osphere, you will have heard of Erewhon – a health store micro-chain which has, in the last decade and despite having ten branches, become the most divisive food retail store in America. The first Erewhon opened in the sixties in Boston, Massachusetts, and was run by Aveline and Michio Kushi. They had come across macrobiotic teachings a few years before, and they wanted to build a miniature natural-foods ecosystem in their adoptive town. At the time, the balance was tipping towards big, bright super-markets selling food grown with pesticides and wrapped in plastic. The store was a hole-in-the-wall, soybeans-in-a-jute-sack, real-heads-only health-food shop, in a tiny unit just below street level. The team went to producers to taste-test oil and, as Kerry Howley has reported in *New York* magazine, grill the Mennonites on whether the grains they were selling were actually organic. For anyone who didn't trust the optimising thrust of retail at the time, Erewhon was an eccentric and lo-fi reprieve.

For a few decades, Erewhon languished in the crustier

enclaves of the macrobiotics scene, which was already crusty even by health-food standards. It was loved by hardcore organics nerds, but it waxed and waned and never gained a following outside the counterculture it served. By 2011, there was a single store left – in Pasadena, California, since the epicentre of the natural-foods movement had shifted to the West Coast. Then it got investment, and under a new regime it began the rebrand that has made it the It store it is today. The prices went up, and the macrobiotic stuff retreated in favour of a vaguer, catch-all wellness where instead of a specific programme, you went by the logic of 'if it wasn't healthy, it wouldn't be in Erewhon in the first place'. The crust was exfoliated (Ursa Major's Morning Mojo Bar Soap, with undertones of grapefruit peel, $14) and glow was dialled up (Hailey Bieber's Strawberry Glaze Skin Smoothie, $20).

This new era of health food doesn't belong to the counterculture. It is status food, which is why Erewhons live in just a few locations around the more Ashtanga-and-a-cold-brew areas of LA. Some people who go there are haters, like I thought I was, but it's all the same American dollars, and we all post about it online. The house wins with every turmeric crush smoothie with organic camu camu and beet juice and add-on $13 probiotic kefir shot.

Despite being born in the first health-food movement over fifty years ago, Erewhon is the first truly internet-age supermarket chain. But here is the thing about Erewhon – it is not supposed to feel like a supermarket. The shelves, as Howley noted in that *New York* magazine piece, are built high and narrow, which makes it feel more like a quaint grotto for twenty-first-century woo. Things are too high to reach, so you have to ask store assistants for help – after a century of enforced retail independence, you're brought back under a retail worker's temporary care. You really can't make a trolley work here, and it's kind of dark, and nobody seems to be shopping for anything that could add up to an actual meal. I'd guess more people go there to get organic buffalo bones for their dogs than to get a weekly family shop. There are thousands of product lines, but only a few of each thing, which makes things feel bespoke, somehow, as though this isn't actually a mass retail operation, and you're not just a sheep with a shopping cart.

When you think about the place of supermarkets in the West, rather than the supermarket subvariant that is Erewhon, you're probably thinking about something like Supermarket USA – the archetype of the great post-war supermarket, with wide aisles and six-foot promotional pyramids of Campbell's soup. It's a feeling. A supermarket is American, anonymous, consumerist, sterile, the ambient vibration of tannoy bossa nova, panopticon, big brands, fugue state, airy, anti-atmospheric, evil, fun. It caters to the vast, undifferentiated middle – to everyone except the fringe movements of modern food culture. It's something you can visit in an industrial park in fifties Zagreb, or in a post-war New Town in Hertfordshire, and trust that it will be the same.

Erewhon is a new-generation supermarket, an anti-supermarket, designed to look and feel as different to Supermarket USA as it can. But it *is* a supermarket. It cleaves, more or less, to the Smithsonian supermarket definitions, but importantly it fits right into the optimised retail systems that the supermarkets built. Below the surface is a vast logistical and economic root system that feeds it. In the age of the supermarket, the middleman rules. There are serious supermarkets and accessorising supermarkets and every signature product from the Erewhon juice through to the indefatigable £1.50 Costco hotdog. There is the Uzbek supermarket in deepest Brooklyn that I went to a while ago, which had mathematically exact arrangements of onions and apples polished to a mirror-sheen, as well as an eighty-station takeout buffet counter. Tesco Extra, Tesco, Tesco Express. Today even the supermarkets have supermarkets. A hundred years of supermarkets. So many temples, and just one god.

The ice cream age

Or, how to invent a hit ice cream

The golden age of British ice cream started with a simple enough gambit – that there had to be a way of packaging the iconic ice cream cone. What if, instead of having to queue up in the sun outside a seaside ice cream hut, you could go into a shop – any shop – and find a cornet waiting for you, pre-made? What if it was fixed so that it was perfect every time – so that a smooth, dense volume of ice cream went all the way down into the cone, and sauce ran through the ruffles, and never fully froze, and never dripped? What if you could build a world in which it was physically impossible for the ice cream to fall off the cone? These are the kinds of questions that we do not always think to ask, but well . . . that's what the profit motive is for.

An Italian manufacturer had got the formula down in 1959. The success came down to the cone: a bias-cut, crisp wafer construction that had been sprayed on the inside with a mixture of chocolate and coconut oil, which forms a damp-proof barrier between the cone and the ice cream. The ice cream was important too. Full dairy ice cream doesn't hold up well when you try to pipe it or store it like this. But the new ice cream was different. It felt colder on the tongue. It melted quickly but smoothly, with the precision of a racer taking a clean, sharp bend. No gumminess, no particular chew. What you ended up with was a cornet of compactly aerated vegetable-fat emulsion, threaded with sauce and serving mainly as a pretext for the chocolate plug. This did well, even in the homeland of granita and gelato. In the ice cream business, they call products like this impulse ice creams. You could be buying a packet of pasta one moment, and have an ice cream in your hand the next.

In Britain, the idea didn't immediately translate. There's only so long that wet ice cream can last in a crisp sugar cone before things start to break down. The turnover of ice cream in a corner shop in Bolton wasn't like in a store in Rimini, and so when Wall's – the biggest name in British ice cream – tried to launch it in the UK in the mid-sixties, it crashed out. It took ten more years of chemical tweaking to get it right. They played with the ice cream so that it could hit that impossible sweet spot: knocked around in a freezer cabinet, it needed to have the physical qualities of Teflon; in the mouth, it needed to melt like silk. Eventually they nailed it, and Wall's parent company Unilever bought it, and in the summer of 1976, the Cornetto entered the British corner shop.

Ice cream heads – engineers, corporate marketeers, technicians, chemists, steely numbers men and product developers – remember that summer of '76 in the same way as hippies do the summer of '69. A while ago, I spoke to Kevin Hillman, a product developer who started at

Unilever on a scholarship in 1958 and didn't leave until his retirement in 2001. For most of that time, he worked in ice cream, doing the imaginative acrobatics that you'd expect from Willy Wonka, but with granular attention to detail in the matter of things like emulsifiers, viscosity and the complex chemistry of milk. 'Ahhh,' he said. '1976. You will not remember, but take it from me – if you ever wanted to launch an ice cream, it couldn't have been a better year.' It was the hottest summer on record, ice cream season extending long into autumn. Then there were semi-luxury ice cream chains Baskin-Robbins and Dayvilles, which both entered the UK that year and so got people used to the idea that you might pay as much as 25p for an ice cream cone. It wasn't even competition for the Cornetto – it was an opportunity. 'People suddenly started showing interest in exotic premium cones,' Hillman explained, getting gently animated about it, nearly half a century on. 'It was a price point we'd never dreamed about.'

There was also a proto-viral marketing campaign – the 'Just One Cornetto' song. Printed ads, too, like the pastiche of the ceiling of the Sistine Chapel, except instead of God and Adam it's a Wall's chocolate Cornetto. 'Fall for the smoothest Italian under the sun,' they said. Unlike kids' Thunderbirds ice creams or Cornish ice cream blocks, which were simple frozen iterations of custard or cream and marketed at children, this was an adult ice cream, maybe even a quality ice cream. In the terrifyingly analytical world of industrial food production, you don't just come up with a decent thing and sell it. You develop a formula, you acquire a patent, you wait for a perfect storm of social, economic and climate conditions. You market hard. Nearly seven million Cornettos were sold during that summer of '76. Within a decade, Cornetto had variants in strawberry, mint, and rum and raisin flavours, and was selling seventy million units a year. It was by far the most popular ice cream Britain had ever produced.

This was, in the world of British ice cream, the inception event – the beginning of a fifteen-year purple patch which spawned pretty much every one of the ice creams you find in the freezers today. Go to a shop or browse the menu on the side of an ice cream van. You see the Mini Milks? 1976. Funny Feet – the ancestor of skinless, sculptural ice creams in the shape of Minions and Peppa Pig – debuted in 1980. The Twister, the coiled ice cream and sorbet hybrid? The format was invented in 1982 in Ireland as a strawberry, vanilla and chocolate ice cream. And the flavours it has today – the lime, pineapple and strawberry trifecta? Allegedly, incomprehensibly, the result of a schoolgirl's trip to the Gloucester Wall's factory in 1987 courtesy of *Jim'll Fix It*. Viennetta was invented in 1982. Calippo came to the UK in 1982, although the orange Calippo wasn't launched by Wall's until 1988. Feast, a horrible ice cream but unkillable in a hard-shelled, cockroach kind of way – that was 1983. In 1988, we got Mars ice cream bars. 1990, Carte d'Or. And then there are two titans at each end of this Big Bang. The first is the Cornetto. The second, drawing the period to a close in 1990, was the Magnum – the most popular ice cream in the world today.

Ice creams are like buses . . . but honestly, this *is* how things work, once food gets to an industrial scale. Change happens quickly, and innovation comes in waves – amplified by economic changes and mergers, acquisitions and low-stakes corporate arms races. And advances in technology are, like it or not, advances in culture too. In the 1930s it was chocolate, giving us Mars bars, Snickers, Milky Bar, Maltesers, Aero, Ritter Sport, Rolos and KitKats – a chocolate-bar formal repertoire that we haven't meaningfully improved upon almost a century later. Something similar has happened in the last few years: an era of unprecedented creativity in crisp flavourings, a revolution in powder-format taste that has yielded everything from beer flavour to lasagne and chilli squid. Or take the recent uptick in wellness beverages. The golden age of ice cream was just fifteen years, roughly overlaying the late seventies and eighties, but it saw the biggest explosion of British food culture in the last half century. Forget the romance of Elizabeth David – a lot of the biggest changes in food today are the work of people in offices, and boardroom meetings, and in furtive, sterile labs.

When ice cream was popularised in the UK in the late 1800s, it would have been hard to imagine that things would go this far. Italian migrants sold penny lick milk ices on the streets, sellers convening on the canals in the early morning to buy blocks of ice, then dispersing across the city. Milk was frozen with sugar, maybe egg; serving glasses were wiped out with an old rag and then refilled to order. Over time, selling evolved, even if the ice cream itself stayed more or less the same. By the start of the Second World War, there were armadas of ice cream tricycles incorporated under the branding of Wall's – a sausage manufacturer that had realised, astutely enough, that people weren't really buying pork pies in summertime, and they probably needed a second income stream.

During the thirties, the catering and cafe empire Lyons, Wall's main competitor, made ice cream cakes – campy things like Trocadero Wonder Gateau and Glace Pompadour, with ice cream moulded like a ball-gown skirt. But there wasn't time to get in too deep. Ice cream was extraneous to the war effort when that all kicked off, so by the fifties, if anything, ice cream was more basic than ever. Most Lyons ice cream – eventually brought under the banner of Lyons Maid – was rigorously functional: bricks, bricklets, cups, poles and rectangular choc ices.

With the end of rationing in 1954, restrictions were lifted on how much dairy and sugar the ice cream industry could use. Spending power increased. During the war, fleets of ice cream tricycles had been sold and scrapped, and these were succeeded by ice cream vans and, to an even greater extent, convenience stores. Wall's, which had once sold 90 per cent of its ice cream on the road, now sold 90 per cent from the more capacious freezer cabinets of brick-and-mortar shops. All of a sudden, and pretty much out of nothing, there was an opportunity to do something new.

The first technologically cutting-edge ice creams were basic by today's standards. Take the Lyons Maid Mivvi – a fruit split with a strawberry or orange ice shell around vanilla ice cream on a stick – which debuted in 1959. It was simple, but undergirded by some of the most complex technologies of the time. Fruit-flavoured syrup was pumped from plastic arteries into moulds, a two-handed manoeuvre in which the rows of moulds advanced in time with the pulse. Mechanical arms swung the moulds through a cryogenically cold brine bath, a motion just smooth enough to be legible to the human eye, during which a crust of fruit ice a few millimetres thick froze to the contours of the metal. After this, the machine began to spin away from time again: the moulds were inverted with the snap of a flamenco dancer's wrist, tipping the unfrozen centres into a vat, then ice cream was piped into the empty shells through exacting metal mouths. Wooden lolly sticks were shot from muzzles lining the sides of the conveyor. A machine like this could make tens of thousands of strawberry splits every hour. After it launched, over a third of Lyons Maid ice cream sold came on a stick.

Over the sixties and seventies, technological change led to ice creams that would've been unimaginable even a decade earlier. So we got Haunted House ice lollies, which had blue ghosts printed into white milk ice. Until this point, ice lollies didn't do anything more ambitious than taper towards the top. But a new blood-red Dracula-inspired lolly had the craftsman's line of a medieval gargoyle. As you licked a Magic Monster lolly, Frankenstein's monster's face came through the ice.

Lyons Maid's Zoom, Orbit and Sea Jet were shaped like rockets and subs. Fab – an underskirt of strawberry ice, a wraparound of vanilla ice cream and an outer layer of sprinkle-beaded chocolate – was inspired by Lady Penelope's FAB1 Rolls-Royce from *Thunderbirds*. By the early eighties, the machinery would be so advanced that it dispensed with straight lines and normal gravitational laws altogether, which is how we ended up with the Twister: that twin spiral of pineapple and lime around an axis of strawberry ice, like a kind of psychedelic maypole.

This particular thread of ice cream – the low-budget, juvenile stuff – was beginning to wear out by the mid-seventies. The ice creams and lollies being produced were popular enough, but they were cheap and mainly bought by kids. Slowly, more people got home freezers, which opened space for bigger, take-home tubs of ice cream and super-market multipacks of their own-brand lollies. Companies like Unilever had to come up with something bigger and better if they wanted to avoid going the Lyons Maid way, which is to say, sliding into total irrelevance. This was the driving force behind the Cornetto – the first of many answers to one simple question: 'How do you sell ice cream to grown-ups?'

In 1980, Kevin Hillman – who by then was a product development manager at the new Wall's production plant in Gloucester – was looking through a *Good Housekeeping* cookbook that he'd bought his wife for Christmas. Inside, he saw a recipe for millefeuille. A millefeuille is a kind of experimental club sandwich: three sheets of puff pastry, each one with around 729 layers of buttery carbs and air, mortared with two layers of thick vanilla custard or cream. The name, which in French means 1,000 layers, is a rare example of the French culinary canon playing things down. Hillman began to wonder what an ice cream millefeuille would look like. You could extrude drifts of ice cream, but instead of sandwiching them with pastry – which would soften and warp – you could interpolate them with the thinnest leaves of chocolate. Until the late seventies, take-home ice cream was a support act, like custard, but Hillman's team had begun to experiment with ice creams that were good enough to work a crowd. Wall's had tried out Arctic roll, wrapping a log of vanilla ice cream in a jam-slicked sleeve of sponge cake. There were also experiments in strawberry- and chocolate-flavoured log desserts, the foundations of a sundae compacted into a 600ml rectangular ice cream block.

The earliest prototypes were basic, the size of a Vesta matchbox, with rigid layers that tasted great but visually fell flat. They found that if you squeezed a length of steel pipe in a vice, until it had an aperture of just a few millimetres, you could extrude very broad, thin sheets of ice cream in an unbroken stream; in time, they also found that if you increased the output speed, the ice cream would begin to pile up in collapsing sine waves. The engineers worked on adapting the machinery so it could do the impossible – using the process of plastic extrusion to make something like art. In between each of one dozen ice cream layers, they sprayed atomically thin, stracciatella-style layers of chocolate, using the technology of car production line spray painters, and the visual reference point of an Elizabethan ruff. The result was a dessert the size of the Motorola 8000X, an early, brick-like mobile phone that debuted the same year. When they drafted the patent they described 'Composite confection products [that] comprise a multiplicity of superimposed extruded thin layers of extrudable e.g. aerated frozen confection, optionally separated by interleaved very thin second confection layers such as couverture thin enough to be at least partly discontinuous.' But on the streets, they called it Viennetta.

If you're talking to anyone about the ice cream greatest generation, Hillman's name will inevitably come up. He was head of product development for take-home ice cream – that is, the big tubs and desserts that you don't eat on the go – at Unilever for pretty much all of this creative boomtime, alongside a team of engineers and chemists and nutritionists and marketers. But if you probe too hard about Hillman's Viennetta brainwave, he gets shy. The Viennetta origins story is the kind of thing that gets constantly brought up and broken down and misremembered. We like to hear fairy tales about these kinds of foods – the foods that are everywhere but which none of us knows how to make. They're bizarre and often beautiful. They are also, it bears saying, painstakingly engineered at costs running into millions of pounds, in order to game our dopamine systems and have us buying more. Hillman knows this better than anyone, which is why, when I probed him on the lightbulb moment, he politely referred me to a corporate history book called *Renewing Unilever: Transformation and Tradition* and left it at that.

But when I got him on to the real lineage of this ice cream – the myriad corporate, commercial, industrial and trans-European forces that led to the Viennetta being invented – he jumped right in. The spray guns for those ultra-thin layers of chocolate couverture were a trick they took from Cornettos. 'Exactly the same technology,' he noted, 'is used to spray chocolate as is used to spray paint on cars.' The ice cream, too, was the same as Cornetto – that bright white, sculptable, continental-style ice cream, made using vegetable fat instead of butterfat. The fat, by the way, is important: it's this that gives the ice cream its plastic properties, arguably at the expense of taste. Unilever came from the merger of a Dutch margarine company and a British soap business. Both were in the business of vegetable fat, which set things up nicely for the rise of highly processed ice creams. Dutch colonial links to Indonesia made coconut oil a sure bet. Then there was the packaging, which was borrowed from Unilever's German ice cream brand, Langnese.

'We had very close links. We could pick up the phone and get anything from Europe,' Hillman told me. This is how Britain came to host the most productive decade in ice cream, globally, ever – because it didn't do it alone. Unilever had been slowly acquiring ice cream businesses from across the continent for decades. That particular white ice cream is a rethink of an Italian ice cream, per- fected under Unilever's Belgian business, marketed in the UK. Sometimes the impetus for creativity is romance, but most of the time it's something more prosaic – a Medici, or a Unilever.

So much of our food culture comes down to things like this – the movements of huge companies to create, and then aggressively enforce, a new agenda. The story of ice cream is one of corporate tactics and injections of cash. It is also about using the law to carve out a space in the market. You can patent a process or a mechanism. You can in theory patent a particular combination and formulation of ice cream, chocolate, fruit, sugar and fat, as was the case for the Viennetta. Look through the patent records and you'll find dozens of patents like this – for ice cream icons that have or have not gone the distance. There's an ice cream inside a brandysnap-style tuile, capped with waxy chocolate at the ends. There's another for a lolly made using tiny pellets of fruit ice, poured into a mould, and then frozen together with a contrasting-flavour ice cement. There's a slumping, sexy, coiling proto-Twister, from a process patented in 1980. This is how things have to be, in an age when trade is, by default, multinational, and when good ideas – even good obvious ideas, like the ample, intuitive curves of a Magnum – are protected and litigable traits.

After Viennetta blew up, Unilever tried to squeeze a few more ice creams from that basic idea. They developed things like Carissima, Romantica, Sonata and Cassata Denice – all Italianate ice cream gateaux with the kinds of names a person would use to catfish on a sugar daddy site. In 1985 the company started 'Project Renaissance', exploring the hypothetical that ice cream could be, instead of a kids' thing, 'a secret affair – a lover to be "used"'. Everyone was doing it. Over at Lyons Maid, they rebranded their choc ice as Figaro and developed Caprice – a chocolate bar with malt ice cream and caramel that now persists only in lore. Nutcracker, a vanilla ice cream bar with toffee sauce and peanuts, joined Caprice in what was marketed at the time as an 'adult connoisseur range'.

Here's the trouble, though, with marketing ice cream to adults – novelty isn't enough. You need things to actually taste great, or at least to taste as luxe as they look. In kids' ice creams, the ingredients didn't matter so long as the thing was fun. But over the eighties, the principles of ice cream began to change. Lyons Maid introduced a Gold Seal range, then Crème de la Crème – seemingly arbitrary grada-tions of luxuriousness. In France, Carte d'Or found a path from wholesale into the retail market. Pillsbury bought and popularised the pseudo-Scandinavian Häagen-Dazs, setting a precedent for the umlaut republic of coffee shops today. Ben & Jerry's, which started as a shop in a Vermont garage, opened its first factory in 1985, sold on the strength of its countercultural credentials and natural ingredients. 'Wanted!' ran one Lyons Maid advert. 'Real chocolate, real goodness, real fruit and double cream.'

Around this time, European subsidiaries of Unilever were developing the simple ice cream – vanilla, enrobed in chocolate, on a stick – that would eventually become the Magnum. It was the polar opposite of Cornetto and Viennetta, despite working towards the same grown-up principles. It had real vanilla ice cream, enriched not with coconut oil but with butterfat. The chocolate also needed to be right. Most of the chocolate that Unilever had been using was imitation – cheap and adaptable, setting either to a waxy cap or the thinnest layer of craquelure. They took inspiration from the United States, where Häagen-Dazs was already huge, along with Magnum-like Dove ice creams. And so they developed a better kind of chocolate – one that could be deep-frozen, and snap loudly into big, angular shards, but still melt in the mouth. They experimented with the recipe, took it back to basics, and gave the lolly a smooth, cursive silhouette. The industry, which for much of the eighties had evolved in the same implausible, molecularly disruptive way as a deep-sea fish, returned to simple forms. It debuted in Germany in 1989, and in the UK the year after.

Ice cream is an iterative process, combining and recasting the same components, with incrementally better technologies and sometimes new ingredients. At the end of the day, a Magnum is a choc ice. But what a choc ice. It's hard to capture just how horny the Magnum was. 'Magnumize your free time', an ad would say, and show a woman lock the kids outside, so she can go hard on her Magnum in peace. 'Magnumize your life': at the office, she has unplugged the telephone landline master socket. If Wall's started selling ice cream to get through the pork-pie-fallow summer months, then Unilever smashed the final frontier by finding a way to market ice cream all year round – any time, any place. It wasn't about the sun or refreshment any more, but just an adult's right to a moment of pleasure. In 1990, for their first big stunt, and the last truly exciting day in British ice cream, Magnums were handed out to thousands of commuters in three major London stations, in rush hour, in November. Within a couple of years, it was the best-selling ice cream in the world.

'Of all the fast foods on sale in Britain,' the food writer Jane Grigson wrote in the *Observer* at the start of 1990, 'I would say that vanilla ice cream represents the most catastrophic fall from original virtue.' But she died just a couple of months later and I have to ask – did she ever get the chance to try a Magnum? There are two lines of tradition in British food. The first is romantic and comes from the countryside, specific to even the tiniest village. The second kind of British folk food is factory food. It is the antithesis of folk food, but it's also the archetype. If the first folk traditions are folk because they represent the hyper-regional diversity of people, these industrial foods are folk foods in another way – because they represent the sum of people, the rough direction of popular will at a moment in industrial time. For better or worse, these foods mean something to us too.

The ice creams that came out of the golden age – from the Cornetto to the Magnum – are as much a part of British food culture as Cheddar cheese. In fact, there are a lot of parallels between the two. Like cheese, ice cream is a dairy product that was given new vitality in the eighties. In the case of cheese, it was down that traditional folk path: wrinkled, mould-tufted goat's cheeses, and precious truckles of nettle-wrapped Yarg. In the case of the ice cream, it was innovation, rather than revival, and it happened on the biggest imaginable scale. But unlike the cheese side of the dairy industry, which has continued to thrive, ice cream has stagnated.

It's not like people haven't tried. In the early nineties, Kevin Hillman was fine-tuning the recipe for a new fruit Romantica – a Viennetta-inspired gateau constructed with stacked rosettes of vanilla and strawberry ice cream and sprinkled with beads of fruit ice. He found that if you used a kind of rudimentary shower head, you could spray globular drops of fruit syrup into a bath of liquid nitrogen, where they instantly froze into hailstones. Romantica never took off, but the idea was eventually recycled as Calippo – and then Solero – shots: tiny pellets of fruit ice that you tipped back like the crumbs at the bottom of a bag of crisps. This was, for ice cream aficionados, a moment of hope, but these were discontinued within a few years and nothing good has really happened since.

We've done this to ourselves. Ice cream is milk, frozen and sweetened. This is all. Britain is a dairy country, with the weather and the pasture for the kind of cows that yield good, fatty milk and lots of it. We could, in theory, have thousands of dairy farmers producing ice cream in small batches with their fresh milk and cream, and selling it patchwork across the country, as regionally specific as a farmhouse cheese. But the battles we wage in food are never just about the food itself. They are squabbles over territory and systems and logistical networks: they are battles that are won not by owning cows, but by owning freezers. During the seventies, when Wall's and its parent company Unilever were approaching their warp speed period of productivity, they had also been buying up valuable freezer real estate. Seventy thousand freezer cabinets, in as many corner shops and tobacconists across the entire country, were owned by Wall's and leased to the stores on one condition – that they didn't use the cabinets to display any rival ice cream brands. In several thousand other shops, Lyons Maid owned and controlled the freezers. There was no room for anything else. A shop couldn't just display a local dairy's milk ices on a random shelf they'd cleared. Without the freezer, there was nothing.

Anti-monopoly laws freed up some of the freezer space for competitors, but still – tens of thousands of freezers, tens of thousands of metres of decals and branding stickers and big-board Wall's price displays. In 1984, when the Milk Marketing Board tried to run a campaign for real dairy ice cream, the multinationals snuffed it out. Even if they had the will, dairy farmers never had a commercial incentive to really do much with ice cream at all. At the huge corporations, they were so busy testing the limits of ice cream that it almost stopped being a dairy product at all – instead, a Viennetta, a beautiful, legally protected formula of plant fats and stabilisers and aerated emulsions designed to chemically delight us. No dairy farmer could make or market a Viennetta. But then again, multinational corporations weren't great at making uncomplicatedly delicious, all-dairy ice creams either.

It says something that the greatest success of the most prolific period of product development in ice cream history is, simply, a Magnum. It is the thing that's arguably closest to what small, dairy ice cream producers could have been doing all along, if they'd had the chance. It's hard to do better than covering a decent vanilla ice cream in chocolate and putting it on a stick – especially once you've ploughed a few tens of millions of dollars into research and development, to fast-track the evolution of the ice cream and the chocolate and the shape to their optimum possible form. The world of industrial ice cream manufacture is incredibly complex, but our tastes are simple.

In the decades since the Magnum we've not made anything good enough to challenge. In a corner shop freezer cabinet, there will be a clade of Magnums: classic, double caramel, white chocolate, almond, mint. The novelties: Starchaser Chocolate Caramel & Popcorn; Gold Caramel Billionaire; Sunlover White Chocolate. Even in the same flavours, Magnums keep on finding culinary synonyms, from vegan Magnums to Magnum ice cream tubs – the chocolate shell turned into an upper crust – mini Magnums and Magnum bites. It never ends. If you want a break from all of this, your option is either that one malformed Twister at the bottom of the freezer, or a Cornetto.

*

Just in case the industry was turning out ice creams that

I didn't yet know about but should, I recently went to a food industry expo at London's ExCel Centre, the home of the national id. The half-kilometre-long space, a building with the lowest ratio of beauty to square footage in the city, hosts expos that are a mix of both specificity and unbelievable scale. For a few days each spring, the IFE, the International Food & Drink Event, takes over and a usually furtive economy comes out into the open.

I wanted to see the prototypes of a new generation of ice creams, the technological and imaginative vanguard. What I saw was a vegan non-Cornetto brand at an unmanned stall. There was a Romanian manufacturer of ice creams modelled after Magnums, making a push for relevance after Unilever entered the Romanian market with the real thing. There were health-food anti-Soleros made from plant juice, fibre and pulp. A Slovenian brand had a product poster that could have been photocopied and transliterated from a Wall's decal from 1989: Everest was a facsimile of a Magnum, Turbo was a MagicIce brand Twister, Free was a Maxibon. The only thing that really spoke to the idiosyncrasies of Slovenian taste was Adore – a mini imitation-Viennetta on a stick. I told Kevin Hillman about it, and he started asking questions that I couldn't answer about exactly how many layers this thing had.

Increasingly, ice creams are fighting giants like Magnum on its own terms, following the luxe-is-more principle but taking it further. In this camp, the uber-luxury of Nuii ice creams, with unnecessary qualifiers like Texan pecan, New Zealand honey, Italian roasted hazelnut, as though the company isn't a sub-brand of one of the biggest ice cream companies in the world. Near the exit of the expo, there was a stall from Jude's, an upscale British brand in the same vein as Häagen-Dazs. Maybe it's a sign of how much things have changed that now British ice cream, like cheese, can sell itself on how British it is. They were handing out samples. It was a valedictory piece, mid-level sales reps with tote bags of brochures, trying salted caramel before catching the DLR. Clotted cream was doing well. Chocolate, always. The salesperson told me they were doing something different to the multinationals. They tried to give me a sample of 'blue vanilla' ice cream coloured with spirulina.

Behind, in the freezer cabinet, there were legally daring Jude's not-Rockets and Mini Milks, indistinguishable at a glance from the real thing. The Jude's version of a Twister was called a Fruit Twist: the same maypole but vegan, smaller, lower sugar. I want to say it's all outdated, but nothing resonates with the current moment quite like constantly reliving, without resolution or growth, the limited victories of the eighties. Their biggest line was a range of ice cream sticks, not Magnums, but not *not* Magnums. They were rounded, slightly fatter at the bottom, with dairy ice cream in a thick chocolate shell. Belgian chocolate, salted caramel, peanut butter – the same as always and, maybe, as good as we'll ever get.

Tonic waters

Or, the rise and rise of the magic wellness drink

I think I must be losing my mind. I just saw an advert. 'You are human on Earth,' the voiceover said, over the top of some old footage of a spacecraft launch. There was music too: electronic beats from 'Only You', a Yazoo song from 1982 that sounds like nostalgia for a future you lost. 'Throughout all of humanity's existence on Earth,' the voiceover continued, 'there have been ideas, strides and accomplishments.' Then there were grainy reels of vintage breakdancing and early automobiles. 'Some have been enormous.' A clunky early mobile phone. 'Some have been small and personal.' Old camcorder footage of a kid's birthday. 'Others have been revelatory – a simple change that redefines everything we thought we knew.' I knew where this was going, but I still couldn't believe it. The advert showed a super lo-fi computer interface – the mouse hovering over the button to *Connect* on to the early internet, into the next frontier of human brilliance. And then, the click – and the frame filled with screengrabs and reels and photos of Poppi, a Millennial gut-health soda brand.

If the eighties was the age of ice cream, we've now entered a new era of food production hyperactivity. This is the age of the functional drink – an expansive, dreamy, multi-million-pound retail category that covers everything from immunity shots to energy drinks and prebiotic sodas. In the last five years or so, these drinks have become inescapable. They're on my Instagram feed. They're in the restaurants where I go to escape quasi-scientific wellness grift. I'm finding cans of CBD-infused pop in the local shop where I buy washing-up liquid and frozen peas. They're even being advertised in the commercial breaks of the Super Bowl – the one I just described, Poppi, took the primetime ad space where you used to see things like the Pepsi Gladiators commercial. This stuff is blockbuster. It is also insane.

I went to a central London branch of Whole Foods to see the real-life implications of this advertising deluge. There had to have been about fifty metres of shelf space, collectively, given over to hundreds of these drinks, across various brands and nutritional sub-niches, and employing every health-signifying keyword you can imagine. For example, smart lemonade. Or pomegranate and rhubarb electric blend. Mango passionfruit organic coconut kefir. Organic Elixir Mix with chaga mushroom and eleuthero. Culture shot. Raspberry probiotic water. Focus water. Cold-pressed ginger booster. Protein soda. Black cherry, guarana and goji Extreme Black plant power shot. Strawberry lime yerba mate zero-sugar clean energy drink. Mindful-blend elderflower and mint. Liquid Death carbonated Alpine water – I am not making this up. Pink grapefruit living soda. Power shake. Prebiotic dosing bottle.

Naturally fermented sparkling raspberry and apple cider vinegar kombucha. CBD soda. Vitamin C sparkling magnesium water. Prebiotic fibre pop.

I was expecting to be annoyed, and I was, but I was also, in a sick way, enthralled. Here were several hundred drinks that were so conceptually debased that they tested the limits of both literacy and common sense. What the fuck is Liquid Death? Why would I pay for it? Why *have* I paid for it? Every one of these drinks invented a problem that I'd never thought I had, and offered a solution in terms that I will never properly understand. What's more, they looked cute while doing it: pop colours, illustrations, infantilising slogans, anthropomorphised fruits and bottles that say things like 'the bottle in your hand symbolizes good health from within', with a Y2K-era smiley face emoticon. It was like 1967 – the year in music that gave us Sgt. Pepper's Lonely Hearts Club Band, the Velvet Underground and Pink Floyd's debuts, and the Doors self-titled, and redirected about 70 per cent of subsequent music history – except for nutritionally extraneous and potentially litigable wellness drinks.

There are some obvious reasons why this has happened. To start with, people – especially younger people – have been drinking less alcohol in the last few years, or at least we've been making a bigger deal about the amount of alcohol we don't drink. And then there's sugar: a basic metabolic building block which has, in the last decade or two, become public health enemy number one. But there's also a feeling, in the culture, that the over-inflated Zeppelin brands – Coca-Cola, Pepsi, and the rest – need to be taken down. And the way to do that? Well, you create another multi-million-dollar soft drinks company to take the Super Bowl slot, and you call it something like Fruitola or Peppy Pop and add a gram or two of soluble fibre, and you say something like 'this will be the last moment you ever think of soda as being a dirty word'.

We are all fluent in wellness by now. Over the last fifteen years, wellness has become one of the most successful ways to mis-sell food. It picks up where old-fashioned diet culture left off, but it's more slippery somehow. Under the banner of 'making people healthier', wellness is pantheistic and politically diverse. It includes people who want you to lose weight, and people who want you to optimise your body mass to muscle ratios, and people who want you to cosmically manifest your ideal self (smaller than you currently are). It can work pretty much any way you want it to work, as long as you accept the basic messaging: that fatness is bad, and health is good, and both are very much your so-called problem to deal with. If you dig around online you'll find everything from hard-line keto content to euphemisms like 'get your glow'. The main difference between dieting and wellness is that diets start with consuming less, whereas in wellness you start by adding on – a self-help book, a vitamin supplement, a melatonin patch, an app, an immunity shot, a silly little juice. This small shift of perspective has turned something that you conceivably do for free (eat less) into a mega-industry that makes everyday living into an extreme sport.

There are bigger cracks in the culture, too – the spaces in which all these anxieties have entered and grown like weeds. What is happening with healthcare? Why do none of us – even scientists – seem to know what's good for us? In the absence of hard facts about how to stay alive, it's tempting to reach for compelling stories instead – stories like a new Poppi cream-soda flavour that you've been conditioned to associate with the 1969 moon landings.

Naturally, wellness culture has spawned a gold rush of food and healthcare companies looking to offer pricey solutions. But for various reasons – not least the fact that soft drinks are regulated less stringently than medicines and cost almost nothing to produce – wellness beverages have become the most competitive part of this market. What could be more relevant to here and now than a gut-healthy yoghurt shot? It's the waters of Lourdes for people with undiagnosed IBS. It asks nothing of you except your money – you don't even have to chew. You just add it on to the shopping bill, on to the cosmic wellness karma tab, and hurry on to your Pilates class.

When it happened in ice cream, it was about technology getting better, expanding the horizons of what was physically possible in the medium of frozen milk. But this is different. Look at the most popular functional drinks and you'll see that the actual recipes are old, even crusty. There's nothing cutting edge about kombucha: it's been made the same way for a couple of thousand years by fermenting sweet tea with a symbiotic culture of bacteria and yeast (SCOBY, for those in the know). Dissolving vitamin C in water is hardly groundbreaking. You can turbo-charge hydration with protein and minerals and energy-boosting sugar, if you want, or you could just have a glass of milk. There are street names for these drinks. We used to call them 'fruit juice', 'yoghurt', 'sugar water', 'vinegar'.

The difference is that this time around, it's not a revolution in production – it's a revolution in marketing. Kombucha, instead of being a centuries-old, historically Chinese, tea-based beverage, is now available in varieties that you could describe as bubblegum Barbiecore, laundry-day goth, softcore triathlon bro and Apple Watch. There's a drink for everyone, and really it's beside the point that once you get past the bottle and the branding and the colour of the liquid, you're basically just drinking solute vinegar. When we're looking for cutting-edge, episteme-bending approaches to food, we usually look at chefs and high-end restaurants. But what if the exciting and explosive changes in food right now aren't happening in restaurants at all, but in retail? What if it's not even what's in the food that matters, but how it's packed?

We have been here before, believe it or not. During the Victorian temperance movement, sweet carbonated drinks were a good alternative to beer. Artificially carbonated water – which had been perfected the century before – was a forgiving medium to work in: bubbles broke the heaviness of the sugar syrup and carried the flavour; and because the fizz was man-made, you didn't have to rely on fermentation that could've produced alcohol. There were fun lemonades and cream sodas. Luxe dispensing equipment reflected how lucrative these drinks could be. One top-of-the-line soda fountain was a ten-foot-tall black marble structure with columns and porticos, a few dozen taps, ornamental lamps, silver detailing and a price tag of what would now be about $200,000. (A century later, Poppi is sending influencers bright pink soda vending machines. We have fallen.) Elsewhere in the culture, there were proto-wellness drinks like naturally fermented, non-alcoholic ginger ale – made and marketed in pretty much the same ways as kombucha is today – or tonic water, whose quinine protected the British colonial middle management against malaria.

When American pharmacists figured out that they could apply chemical know-how to something more fun than pills, soda fountains became even more popular. The drugstore shopkeeper could pull you a half-pint of cocaine-based soda. As the tonics started tasting better, and soft drinks started grafting, the two great soda traditions of the Victorian era began to work as one. Starting in 1885 and within the space of a decade, pharmacists invented Dr Pepper, Coca-Cola, bottled root beer, and Pepsi. Each got the kind of hard sell a person used to hear from the travelling medicine man, a ye olde hyperbole parade that would seem unhinged to us, I think, if we weren't reliving history right now. Pepsi – the OG gut-friendly tonic – was named after the peptide enzymes it contained that were supposed to help digestion. Dr Pepper – 'the king of beverages' – was marketed as 'liquid sunlight', 'a great natural law', vim, vigour and vitality, and was supposed to be good for your gut.

Or how about another drink popularised in the late 1800s? 'A non-alcoholic life renewer', it was called. 'A combination of Vegetable Tonics and delicious Aromatics, enriching and strengthening the blood, muscles, brain; regulating the stomachic and nervous system; relieving headache, nausea, dyspepsia, sleeplessness, general debility, and on account of its life and health renewing properties the most valuable tonic and delicious beverage ever offered to the public.' It was based on a recipe from a renowned physician. It was branded with big flexed biceps on the labels, and pictures of a strongman Highland athlete with a Tom Selleck moustache. It was iron brew. It's hard to know now exactly what this iron brew was – whether it had the same long, lush ferrous tang of the A. G. Barr Irn-Bru we know today, that penny-with-a-hint-of-bubblegum flavour we've come to love. We only know that this was called iron brew, and that the strongman marketing was the same. But maybe this is all there is: the marketing. These things are what they say they are. They are the sum of the promises they make to us.

How gullible must people have been back then, and then you remember where we are now, with a hundred extra years of history to learn from, spending more money on this shit than ever. 'Solar energy-liquid sunshine' – that's what they called Dr Pepper in an early-twentieth-century ad. Now, you've got 'a hug from the sun' – Humble Warrior's mango turmeric can, with '3 kick-ass plants and natural vitamin C to make you strong like a warrior'. It's vegan, by the way.

These drinks promise a solution to the most boring and inevitable problem we face in our pursuit of wellness: that medicine is not nice. Well – not any more. Right now I've got a peach, rosemary and ashwagandha sparkling magnesium water on my desk. It's a tall, slim, pastel orange tin of aggressively aspirational wellness. It resists making any claims that it could be sued for or held to, instead relying on aesthetics that imply it will stealthily overhaul my life. 'Pure sparkling water infused with bioavailable Magnesium, natural fruit extracts and botanicals, and that's about it . . . simple!' I don't know what it does.

You'd think that advertising regulations would have stymied the old-fashioned quack, but a couple of years ago the delusion economy gave us Moon Juice, an LA-based health-food and supplement company and one of the most extreme manifestations of New Age wellness. Moon Juice sells dissolvable powders for what it describes as 'cellular waters'. One of them, called Ting, is an energy- and serotonin-boosting infusion with a B complex derived from tulsi and guava. It 'provides cofactors' and hacks 'cellular currency'. Another rhetoric infusion is a night-time shot that helps you to microdose melatonin and tastes like organic blackberries. I went to the Moon Juice store a couple of years ago while in Los Angeles out of a sick curiosity. I drank something described to me as shilajit resin – a short, vile drink with the aromatic profile of topsoil crossed with tar.

When Moon Juice came on the scene, people rightly dragged them to hell and back, but that doesn't seem to have done much. Now, not only does Moon Juice stand its ground in the more acutely wellness-addled parts of the LA health world, but it's also totally moved the Overton window on what reads to us as mad, which is how I came to pick up a bottle of cold-pressed raw greens virgin smoothie in Whole Foods and think, with total sincerity – 'Finally, something normal.' I've lost all perspective. I'm told that you'd have to be out of your mind to fill your body with a chemical weapon like Diet Coke. What you really need is volcanic black water – actually a solution of alkaline water and fulvic acid, which is supposed to be anti-ageing and became famous off the back of *Real Housewives*.

Just thinking about it all makes me weary, but then that is how this works. The wellness drinks explosion feeds on the way the world is set up right now. In the eighties, you needed multinational megacorporations, and the free market, and mergers, and acquisitions, and intense industrial food production technologies to give us the Twister. But capitalism today is weirder and more fragmented. The retail world has been totally reconfigured by the internet – you don't need to start out as a Unilever-size company to hit the market, you just need to have a look, and a brand, and a perfectly calibrated list of SEO-friendly ingredients to help you look good online. Then, you get the investment. If you can do this, you will find a path into the stores. And so it's marketing – not production – where the biggest battles in food are currently being fought.

You end up with a company like Poppi – a soda company founded by Allison Ellsworth, formerly in the feel-good world of oil and gas. Poppi used to be called Mother Beverage, after the raw, unfiltered 'mother' apple cider vinegar in her drinks – but who's going to buy that? They got investment on the American show *Shark Tank*, and used the few hundred thousand dollars to rebrand the drinks as Poppi. They got big on TikTok. Paris Hilton DJ'd their new flavour drop in LA. They had that advert at the Super Bowl. Poppi has been the best-selling drink on Amazon and is also, as it happens, being sued for making supposedly misleading health claims. And what is it? What does it do? Damned if I know.

And then recently, as sure as the sun will rise, I saw the announcement that any astute retail maven will have seen coming a mile off: at a price tag of $2 billion, Poppi was acquired by Pepsi. The drink and its doppelganger – the uncanny sameness of these wildly different tonics. 'It will be the soda your kids and grandkids think of when they think of soda,' the adverts tell me. 'The future of soda is now.'

Fast food

Fast food

The automat is dead

Or, on the past and future lives of food machines

Last summer I went to Aix-en-Provence, a small town in the south of France with the kind of markets that could make a Londoner cry. On market days, the town rearranges itself as if doing some kind of medieval Tetris: the dozens of squares and courtyards fill with tables, makeshift gazebos, crates, clapped-out Renault vans, and every delicacy you can imagine. I thought I was above being a Francophile, like it was all too obvious, but it turns out you can't know how you'll react to a French market until you're there, looking at a small, round cheese coated in dried herbs, or big bulbs of garlic stroked with lilac, or a rôtisserie chicken stall where the potatoes are basted in the dripping juices.

I always think my French is functional, but conversations only work if everyone else sticks to the script I've written for them in my head. If they don't, I end up saying 'oui' when someone asks me how many apricots. Still, it felt dignified to have honest interpersonal friction, especially considering how much of my shopping at home is done at a self-checkout. No matter how much I embarrassed myself,

I kept going back because I knew the payoff – a fresh-baked fougasse – was worth the risk.

After eating, we walked around and looked in some old churches. We saw some paintings, we looked at Romanesque towers and Gothic art. Then, just on the shoulder of the old town, we came across a pillar-box-red, pizza-vending machine. You could get a margherita pizza, or tartiflette, or Maxi Burger flavour – which has fried onions, cornichons and burger sauce. A kebab pizza would cost you €12.50. Twenty-four hours a day, seven days a week. Three minutes for a hot pizza. Thirty seconds if you want it cold.

All you had to do was scan through the photos on the touchscreen, choose, then pay with the tap of a card. A pizza would slide out of a thin, wide aperture, like an ejected DVD. I was fascinated by this vending machine. Like finding a giant, out-of-town Carrefour, or thinking about French tacos – which seem to cross a burrito and an Algerian merguez-frites sandwich, but with the good characteristics of neither – it's nice to be reminded that, for every beautiful thing French food culture has to offer, it follows up with something more ridiculous and chaotic than the Académie could ever have feared.

The company that owns the machines – there are a few in towns across the south of France – is open about what happens behind the scenes. On social media they post videos of the team smoothing tomato sauce on pizza bases and slinging cheese. By the time the pizzas get to the back end of the vending machine, it's just a question of the machine reheating them to order. In a town of tourist restaurants, bar-tabacs with idiosyncratic opening hours, and something like six ornamental Amorino stores, it was a relief to find that you could plausibly get food that was better than a Carrefour Dr Oetker, but without the sometimes uncomfortable necessity of being served.

I had to respect the vision of putting a pizza-vending machine a few doors down from an actual pizza restaurant and within earshot of the bells of Saint Sauveur. I liked knowing that even in the emptiest hours of the night, the machine would be there. My French didn't matter. I could get handmade food, without a moment of human friction, whenever and however I wanted. But did I get a pizza from the hole in the wall? Did I fuck. We all draw a line somewhere. Maybe under the right circumstances, but as things stood I was happy for it to stay in the good-in-theory lane.

Honestly, though, I shouldn't be weird about this when so much of my food – like anyone's, if you live in a city today – relies on machine-led convenience. I know the sinking feeling of getting a coffee from a push-button Costa machine in a Tesco Express. Maybe you know what it feels like to hang your hopes on a Huel vending machine. There are Deliveroo, Resy and Google Map reviews. The average meal isn't a communion between the cook and the eater; it's a conversation that's mediated, and complicated, by tech. It feels so modern, to have food culture contained in touchscreen, or the few square inches of the average smartphone. But really, this is only the latest episode in a century-long, convenience-centric ordeal. The nadir is the pizza-vending machine, and the blueprint was the automat.

Walk into a New York automat in the 1940s, and you'd find a crowd of people in front of a wall of glass-fronted lockers. Imagine: the windows are arranged in blocks – Pies,

Sandwiches, Pastries, Bread and Rolls, Hot Platters – and alongside each is a chrome coin slot and turntable knob. One locker has a slice of peach pie on a small white plate; another one has a bowl of franks and beans. Each of these dishes is composed like a museum diorama, under a spot-light and with a caption card alongside. 'Apple cake, 2 nickels', 'Chicken pie, 50c'.

Taken together, the lockers are a complete picture of the modern American table. Deluxe bologna sandwich, fish cake, prune bun, beef pie, corn muffin, club roll. Every one of these is in its own locker, as though it's the only one, as though it's been waiting there for you. Grease the palm of the machine and the window will swing open. You take your food, find a seat, eat and leave. You haven't had to deal with a single person. Inside the locker, as soon as you walk away, a rotating drum brings a fresh plate into view.

The first American automat opened in Philadelphia in 1902. Joseph Horn and Frank Hardart had a small chain of luncheonettes where workers could get a hot but simple meal and the organising principle was convenience. There were no tables, just a long counter where servers could get the food and then the eaters out as quickly as possible. On a trip to Europe, Horn noticed machines that could vend drinks – coffees, juices, sodas – automatically, on a coin-operated basis. It cut down on labour costs, and it felt like it should be quicker than being served, even if it wasn't. Horn and Hardart worked on getting the machines to Philadelphia and converted a few luncheonettes so that instead of servers and chatter, there would be an unbroken wall of metal, and the quiet percussion of levers and falling coins.

People had tried to make dining machines before. In the late eighteenth century, Café Mécanique in Paris had tables with metal trumpets through which you placed your order with the kitchen below, and hollow mechanised vestibules that brought the food up to you. But these new vending machines didn't feel like pure novelty. They were plausibly useful, and then they got better, and soon they were all-rounders that could just as easily present you with a cherry pie as dispense a cold juice. It was a weird place, but in the way you'd expect things to be weird when the culture is shifting into a more efficient, more future-facing gear. In Philadelphia, it was hard to balance the books, the technology cost so much, but the city was still small and not everyone was in that much of a rush. Serving sandwiches out of quickfire, mechanised lockers was like using a JCB to plant a rose.

But New York, which got its first Horn & Hardart automat in 1912, had Goldilocks conditions. There were offices on offices on offices. Fewer people lived south of 59th Street, where the actual work was, while subways were serving commuters from the boroughs. If you couldn't go home for lunch, it was a scramble to find whatever place would serve you as much as possible, for as little as possible, and in the minimum possible time. And then in seemingly no time at all, there were Horn & Hardart automats on Broadway, Sixth Avenue and down to 33rd Street. They figured out what Pret A Manger would retap many years later – that if you take the urban density of stores to its limit, people come to think of these places not just as one option, but the default. According to the ads, these were 'as famous as the New York skyline itself'. By the late 1940s, there were a few dozen Horn & Hardarts in Manhattan, serving tens of thousands of customers each week.

There's only so fast a lunch can be. The limiting variable is always going to be the eater, a reality that even a few tons of highly articulated, proto-space-age control panel can't mitigate. And really, despite appearances, the technology of automats was basic – something like the sum of a Lazy Susan, a set of mechanical scales and a mortise lock. You wouldn't have to queue at a counter at the automat, but if you weren't waiting, you were moving that dead time elsewhere – pacing the length of the wall, being immobilised by choice, looking for a seat, waiting for a new portion of cherry pie to be swivelled around the wall, and eating. If automats were machines, they were less like steam engines and more like wurlitzers.

There were already countless ways to lunch in New York. The most famous Manhattan lunch is *Lunch atop a Skyscraper* – the 1932 photo of ironworkers on scaffolding with the then-incomplete Rockefeller complex. Eight hundred feet below, you could go to a counter like the Exchange Buffet and eat standing elbow to elbow with finance guys. There were self-service restaurants where instead of table service you had trays that you pushed along the rails, like an Ikea canteen, or you could go to any standard luncheonette or diner and get eggs, a burger, or a slice of pie. New York, one of the most street-food-literate cities in America at the time, had countless hotdog carts and as many slices. Even Horn & Hardart restaurants had a dual-format set-up – cafeteria-style on one side, automat on the other. None of these options were slow or expensive, but there was something about the experience of going to the automat – a swagger that set it apart.

To start with, it was clean, or at least it felt like it, when the food came from a metal box and you never had to see other hands on it. You never had to see it dished out from a bigger chafing dish. You never saw the kitchen or the prep. You only saw the food in the sterile antechamber, and then it was yours. This mattered in the early automat days, when 'free lunch' – a sleazy beer-for-cash, food-for-free lunch deal in some of the city's dankest taverns – was within living memory.

There was also the matter of style. We've got used to the idea that the quicker and more casual a place is, the more dismal the ambience has to be, like this is the spiritual toll of convenience. But there were automats with marble frontage and mosaic floors. The self-service drip coffee – a Horn & Hardart signature brew – flowed from a tap modelled on the mouth of a Pompeii fountain. The first automat in the city had a twenty-foot-tall stained-glass facade. Even the tech was meant to be beautiful – an architecturally expansive art deco vending machine, an interrupted plane of ornament, the Doge's Palace of American fast-casual dining.

More than anything, though, you can't understand automats unless you understand just how much, in the early twentieth century, Americans hated waiting staff. According to *The New York Times*, they were 'one of the necessary evils of an advanced civilization'. Tipping was seen as 'offensively un-American'. The art of service was a European thing – uncomfortably subtextual and too delicate for hard American business. The entire point of early automats was that they were waiterless, not just because it was quick, but because it was a relief. If tech can't give us anything we don't already have – quick food, cheap food – it has to sell itself on asking for less. The automats gave people service without the interpersonal weirdness of being served.

You can't destroy energy – you can only move it around. You can outsource a contractor, you can move the IT department into the basement, you can silo the work of cleaning the office or buy in the onions pre-chopped. You can do all of this, and add a touchscreen or a sushi conveyor belt somewhere into the workflow, and have things seem to happen by magic. You can hide a platoon of servers and prep chefs behind a wall of automat machines.

The shadow world of automats was like this: on the other side of the wall, there was a tight galley kitchen, with the punitive lighting and pressing walls of a submarine. There was no art deco detailing here, just a row of workers facing the back side of the metal wall. From this angle, the vending machines were columns of stacked steel drums, each rotating around a vertical axis. Sometimes they were more boxy – a cat-flap aperture – and if someone looked through the locker window at the wrong time they saw a hand putting a fresh plate in. Paintings and photos show how efficiently lonely it could be to eat in a place like this, even if they didn't show the purgatory behind the wall.

It was here, the human world behind the wall, that the automats really did their work. Most of the food was produced in a central Horn & Hardart commissary on Manhattan's West Side, and up to five deliveries went out to the restaurants each day. It was cheaper than splitting this work across individual kitchens, and more consistent. For thirty-seven years, the recipes were developed by a French chef, Francis Bourdon, whose mission wasn't just to make the cooking good, but to make it good every day, without variance, without being worse or even better on any given meal. He standardised the process of making broth, developing recipes that would yield the exact same 300-gallon stock pot every day. The drip coffee was the first widely available drip coffee in the United States, and it was taste-tested each morning at HQ, and it was identical across each of the dozens of Horn & Hardart shops. There was a 400-page manual about how to cut the bacon into uniform squares before putting it on top of beans, and the precise trigonometry involved in slicing the coconut pie.

It's this sameness – which you can only really get if you treat humans like machines – that made the automats. You only see it at the very highest and most chainified ends of the spectrum. In Michelin-starred restaurants, consistency matters because every person who walks through the door – including critics – should experience the same quality, and because when you are talking about the very best, there's only one way to do things. In the case of fast-food chains, it's because you should be able to walk into any branch, on any day, and never taste anything you don't expect.

All this was done by hands behind a metal edifice. When a meal was ready, the plates were quietly cleared and cleaned by more workers. After hours, more workers came and scrubbed the tables and mopped the floors. There were small armies of cooks in the centralised production kitchens. All this labour had to be done as quickly and cheaply as possible, but without letting on that it was any work at all. The machines got the credit for a human system, which reminds me – do you know those Amazon stores? You're monitored by cameras that track what you pick up. Then you just walk out of the store, without going to a cashier, and you're automatically billed for the right amount. There were reports last year that a lot of these images weren't being processed by AI at all, but by legions of 'data labellers' staring at remote video feeds on computer monitors halfway across the world. But then, what's a worker supposed to do? In the 1930s, the automat behind-the-wallers – many of them African American and Latino – went on strike over pay and working conditions. They lay down in the road and gridlocked Herald Square, making themselves unignorable. But the union can't take on the catering giants. Most people just got arrested, or lost their jobs, and that was that.

This is the thing: the machines themselves were the least important part of the system. It was the human work behind the wall that was unprecedented. The logistics and the centralised control, the systematisation of service, the routines for quality control, the total oversight at HQ. It was the way that power was distributed. The chef wasn't boss any more – up the food chain was the branch manager, then the regional supervisor, then the guys in corporate. No food business had ever turned food service into an industry like this, at least not so successfully. At one point, Horn & Hardart was the biggest restaurant chain in the world.

*

In the 1950s, automats started looking tired. Various New York corporate headquarters moved to the suburban areas that gabled the city. The Manhattan lunch rush got less intense. The clientele changed. In a Diane Arbus photo, two older women, one in a fur leopard-print hat and a stack of three heavy curb-chain necklaces, the other in a high-rise black pillbox, smoked at an automat table with the air of queens holding court. People started using automats like living rooms, and the company had to bring in both doormen and a minimum spend. It was already looking old, this particular vision of the future, so Horn & Hardart tried to roll with the kitsch. Nothing really worked to make automats make sense. Before long, the machines didn't run on real currency but on tokens that you had to buy from a cashier: go in, feed the machine, mash some buttons, play.

The trouble was that there were other places now – less flashy but more modern – where you could grab a quick lunch. Fast-food chains had been growing in popularity and size in the 1930s and now they were moving out of their suburban heartlands and into the city. McDonald's, Burger King and KFC muscled in on the automat's economic niche, but they were smaller and more agile. They were also easier to run, because everything that needed to be cooked could be cooked then and there, in a couple of minutes on the line, instead of doing cross-city logistical juggling with vats of soup and fresh-baked pies. It helped that the primary income stream didn't come from kaiser rolls.

You could say fast food killed the automat, but it'd be more accurate to say the automat birthed fast food. The unbendable maxims of fast-food chains – consistency, cleanliness, convenience, control – weren't invented by Horn & Hardart, but it was the first time these things had been done together so well, and for so long. Automats took the language of subs, soups and franks and transformed it, not by touching the food itself but by totally changing how it got to you.

Everything the automats pioneered eventually became part of fast food. In Kansas during the 1920s, White Castle lined its interiors with stainless steel and put the kids behind the counter in clean, anonymous uniforms. An early McDonald's mascot, a guy with a burger for a head, was called Speedee. Burger King became what it is because it pioneered an automated broiler system. Every one of these places, through careful micromanagement, developed structures for absolute sameness, and eventually became chains. You can see the logic of the automat in all of this. The systems were in place. The mood had been established – for sameness, for ease. 'Fast food' stopped being an adjectival phrase and started looking more like a philosophy. The only thing the fast-food joints did differently is they gave you the kind of food you'd eat on the road, whereas the automats never really got past just speeding up the food you got at home.

Maybe all this would've been OK and automats could've coexisted with fast food, but the insurmountable hurdle, in the end, was the machines themselves. It was hard to talk about this – the fact that when you really got down to things, the machinery wasn't all that useful. The cabinets got jammed, and the slots backed up with old nickels and bung coins. People got frustrated with the effortful theatre of this supposedly labour-saving device. Labour-saving for who exactly? 'This kind of restaurant underlines one of the greatest confusions of my life,' as Alfred Hitchcock put it. 'I frequently find myself trying to tip slot machines and tilt waitresses.' In the seventies, Horn & Hardart started converting the compact square footage of its automats into Burger King franchises. In 1991, the last New York automat closed.

'When one dies with this world in this meltdown,' asked Merce Cunningham, a dancer and choreographer, and the life partner of John Cage, in his late diaries, 'is one missing something grand that will happen?' Maybe transit would overhaul the fabric of the city, the reinvention of the subway. Maybe manufacturing would revive the South. Maybe something wild could happen, something completely new, made from the stuff you already know. It would have the feeling of an old dream. Maybe, he wrote, 'the automat could return.'

And so it is. I saw recently that Horn & Hardart are back. They're trying to bring back the automat, to open a fresh Manhattan branch. But why? We live in an automat world. The spirit endures in the quasi-industrial systems behind fast food. It also lives on experientially, when it comes to how you navigate – or avoid – the uneasy interaction between the person who's eating, and the people who serve. We barely had any automats in the UK, at least not in any meaningful way, but the impact of these Americanised food systems, and the logic of the wall, is in every one of the techy interfaces we've come to rely on. Have you been to a McDonald's any time in the last five years? A complex of screens to rival the New York stock exchange will supposedly simplify the process of getting your food. They stand around the restaurant floor, with the perfect, receptive posture of a waiting maître d'. They're silently obliging in every way, except they refuse to issue a receipt. No chat, no conversational weaving, just a person and a screen. Even when it comes to getting the order, the person at the counter calls a number, and the number is you, and that's it.

During the pandemic, this tech became genuinely mainstream. Let's say you order tacos on Deliveroo. The wall of automat machines – an almost televisual grid – has turned into the app. Once you've chosen something, the distance this idea has to travel is a few thousand miles' worth of cellular and broadband vibrations, pinging back and forth between phone, servers and business; plus a circuitous path on the back of a moped to your door. Go into a branch of a casual chain restaurant and you'll find QR code menus, maybe even a way to pay by going to a website and entering your table number – a system that makes avoiding servers, and tipping, as easy as it's ever been. Restaurants don't even list telephone numbers any more, because why would you, if you can have a quick and wordless interaction via a third-party booking app? You could order from Five Guys a dozen times without ever stepping foot in one, without ever experiencing it first-hand. The restaurant pass – the thin, busy interchange across which food is ferried from the kitchen to the table – gets wider every day.

This is the age of the interface, even if it started a hundred years and a few thousand miles away. This should make things easier, but a lot of the time these interventions aren't actually that time-saving at all. Even the McDonald's screens – especially the McDonald's screens.

I was in New York last year and went out to eat with new friends. Our night started at a kerbside stall where we had chalupas topped with green and red salsas and fresh onion. The money had barely changed hands before the chalupas were ours, fresh from the comal – they'd been fried in hot lard – and about hot enough to blister your fingers. It was the quickest food, and the most convenient, and frankly some of the best food that we had during the trip, and we saw it all – how the cook manoeuvred the tortillas between the hotspots and the edges of the comal, the deftness required to speed-ladle salsa with precision. New York is a city full of places like these. And hotdog stands. And pizza slices that don't come from vending machines.

I have no delusions about the social conditions behind this work. Or the economics that lead to many vendors having no choice but to go analogue. Some vendors like it this way, others just can't afford a bricks and mortar store or streamlining tech. How did this stuff – the quickest, most necessary stuff we eat – become so convoluted? I appreciate factories and machines and tech and social media and the ways that these things are reshaping the culture. I don't think there's anything wrong with modernisation. But there are cases where you have to wonder who it really serves. Our night ended in a tiny, almost-empty dessert cafe in deepest Queens – miles from Manhattan and decades from the automat – where we ordered a ready-prepared dessert using an iPad interface, and then waited while some invisible levers and buttons were pushed, and waited some more, and didn't dare ask because the whole system was set up to strongly discourage things like asking – that is what the screens are for. In any case, the dessert was sitting in a glass cabinet six feet away the whole time. The automat is dead, long live the automat.

There are reasons why we're here – there is labour saved, there are journeys shortened, some things are easier, others are not. This is all fine, I guess, so long as we don't kid ourselves. The screen isn't just an interface to connect the eater and the cook. It is also a wall. It's a wall, just like a wall of coin-operated lockers behind which a busy kitchen sweats. Still, I use these antisocial platforms, as we all seem to these days. It's not always good, but it is human – this desire to have your needs instantly and silently met. It's the anxious eater's Valhalla. 'Man is God's likeness; a thing is man's likeness,' Vladimir Nabokov wrote in 1928. 'An automat is in many ways most similar to man.' Somehow, history has intractably led us to the pizza vending machine.

Wimpy

Or, the good, the bad and the ugly of British American food

I will say it: I like Wimpy. I grew up in Southend – one of a series of towns suffixed with '-on-Sea' even though the sea is actually the Thames and you can see the opposite shore in clear weather. If you're from here, you know how to lean into how naff it all is, to make the prosaic into a strength. The Wimpy restaurant, or at least one of them, is in a perma-shadowed corner of the town's tiredest shopping centre. Looking across from Next, which for better or worse is the most ambitious thing in here, the Wimpy is struck from view by two escalators to the largely abandoned upper floor. The only time that you are likely to see it is gliding down the other escalators to the exit below, by which point you're already gone.

This Wimpy is the kind of place you could walk past a hundred times without noticing it was there, but if you did notice it, you'd notice that it's a scene from that Edward Hopper painting: a rectangle of yolk-coloured light, the silhouette of someone sitting alone with a coffee. There are faux leather banquettes and granite-finish tabletops in an uptight grid. Along the right-hand wall, a long counter. There's a grill where a guy attends to patties, a vibrating soft-serve dispenser, a soda fountain. You feel it – the quiet skill that goes into this place. The machines are buffed until their steel has the texture of satin. It's a sharp-edged replica of an American burger bar. Like all Wimpys, it seems to sit outside of normal space and time.

Southend has a lot of Wimpys. There are five if you count the contiguous suburbs like Benfleet or Rayleigh – suburbs that are very clear about not being part of Southend, but *are* part of Southend, and if they want to address the allegations then they'd do well to have fewer Wimpys. It also has a lot of almost-Wimpys. There's an 'American themed restaurant' with a decorative red fire hydrant inside and a Statue of Liberty wearing the Stars and Stripes as a wraparound. There's a place themed around the American frontier. Each eerie American-themed restaurant is eerie in its own way, but the strength of Wimpy is that it accepts what it is – a timewarp restaurant, with the vibe of an American diner, and the mannerisms of a caff.

The menu is uncomplicated. There are grills, shakes and sundaes. There are over a dozen iterations of burger: the modular beef options, with or without various toppings or extra patties, going all the way up to a triple quarter pounder with bacon and cheese; there are chicken burgers and a chicken-esque Quorn burger; there's a Beyond Burger; Wimpy must be the last place in the world that you can still get a bean burger. The most famous thing on any Wimpy menu is the Bendy: a frankfurter sausage with deep, methodical lacerations along one long side, curved in a circle as if chasing its own tail and then fried. This you can have in a bun or as a grill, though what nobody will tell you is that although a sausage can be bent to fit into a hamburger bun, it shouldn't, because the geometrically inevitable circle in the middle then has to be filled – in this case, by a thick slice of tomato.

And then, there are the English breakfasts and buttered, toasted teacakes. The fries look and taste like fries, but they are called chips. Every time beans are mentioned on the menu, it says Heinz Baked Beans, in the same way that you might capitalise God. Not only can you get a cup of tea in this sharp-edged replica of an American burger bar, but it comes in a teapot with a cup, saucer, teaspoon and complimentary Lotus biscuit on the side. There was a story a while back that Brad Pitt had been filming in Essex and got himself a cheeseburger meal at Billericay Wimpy. This was all backwards, like Nero hitting up Caesars Palace. You couldn't help but wonder – as an Essex person, as a Wimpy person – what it looked like through his eyes.

'Our kitchen has more in common with America than with any other country,' Florence White wrote in the introduction to her 1932 book, *Good Things in England*. She was looking backward when she said it – to colonial roots and shared culinary grammars – but I don't think she could have known just how true this would turn out to be, and in a way that she almost certainly would have hated. In case you missed it, American food is huge in the UK. Even the most vibeless high street has half a dozen fast American-ish food places. There are American-style barbecue festivals and chefs giving soul food concepts a go. We've moved into the smashburger era, with super-thin patties that are basically reinventing McDonald's, but giving it the look of a roadside diner. It feels like every day some American fast- or fast-casual chain opens its augural UK store, usually in some kind of new and oversized mall, where the cultural landscape is a Petri dish for recycled American ideas. And then, in the shadows, there is Wimpy – the original British burger bar, and the place where all this began.

Wimpy, the least relevant burger restaurant chain in the UK, is the scion of a tearoom dynasty. In the first half of the twentieth century, J. Lyons and Co. was Britain's largest restaurant group. It had Corner House cafeterias in prime London real estate, tearooms, Maison Lyons restaurants, and factories that produced 36,000 miles of Swiss roll a week. Lyons delivery vans were as emblematic of the British roads as Eddie Stobart trucks or Royal Mail vans.

Even when they were new, they were dated. The wait-resses were called Nippies and had to wear ugly grey dresses and had bonnets which, for real, had embroidery in the shape of an L on the forehead. You got the full white tablecloth treatment, even if you were only there for a ham sandwich. 'I must think kindly of the Corner Houses and Maison Lyons,' ran an article in *The Times*. 'Not because I find pleasure in them. I do not. But I recognize that these Corner Houses do give to thousands of people something that they very much like.' This something was affordable grandeur, maybe getting the chance to have tea under a chandelier instead of in a caff. People remembered being taken there as a child, and they took their children and grandchildren in turn. The article was an advertorial and it was paid for by Lyons. The obsolescence was half the point.

During the Second World War, Lyons had to streamline and converted a lot of the tearooms to self-service cafeterias. After the war, they tried a bunch of concept restaurants to work the post-war energy to their advantage, because even if you could go back to the way things were before, why would you want to? So they tried a chicken restaurant, as well as a place called Chips on Everything and a casual spot called Haversnack. There was a high-concept restaurant called Upper Crust where you could get steak and wine on a London double-decker bus, but then it turned out it was illegal to serve alcohol on the bus when it was parked, so the bus could not legally stop while you ate. The menu of an Angus Steakhouse, and the plot of *Speed*.

Lyons Corner Houses were perfect testing grounds for concepts like these. Each level worked the Lyons brand in a different key, with a yassified greasy spoon called the Bacon and Egg on one floor, a more formal restaurant on another, a jazz bar higher up. Lyons figured out early that what distinguishes tiers of restaurant, maybe even more than taste, is just speed. Do you want a quick steak or a boozy business-lunch steak? A romantic and long-winded steak? We have a steak for everyone. Restaurants still work like this, and maybe now more than ever – a chain fast-casual ramen place has a lot more in common with a chain fast-casual peri-peri-chicken place than it does with a kaiseki restaurant.

In 1954, the year that meat rationing ended, Lyons trialled a new concept – a burger bar, in collaboration with Wimpy, a small chain of restaurants founded in Indiana. A full fifty years before burger pop-ups became a thing, they turned up at events like Wimbledon and the Chelsea

Flower Show. At the Ideal Home Exhibition, they shifted 10,000 burgers in a week. It was a moment of American fixation. Even if you didn't live it, you can imagine it: Americanised supermarkets were spreading; there were the movies coming out of Hollywood, their main job being to sell America as an idea; and teenagers were suddenly a thing, with languages and subcultures of their own, instead of just being big kids or small adults.

Wimpy isn't a burger bar, as it was in its Midwestern prototype form, but a capital-B burger bar, a pastiche of something the English understood almost nothing about. In the United States, Wimpy had been the kind of moderately successful but ultimately small-time burger restaurant chain the Midwest was built on. In the UK, it was unprecedented: the predominance of the grill, the thickness of the milkshakes, the burgers themselves. A huge Wimpy opened on Coventry Street in 1955, selling tens of thousands of burgers a week. Reporters visited, and prefaced their articles by saying that they now knew the difference between a burger and a hotdog. And so, on the fourth vertex of one of the busiest crossroads in London, Britain's tearoom dynasty started flipping patties. It was the first burger restaurant in the UK.

I don't think I need to explain why people liked burgers once they tried them. Wimpy spread quickly, first as a chain and then as franchises, moving more or less evenly across the UK. One by one, the old Lyons tearooms and Corner Houses were replaced by this new generation of burger bars. Tongue and pressed beef were lost, along with Bovril and biscuits and Nippies. Crooning entertainments – ladies' symphony orchestras and jazz singers – stopped and the easy percussion of the grill station started up. The afternoon tea and cake crowd vacated and young people moved in, relaxing in groups in the banquettes, pulling the grainy milk-slush of a Wimpy 'Whippsy' up through a straw. You can imagine the cultural dysphoria that the Lyons old-timers must have felt, seeing ham and mustard sandwiches and white tablecloths replaced by Bendys in a Bun. Wimpy Grills was named after J. Wellington Wimpy, a burger-mad Popeye character. By the mid-sixties there were over 500 Wimpys in the UK.

You'd be hard-pressed to find a British person who was a teenager any time between the fifties and the eighties who doesn't have some story to tell about Wimpy – about how much time they killed there, or how many small, pointless, landmark teenage moments happened in those booths. Everyone ate burgers. Everyone liked Americana, which they mistook for actual Americanness. The United States was an imaginary place, and you could find it on the high street in Hemel Hempstead, seven days a week. In a single generation, hamburgers went from being a novelty to becoming England's second national cuisine.

It's extraordinary how quickly this happened. It's even more extraordinary given that the burgers were mid. In his 1976 survey of American food, Waverley Root wrote it was speed that defined American cooking the best. In America, restaurants came of age at the same time as the railroads; and diners co-evolved with highways. But we never really understood this over here. For the most part, Wimpy was just as slow as the silver-urn, white-tablecloth tearooms it replaced. These Wimpys, unlike the American ones, were table service. They set up in places of sleepy English leisure: suburbs, high streets, malls. Through some kind of protracted transatlantic game of telephone, Lyons took the idea of the hamburger bar – quick, casual, coherent with the country it was born in – and turned it into a more parochial, hybrid space, where the 'Delta burger' could have as easily referred to the Thames estuary as the Mississippi.

The thing is – and there's really no way of getting around this – for all the ambition and the vision that Wimpy had in those early days, the food has never been all that. The thermic foundation of American short-order cooking is the grill, but in Britain we've historically relied on deep-frying instead. Line cooking in that specific American way is not our strength. There were so many mistranslations, so many things that were almost right but so, so wrong. It's hard to imagine that a Wimpy burger – that voluminous, matte-finish English bread roll, the underseasoned patty, the unforgivable mistake of including tomato slices as standard – would've been such a popular burger if it hadn't been the first.

In 1974, the first McDonald's in Britain opened in Woolwich in South East London. In some ways it looked like a counter-service Wimpy: the same static banks of chairs bolted to the floor, the same overhead menu boards, similar prices. Still, it felt new. Wimpy was an American-flavour revival from a legacy caterer, many of its branches left in the care of local franchisees who set the prices how they wanted and could either serve you the best or the most vile chips of your life on any given day. McDonald's was a direct American import where the hamburger, fries and shake combo was marketed, at the start, as the 'United Tastes of America'. The burgers came out quicker, the systems were cleaner and the prices were lower. In Wimpy you could bank on the tomato-shaped ketchup dispenser and the ashtray on the table, but in McDonald's you could bank on absolute sameness in the food itself, from site to site and week to week. And it tasted better. You couldn't try the coarse-ground pure-beef McDonald's patties and then realistically go back to the texturally undifferentiated pulp of the Wimpy ones. Think about the golden ratios of the double cheeseburger – for all the evils of McDonald's itself, it's one of the most delicately constructed foods in modern history.

This McDonald's was the beginning of a new wave of British Americana. The Wimpy generation, from the seventies, started with the aesthetics of American fast food and fitted this stuff into existing British food culture – the tearooms, the caffs – however they could. But the second wave started with systems: the corporate autarkies that you really need if the burgers are going to be the same every single time, globalised logistics networks, an economy where multinationals are encouraged to spread, the intricate food mechanics required to get meals out as cheaply and as quickly as possible. The actual chips and burgers and milkshakes were only the consequences of a pure American business concept. Within a couple of years, the UK had its first Burger King. By 1980, there were also American imports Huckleberry's, Wendy's and KFC. Domino's came in the mid-eighties, along with the first McDonald's drive-thru and franchise locations.

In the late eighties, the number of McDonald's surpassed

Wimpy for the first time. There were corporate take-overs, and table-service Wimpy branches were converted to counter service to try to match the speed and slick of the American fast-food brands. It was too late. In the big-gest English cultural reshuffle since Thomas Cromwell's monastery cull, Wimpys started closing down and their cultural capital was reassigned to the incoming, genuinely American chains. Successful Wimpys just about survived, but the smaller, more vulnerable branches were converted to new-wave Burger Kings, which opened seamlessly in the same spots on the same high streets, as though nothing had happened.

It's hardly surprising that Wimpy – less swag, more 'How do you do, fellow kids?' – was collapsing by the late eighties. As the cull continued and the Burger King takeover went on, the demographics changed. The pleather banquette crowd started skewing older, and you'd find more people in there killing time alone with a tea than in a pack with a Wimpy milkshake. It's funny – the Wimpys that actu-ally survived were the intransigent, table-service ones that refused to change with the times. They didn't try to fight McDonald's on its terms. Instead they relaxed into what they really were: a cultural hybrid, more English than actu-ally American, that ran on nostalgia, affordability, and being a reliable hideaway for people with nowhere better to go. There are fifty-nine Wimpys in the UK now, down from the sixty-one when I first drafted this chapter, and way down from the 600-plus in the pre-Golden Arches golden age.

A while ago, I went to a food festival in South London, where – in a smoky, concrete atrium between two runs of railway arches – about a dozen barbecue stalls were set up. You can find barbecue and grill cooking easily enough in Peckham. There is suya, South African braii, skewers of chicken kofte, all of which use direct heat in a way that Britain hasn't done properly since the suckling-pig era. The barbecue festival was different. Instead of barbecuing – a verb, a way of cooking – it felt like people were *doing* barbecue, in the same way that your uncle will *do* Sean Connery when he's taking impression requests.

Of the dozen or so vendors, most were doing non-specific, seemingly American-inspired barbecue: slow-cooked brisket piled into burgers, burnt ends, actually burnt ends, cheeseburger wings, beef sliders, ribs and ribs and ribs, Texas-inspired massaman curry. Even when the flavours were global, the foundations cleaved to certain barbecue methods, and the basic units of North American culinary vocab. 'Cherry smoked char siu glazed kurobuta pork belly taco.' 'House brined & cherry smoked short rib pastrami slider.' 'Hickory smoked brisket.' 'Crack pork' – in a pork-crackling 'taco'. The crowd was full of people on pilgrimage from Essex, Surrey and Kent, where America is still about the most exciting thing anyone can think of, fifty years after the first British McDonald's. People were doing pitmaster roleplay – LARPing for meatheads – over mid-range hibachi grills. Everyone had trained under the most renowned barbecue chef in Texas. The master of ceremonies was a TikTok influencer with the mien of Henry VIII but the gravitas of Harry Hill, who has become famous on social media mainly by posting hyperbolic, uber-meaty videos of pseudo-American food.

You'd think we might have gotten bored of America, as

an idea, by now. But in the UK American food is bigger now than ever. Even foods that aren't originally American have come to us triangulated through the United States. Talk about pizza with anyone who was born after the first British branch of Domino's, and you're as likely to hear about New York slices, Teenage Mutant Ninja Turtles, and orgiastic stuffed-crust options as you are to hear about Italy. In most of Britain, if you talk about tacos you'll be talking about an American-Mexican fusion style, indigenous mainly to Taco Bell. London's traditional bagel culture, which survived in the East End until relatively recently, has lost ground to New York bagels, to the extent that the default now isn't salt beef, but American-style salmon and schmear. Big, orb-like filled doughnuts have been sidelined in favour of American ring doughnuts. I love all of these things, even though the doughnut also loses something when it gains that hole. We talk about how much of an impact French cuisine has had on dining, but when it comes to ordinary eating out, it's America that sets the bar.

The good thing about this third wave of British American food is that it's no longer just one thing. Under the Wimpy hegemony, American food was a type – namely, burgers, badly done but misted with romantic ideas about what the food of the United States might be. During the McDonald's wave, American food was more of a mood – super quick and ultra cheap – and came to you courtesy of some of the biggest corporations in global food. You start with imitation, then you have big-business proliferation, but the latest wave is lighter, more absurd. The barbecue festival was just one drop in a deluge of American cultural food that crosses my social media feeds every single day. It's mostly happening at a smaller scale – individual businesses or very small chains, taking what they've seen of nü-American fast food online, and reimagining it for wherever they're at. This means places in Wolverhampton trying New Orleans-style food, or dessert bars serving banana pudding as though this is Charleston, South Carolina, and not Ilford. It means Instagram-hyped businesses in the Midlands serving 'soul food'. It's not even a contradiction – soul food, as a concept, was invented in northern American cities in the sixties and seventies, to understand the food of the South. Its foundations were always different to its roots.

The most creative work being done right now is in the halal food scene. No sector in British fast food is doing more, going to such extraneous and sometimes counter-productive lengths, to reimagine the burger. In Manchester, you'll find a new and fiercely contested empire of spicy-dip burgers, created by a new generation of primarily British Pakistani restaurateurs. Dessert parlours like Creams and Kaspas, where the menu is heavily weighted towards brownies and cookie dough, have taken over from Italian shops as *the* places to get ice cream.

I went to Birmingham recently, to Ladypool Road in what used to be known as the Balti Triangle, but is now basically ground zero of postmodern British Americana. Along a 100-yard stretch, there was the following: 3 in 1 Burger, Flamin' Burger, Rockaburger, Donm Tacos, Stack Shack, Dixy Chicken, Pepe's fried chicken, Shake Bees and Mr T's, between them selling Nashville wings, Five Guys-style fries, watermelon coolers, the Mexicano Smash Burger, Louisiana rub wings, and a chicken fillet burger seasoned with crushed hot Cheetos. (When we tried it, it was clear the seasoning was actually Wotsit dust.) One restaurant had Houston, Chicago, Boston, Vegas and Miami burger variants. We've come a long way from the ABC-format KFC ripoffs – Aberdeen Fried Chicken, Basildon Fried Chicken, Carmarthen Fried Chicken and the like. A lot of these restaurants are reinventions of American chains which don't, in their original format, cater for halal diners.

It used to be that Brits learned about American food culture from the movies; now it's the phone screen – Instagram and TikTok helping a pervasive and weirdly anti-geographical Americana to take over the world. This is where the influencers have come in handy, creating an entire secondary economy of unpaid hypemen for average burger joints. Things have never been better, if you're an American food fan in the UK. Every America, real and imagined, is represented: you've got the imported chains, the deep-knowledge regional American cooking, the technique hounds scouring sub-Reddits for smokehouse tips, the fun hybridised creations of the British halal new wave, the high and low and everything in between. And then, like a forgotten toy, there is Wimpy.

Look at a map of the remaining Wimpys and you'll see they mainly stick to a few social niches: there's the Hampshire barracks belt, carving from Farnborough down to the Navy outposts at Southsea; or the fading Wimpy clusters of the high Home Counties like Buckinghamshire or Surrey – places too affluent, if anything, to support a Wimpy, but too stagnant to let it go. There is a ring of Wimpy restaurants that follows almost exactly the path of the M25, in satellite towns caught between the city and the country and loyal to neither. Along the coast, in Birkenhead, Eastbourne, Swanage, the seaside Wimpys, a peripheral terrain built almost entirely on nostalgia. The social terrain is broadly conservative: army bases, outposts of the Royal British Legion, coastal resorts, each place not entirely willing to move past history. There's a balance to be struck – too green-and-pleasant and a place won't sustain a burger bar; too cosmopolitan, and there will be chicken shops, TikTok-viral halal burger joints and McDonald's that have battled Wimpy on relevance and won.

The most concentrated Wimpy heartland is the wedge of land that cuts east from London, following the path of the Thames towards the North Sea. You can plot it as a scalene triangle: its anchor in Bermondsey, up to Clacton-on-Sea on the eastern edge of Essex, with its lower tip in Southend-on-Sea, skirting the estuary. This is my Essex: statistically speaking, the Wimpy capital of the UK. Nearly a quarter of all British Wimpy bars are here, and the epi-centre of this melancholic empire in decline is Southend. You can read the dregs of Wimpy like tea leaves. French scholar Michel de Certeau wrote that 'Only the end of an age makes it possible to say what made it live.'

Wimpy lends itself to nostalgia. I feel myself doing it too, even though I'm trying to be clear-eyed. On Facebook, there are back-in-my-day pages with discussion threads about Wimpy memories. Local newspaper stories about a menu someone found from the 1970s. In Google reviews, one of the most praised things about Wimpy is that you get a knife and fork with your burger. Chips are chips, not fries, and there is vinegar on the tables. It's funny just how native this place feels – Wimpy used to be successful because it channelled the United States, now it's successful because it is as close as we have to a PDO-certified British restaurant, one that almost definitionally could never exist elsewhere. Sometimes I think that everyone is sleeping on Wimpy: that there's a ludic, postmodern burger chain with an architecturally significant frankfurter, and it's nearly empty. But then I remember that despite how much I think about Wimpy, I've only actually been a handful of times. I remember that this isn't my era. I remember the Five Guys shake, the Shake Shack burger and that given a choice, I will always go for the timeless silhouette of a McNugget.

Still, Wimpy does cling on, across its small empire. You can see it trying to modernise – a digital ordering system in Southsea, fresh new fit-outs. Sometimes, in doing so, it loses something, like the fish finger burger – a movingly naff but exceptional choice which in recent years has been replaced by a dupe of a Filet-O-Fish. Wimpy has even, in the last year or two, shown signs of growth. Look, you can't read the future on the basis of a new Eastbourne branch and the headline 'Wimpy makes a triumphant return to Tonbridge'. But I am hopeful, I guess, in an uninvolved kind of way. All of these are franchises, and there's something heartening about how, for all the global ambition of the original Wimpys, these restaurants feel so . . . local. These are community places, which is why the first franchise branches are still Wimpys today, while the central London flagships died years ago. The Southend Wimpy has been in the care of the same family for nearly fifty years.

I went to the Southend Wimpy a while back, to check that I hadn't just imagined it, and to get a Brown Derby. Like the Bendy, the Brown Derby is a Wimpy hallmark – synonymous with Wimpy in the same way as a Big Mac is to McDonald's. Unlike the Bendy, it is wonderful. How do I explain this thing? Well, it's a pyramid-like structure. The foundation is a still-warm sugared ring doughnut. Next, following the contours of the doughnut, there's a swirling crown of soft-serve ice cream. On top, chocolate sauce and small, almost parsimonious, cubes of fudge. Like any adequate sundae, it tastes exactly the sum of its parts. Look at the earliest Wimpy menus and you'll see it used to be called a 'Chocolate Bowler'. The bowler wasn't American enough, I guess, because by the 1970s they'd renamed it 'Brown Derby', the transliteration of a name that neither described nor did justice to the thing in the first place. I like to think that they were thinking of Los Angeles, though – the mythic Brown Derby restaurant was built on Wilshire Boulevard in 1926, and it had a hemispherical dome like a derby hat.

There's no accounting for how much I think about this – a dessert that I have ordered only a couple of times but feels like it was made just for me from the remnants of a dream. And so I ordered one, for old times' sake. The restaurant was quiet. Older couples drifted in, and their usual order was called to them before they even had a chance to sit, and they were pleased to have been remembered. At one table there was a forty-five-minute-long Chuckle Brothers bit – to-me, to-you with a £20 note over who got to treat who. The invisible threads of habit are what make this place run so easy, but you can be tripped up by them too, and you know if you've sat at someone else's table, as I did, when you feel eyes on you. Nobody just ends up in this Wimpy:

if you're here it's because this is your own private Wimpy, the most special ordinary place you know. The burger is what it is, but order a Brown Derby and it'll be put on the table tenderly, like a precious relic of a time gone by. It's gorgeous and irrelevant. I love it.

Author's note: To refresh my memory when finalising the edits on this book, I went to a different Wimpy – the identity of which I will not disclose – to have the Brown Derby again. It was disgusting. The nuts were rancid and the doughnut turned into a gummy mass under the lightest pressure from my fork. I didn't even know a doughnut could do this. But the man who served it to me was so kind that I ate the whole thing out of guilt and have spent the past few weeks digesting it and trying to talk myself around. I am doing my best to see the bright side. The idea of the Brown Derby, at least, is still beautiful to me. And that is Wimpy, through and through.

Epilogue

I learned a lot while writing this book, but the main thing is this: the more I think about it, the more I wonder whether I've ever had an original craving in my life. I go online and I'm met by an endless stream of recipes and reviews and food opinions, often incorrect. I go to the supermarket and enjoy that stoned, bedazzled feeling of walking through a dream. It is a dream that has been meticulously curated, over the past 100 years, to micromanage the delicate process of 'following your gut'. I go to a burger pop-up with a few dozen other people who are just as much Too Online as I am. It can be overwhelming, but it's also electric – the connectedness of it all, the absurdity, the way the modern food world refuses to stay still for any longer than the few seconds it takes you to film that reel.

Could Florence White, writing about English folk cookery in the thirties, have anticipated the arrival of the Dorito-dusted spicy chicken dip burger in Manchester? Could a foodie in the eighties have imagined that Britain would U-turn from tapioca-phobic to a bubble tea republic? Probably not. The pace of change in food culture is increasing, mostly down to the changing ways that media works. Every time that the medium changes, so does the way we talk about food and the kinds of food we value. Cookbooks change. The way we hear about restaurants changes. It's not just reality and representation any more. Modern food *is* its media.

But writing this book also revealed moments of unlikely connection, slower and more meaningful than the frenetic changes we see. The closer I looked, the more I realised that this food culture, even though it has been intensified by the internet, has deep, human roots. I thought that someone like Keith Lee was a singularity – the kind of pop restaurant mega influencer that could only have come from social media. But then I learned about guidebook writers like Duncan Hines and Victor Hugo Green, and the constant movement of critical power from the middle-brow to the elite and back. I learned that there have long existed Wife Guys who like road trips and who, in one way or another, become the arbiters of normal contemporary taste. From the earliest days of the internet, people were searching for cookie recipes, and when they couldn't find a recipe they uploaded their own. And so community cookbooks – which had been a kind of small-time, church-pamphlet, Girl Scout-binder kind of thing until this point – started to adapt for the digital commons. You got sites like Allrecipes, and what you learned from these is that lots of people can't bake for shit, but that those who do bake *really* bake, really care about food and the stories we tell about it.

Epilogue

'Refuse to climb aboard this ship of fools,' Christopher Kimball wrote, in his essay about the online food media free-for-all. But you can choose to self-isolate, or you can plug into the synaptic, capricious, semi-democratic, multivalent realities of food culture right now. There are so many stories about food that the guardians of the culture do not know how to tell, or don't want to tell, or even actively suppress. We need to notice, and archive, and shape our shared food cultures – and do so with the same collective outpouring of energy that gave rise to them in the first place. Besides, as Bee Wilson pointed out, talking about cookbooks: 'People have predicted the death of cooking almost as many times as they have predicted the death of reading.' And the same goes for criticism. The same goes for factory food versus homemade, and restaurants, and offal, and recipes. You name it. You can't trust food writers to predict where the culture is headed. This includes me.

Food is so intimate. I am self-absorbed, maybe even more than most. A lot of my work has been about my personal relationship with food. Even when it's not truly intimate, I've been interested in emotions and narrative – something like using food as a biographical aid. I, like a whole generation of food writers, have been guilty of taking the aphorism 'You are what you eat' more seriously than Brillat-Savarin ever meant it, and besides – he was just some guy who, if he was born in another century, would've had a Tumblr. There's a market for biographical food content, as the cottage industry of food memoirs and personal essays goes to show, but the thing that's most surprised me about writing this book is that I'm now less sentimental about food than I've ever been. Advertising, trends, discourse, TV and words act on me just as much as they do on anybody. But now that I've watched how they do, I find myself taking it all a lot less personally. People often cite Laurie Colwin – 'No one who cooks, cooks alone' – and the same is true when it comes to eating and thinking and talking about food.

For anyone who has ever been anxious about food, getting pulled over the event horizon of your feelings, I have to tell you – it feels amazing when you realise that your appetites don't just belong to you. God, is it a relief to have joint custody over your neuroses. And when you do this, you also get to share in the joy. We're connected. People's emotional landscapes can be impenetrable and despotic. And yet you have to try to know them anyway, first because these attempts at connection are all we have but also, on a selfish level, because that's how we get to know ourselves. This is an empathy that we all need to come around to. Especially now. Isn't it good to know that you're part of a food culture that's bigger than you? Isn't it a relief to know that it shapes you? And that you – by wanting anything at all, just by knowing food and liking it – can shape it in turn? You're in it, I'm in it, Guy Fieri is in it. *It* being a connective, anarchic web of desire that somehow joins us all.

I've thought a lot about something James Baldwin once said about Shakespeare. He talked about how Shakespeare mined the full breadth and weirdness of human experience and found poetry there. 'He could have done this only through love,' Baldwin wrote. We can all try this, and we have to. 'By knowing, which is not the same thing as understanding, that whatever was happening to anyone was happening to him.'

Further Reading

Here are a few resources that you may enjoy if you enjoyed this one – some because they riff on similar themes, others because they fill in the gaps that I've left. First is a general overview of useful materials. After that, a topic-by-topic breakdown of some of the books, websites, magazines and blogs that I consulted during the writing of this book. This isn't a comprehensive or academic list, but a snapshot that I hope will serve as a starting point for your own investigations as you travel along tangents through the culture. If you need more help tracing back to the source of specific references in this book, you can contact me via my website: rubytandoh.co.uk

General

For the history of British food, *English Food* by Diane Purkiss is invaluable. Also: *All Manners of Eating* by Stephen Mennell, *Good Things in England* by Florence White and

The English at Table by Jill Norman. Digging into the last seventy-five years of British eating, *The British at Table* by Christopher Driver, *The Bad Food Guide* by Derek Cooper and various back issues of the *Good Food Guide*, especially those from the eighties and edited by Drew Smith. Looking at London specifically, *London Feeds Itself*, edited by Jonathan Nunn, and *Food Lovers' London* by Jenny Linford both offer loving and exceptionally detailed snapshots of a food scene in constant flux.

As for general books about American food culture, they're already far better recorded than British ones, so I won't expand on them here except to say that Toni Tipton-Martin's *The Jemima Code* is unmissable, and I found *Paradox of Plenty* by Harvey Levenstein informative.

To learn things that you never ever knew you were curious about, journals, magazines, websites and Substacks tend to be more specialised and reactive than books. *Petits Propos Culinaires*, proceedings from the Oxford Food Symposium and *Gastronomica* are excellent for academic deep dives and hyper-niche research. Back issues of now defunct publications like Tom Jaine's *Twelve Times a Year*, *Lucky Peach* and *Fire and Knives* have all been helpful to me too. *Vittles* (now also a print magazine) is one of many Substack newsletters that cover the minutiae and the big picture of food culture today. Jonathan Gold's old reviews, many viewable through the *L.A. Weekly* and *Los Angeles Times* backpages or via archive.org, are evergreen reminders of the beauty, sinew and physicality of food.

The finest food writers are often only accidentally that. Ntozake Shange's *If I Can Cook, You Know God Can* is one of the most lyrical food books of the last fifty years. Nora

Ephron's many essays about the hopes and contradictions of foodies. Reyner Banham's reminders about the architecture of food spaces. Laurie Colwin's kitchen chronicles in *Gourmet*. Some of the most enticing food descriptions I've read in recent years were from Hilary Mantel's *Wolf Hall* trilogy.

For contemporary writers who cover food culture either specifically or incidentally but with great insight, I can recommend: Helen Rosner's kitchen dispatches and restaurant reviews in the *New Yorker*; Aaron Timms' essays about food, capital and influence; Rebecca May Johnson's writing about cooking and kitchens; Jessica Carbone on American food culture; Tammie Teclemariam, Chris Crowley, Pete Wells and Ryan Sutton's dispatches from the food and culture of New York City. Yẹmisí Aríbisálà is one of the most brilliant and stylish writers on food today.

If you want the joy of reading about petty food-industry gripes and score settling: *Is There a Nutmeg in the House?* by Elizabeth David and edited by Jill Norman; *Out to Lunch* by Paul Levy; *The Official Foodie Handbook* by Ann Barr and Paul Levy; *Crazy Salad & Scribble Scribble* by Nora Ephron.

Finally, you'll find dozens of cookbooks mentioned here, most of which are easily available through second-hand bookshops, and many of which you can borrow from somewhere like archive.org. I won't list them all again now, but I will say that if you're interested in going beyond what's available on the shelves of Waterstones, the British Library, Oxford Brookes and the Brotherton Library at Leeds University all have excellent food collections.

Craving content

A lot of my research for this chapter was conducted online, in the constantly renewing websites and social media feeds of recipe factories like Mob, the *Guardian*, *The New York Times* and *Bon Appétit*, not to mention chancing upon some of the many hundreds of individual recipe creators, blogs and Substacks online. But in order to understand the particular energy of what's happening right now, you also need to understand where recipes came from and how they used to work. To this end, a number of resources are helpful: Polly Russell's articles for the *Financial Times*; *Culinary Pleasures* by Nicola Humble; *Eat My Words* by Janet Theophano and *The Recipe Reader* by Janet Floyd and Laurel Forster. Anthropologist Arjun Appardurai's essay 'How to Make a National Cuisine' can be found online and is informative on the geopolitical role of cookbooks.

To get a sense of how food photography has evolved, I turned to: *Food in Vogue*, with an introduction by Arabella Boxer; *A Visual Feast* by Arabella Boxer and photographer Tessa Traeger; *The Cookbook Book*, by Florian Böhm and Annahita Kamali; as well as old issues of British *Vogue*, *Marie Claire*, the *Observer*, the *Guardian* and *À La Carte* (the late-eighties British fever-dream magazine). That said, the greatest resource is just cookbooks, lots of them, many hideous.

It's often fruitful to look at past cookbooks not from here and now, but through the eyes of the people who had to endure the worst of their hype. Michael Field's old cookbook reviews in the *New York Review of Books* clarified my views on a few books that are now considered classics. The

Times and *Guardian* newspaper archives are occasionally useful for this, too, as well as *The Official Foodie Handbook* by Ann Barr and Paul Levy.

On the seventh day, they cooked

The best way to research supplements is to read supplements. Most can be found online and in the British Library. Many of the older *Observer* magazines have not been digitised, but I found the *Guardian* and *Observer* archives useful in those cases. Helpfully, newspaper supplement recipes often end up recycled in books, which makes things easier. From Jane Grigson, *Good Things* as well as the *Observer Guide to British Cookery* are a couple of her compilations. Margaret Costa's *Four Seasons Cookery Book* does the same, as well as Robert Carrier's *Great Dishes of the World* and, much later, *Real Good Food* from Nigel Slater. For background on the supplements, the newspapers have self-mythologised in their own coverage, and you can also consult 'Supplemental Income', a paper by Richard Farmer in *Media History* journal. *Lifestyle Revolution* by Ben Highmore is a broader look at changing taste and class in post-war Britain.

Allrecipes

The OG internet slips like water through our fingers. Luckily, sites like archive.org are working hard to catalogue and preserve web pages so that you can travel back in time and see a site like Allrecipes as it was in the early days. And to understand its social underpinnings, check out *Recipes for Reading* – all about community cookbooks – by Anne L. Bower. Christopher Kimball's essay 'Gourmet to All That' in *The New York Times* remains an object of grim fascination for me.

The critic hits the road

Dining Out, by Katie Rawson and Elliott Shore, is a good primer for how restaurants have changed over time, including in relation to changes in travel and tourism. So are *Paradox of Plenty* by Harvey Levenstein and *Fast Food: Roadside Restaurants in the Automobile Age* by John A. Jakle and Keith A. Sculle. *Duncan Hines*, by Louis Hatchett, is the best biographic resource for the great eater, while Damon Talbott's paper 'Recommended by Duncan Hines' is an excellent discussion of Hines' place in the broader culture. Not much has been written about Keith Lee so far, save for C. T. Jones' profile in *Rolling Stone*. Frank Norris' paper 'Courageous Motorists: African American Pioneers on Route 66' gives a little more background on Victor Hugo Green. Perhaps predictably, the restaurant guides of both Green and Hines went quickly out of date and are now very hard to find, but some are viewable online and others periodically appear on second-hand book sites.

Robert Sietsema's article 'Everyone Eats . . .' for *Columbia Journalism Review* is illuminating on the state and future of criticism, as are a great many of Pete Wells' articles for *The New York Times*. On Craig Claiborne, there's *The Man Who Changed the Way We Eat* by Thomas McNamee.

You can find old Craig Claiborne reviews in *The New York Times* archives, but there are also some lesser-known gems available to those who seek – Clementine Paddleford, Gael Greene, Nigella Lawson, Jonathan Meades, Michael Winner, scattered across various newspaper archives and fan sites, the good, the bad and the ugly. The best was of course Jonathan Gold, whose writing you can find very easily and should read if you're at all interested in restaurants or, indeed, in writing.

Anatomy of a queue

Food and Social Media: You Are What You Tweet, by Signe Rousseau, is a good overview of how blog culture helped to create a world of online food hype, but it came out before the Instagram heyday and long before TikTok. For analysis of these newer platforms, *Filterworld* by *New Yorker* writer Kyle Chayka is helpful, as is the writing of Aaron Timms. But for the most part, these foods are inextricable from their native media, and you have to get hands on with the blogs, geriatric Tumblr accounts, Instagram grids and TikTok demagogues to really understand what's happening. What I found particularly illuminating were the rare moments of overlap between establishment food media and the insurgents – some food writers and critics, like Pete Wells and Helen Rosner, cover these intersections with particular care. If you want a cautionary tale about being tech-reactionary, search newspaper archives for 'food bloggers' scare pieces from the late noughties and see how well they've aged.

I like bubble tea

Much of the media about bubble tea follows digital pathways: through TikTok videos, on Instagram, in deep-archive blog posts and Flickr posts from 2011. Some writers who have written about bubble tea with care and insight include Angela Hui for Vice, and Jenny G. Zhang for Eater, while Clarissa Wei has talked about the drink's Taiwanese origins. For general explorations of East and South East Asian food cultures in the UK, Jenny Lau's *An A-Z of Chinese Food* is informative, as is Angela Hui's memoir *Takeaway*.

Dream home

The *Ebony* archives are accessible across certain corners of the internet and I'd encourage you to see them for yourself – Freda DeKnight's writing is best understood in its contexts, where it gains particular resonance. To learn more about Black magazines in the United States, *Ladies' Pages: African American Women's Magazines and the Culture That Made Them* by Noliwe M. Rooks is crucial, while *The New Noir* by Orly Clerge is a compelling examination of Black suburbia and its socio-economic drivers, as is *Places of Their Own* by Andrew Wiese. Katharina Vester has written about *Ebony* magazine's food pages in the anthology *Dethroning the Deceitful Pork Chop*, edited by Jennifer Jensen Wallach.

The seminal history of Black American recipe culture remains *The Jemima Code* by Toni Tipton-Martin. *Vibration Cooking* by Vertamae Smart-Grosvenor is a wonderful, lyrical exploration of cooking both within and beyond the domestic kitchen. Smart-Grosvenor also writes about food in *The Black Woman*, an anthology edited by Toni Cade Bambara. For other writing on food, bodies and Blackness, I strongly recommend *Eating While Black* by Psyche Williams Forson and *Fearing the Black Body* by Sabrina Strings. *Black Hunger* by Doris Witt is also useful. *Turning the Tables*, edited by Sue O'Sullivan, is a feminist recipe collection and a wonderful look at how the form can be subverted. There are echoes of this in Rebecca May Johnson's *Small Fires*.

How not to use a cookbook

You may want to refer back to some of the resources referenced above for 'Craving content', many of which I also used in researching this chapter. If you want to learn more about Elizabeth David, there's an abundance of (some would say too much) literature on her life and work, including countless essays, and biographies by Artemis Cooper and Lisa Chaney, but the best resources remain her own writing – in her cookbooks, but also scattered across her journalistic work. Many of her essays have been compiled by her editor, Jill Norman, into books: *An Omelette and a Glass of Wine* and *Is There a Nutmeg in the House?* For extra background on the series she co-edited for André Deutsch, see *Stet* – the autobiography of editor Diana Athill, who worked with David on the project. The full collection of Sainsbury's cookbooks can be found in the Sainsbury Archive in London. Sales figures from *The*

Times bestseller lists, the *Bookseller*, *Publisher's Weekly* and Nielsen Bookscan are all useful references if you want to separate out the food writing that is good from the writing that actually sells. These are seldom, I'm sorry to say, the same.

'Cook remaining 100 lobsters'

You will probably not be able to find a cheap copy of Martha Stewart's 1982 classic, *Entertaining*, but this should not stop you from trying. After months of obsessing, I eventually got one on eBay for £40. I wish you the same good fortune. To understand the deep insanity of dinner party culture, you will want to look through old copies of *Gourmet* magazine, many of which are (for now, blessedly) available on archive.org. *Martha Stewart Living* magazine back issues are also fruitful. As far as secondary sources go, Nora Ephron's 'Gourmet Magazine' and 'The New Porn' essays in *Crazy Salad & Scribble Scribble* are all you need.

Supermarket fugue

On the topic of supermarkets, the Sainsbury and M&S archives are both helpful if you want to see the evolution of packaging, supermarket archives and branding. *Own Label* by Jonny Trunk is a beautiful collection of some of the work of the Sainsbury's Design Studio. *Supermarket USA* by Shane Hamilton is a wonderful deep dive into the deployment of supermarkets as political propaganda during the Cold War. *Shopping at Giant Foods* by Alfred Yee covers the history of Chinese American supermarkets. *Look at the Lights, My Love,* by Annie Ernaux, is an often problematic but occasionally beautiful look at the experiential qualities of supermarkets. *Carried Away* by Rachel Bowlby and *Grocery* by Michael Ruhlman are both useful histories of modern shopping. *Building Houses Out of Chicken Legs*, by Psyche A. Williams-Forson, touches on the systemic barriers to Black trade and commerce, as does *Black Food Geographies* by Ashanti M. Reese. *Food Co-ops in America* by Anne Meis Knupfer reminds us that there are other ways of doing things. I also came across a small feature in *Ebony* magazine, from September 1955, about Black-owned supermarkets – this is the kind of archival find that a researcher dreams of, and I wish I could have written more on this specific topic. Delightfully, *Letters of the Century, 1900–1999,* edited by Lisa Grunwald, contains Michael Cullen's initial supermarket-dream pitch in full.

The ice cream age

Licks, Sticks and Bricks by Pim Reinders is *the* resource for all your ice cream needs, with a focus on Unilever brands. The patent collection at the British Library turns up occasional treasures, such as the Viennetta patent, and is well worth investigating if you want to see more behind the scenes. The Unilever Archives at Port Sunlight contain all back issues of in-house Wall's magazines and Unilever

end-of-year reports – these are invaluable. The London
Archives holds a collection of Lyons materials. An exqui-
sitely dry but informative book called *Renewing Unilever:
Transformation and Tradition* by Geoffrey Jones filled in a
few factual gaps for me, but people's relationships with these
products are often so strong that the greatest collections of,
say, Twister adverts, will be on Facebook throwback groups
or fan sites. These are the people's archives.

Tonic waters

Wellness discourse moves faster than most of us can ever
hope to keep up with, but there are a few resources to help
to make sense of this wild phenomenon. *Maintenance Phase*,
a podcast from Aubrey Gordon and Michael Hobbes, is a
meticulously researched dive into the contradictions and
harms of diet culture, in all its forms. Snaxshot, a Substack
from Andrea Hernández, is an incisive resource on postmodern food retail, and gets into the particular weirdness
of wellness products better than anywhere else. For work
that grapples with bigger ideological shifts, *Doppelganger* by
Naomi Klein is instructive if you want to understand some
of the political underpinnings of wellness, as is *Trick Mirror*
by Jia Tolentino. It was beyond the scope of this essay to
get into the broader politics of sugary drinks – from the
power of brands like Coca-Cola to racialised ideas about
sugar and sweetness – but for a closer read of this side of
things, see *Fearing the Black Body* by Sabrina Strings, or
Tasting Food, Tasting Freedom by Sidney Mintz.

The automat is dead

The Robert F. Byrnes collection of automat memorabilia at the New York Public Library is unparalleled. Angelika Epple, Nicholas Bromell and Danya Pilgrim are just three of the people who have written academic papers wholly or partly about automats, and Pilgrim's is particularly interesting for its coverage of modernisations in dining and the Black hospitality trade. Jan Whitaker's website Restaurant-ing Through History is an excellent resource for all kinds of restaurant esoterica, including but not limited to automats. *White Burgers, Black Cash* by Naa Oyo A. Kwate is a book about the racialised inequities of fast-food culture. Fordham University's Bronx African American History Project has a couple of oral histories that touch on life in the age of automats, both sides of the lockers. In *The New York Times* archive you can find coverage of the Horn & Hardart strikes, as well as in Stephen H. Norwood's academic paper 'Organizing the neglected worker: the Women's Trade Union League in New York and Boston, 1930–1950'. Vladimir Nabokov's essay 'Man and Things' can be found in the *New Yorker* archives.

Wimpy

Legacy by Thomas Harding is a great history of Lyons, and you'll find more in the London Archives as well, but really a person needs to experience a Wimpy to understand it. If you want to learn about the strange social geographies of Wimpy, *The Invention of Essex* by Tim Burrows is a good place to start.

Acknowledgements

Huge thanks to Cecily Gayford and Stuart Cooper, without whose extraordinary patience, generosity and understanding this project never would have seen the light of day. To Jenny Dean for stepping in with a title and unparalleled editorial tenacity under pressure. To Annie Lee for copyediting with such care, to Sarah-Jane Forder for proofreading and Emily Frisella for getting this project over the line. Thank you to Jack Smyth for the cover design. To Dahmicca Wright and Valentina Zanca for your energy and dedication to marketing and promoting this project.

To everyone who shared their stories, experiences and expertise with me for the research of this book: Shara Alexander, Cindy Carnes, Jerry Cheung, Jo Yee Cheung, Molly Fergus, Glenn Fleishman, Louise Haines, Amanda Hesser, Chris Hillman, Kevin Hillman, Tim Hunt, Allan Jenkins, Shelia Johnson, Eric Khaw, Arie Knutson, Ben Lebus, Jenny Linford, Carl Lipo, Mark Madsen, Yohannes Miller, Bill Moore, Jill Norman, David Quinn, Pim Reinders, Chloe René, Claudia Roden, Nicky Ross, Dan

Shepherd, Nigel Slater, Kaila Stone, Pete Wells, Sophie Wyburd and Ali.

To every friend who read the early drafts of this book and advised, encouraged or tactfully ignored them; to others who have talked to me about the book and offered a new perspective; to a special few who simply kept me company or offered welcome distraction while I was miserable about it: K. Biswas, Oliver Costello, Bel Davies, Ane Engelstad, Åsa Engelstad, Feroz Gajia, Linnéa Haviland, Tessa Hellett, Rukmini Iyer, Rachel McVeagh, Nadia Mehdi, Sinae Park, Maja Radosavljevic, Guillermo Ruiz de Loizaga, Polly Russell, Molly Pepper Steemson, Kaila Stone, Natalie Tandoh, Rosa Tandoh, Kasia Tomasiewicz, Wong Binghao and Sheila Yates. My love and endless gratitude to Jonathan, for the edits, patience and care.

To the Lopud Foundation and everyone who made my stay on Lopud so restful and productive, including Lucien Rees-Roberts, Colin Groundwater, Nikolina, Dragana, Esad and Zeljko. To Draško Adžić, Kadri Koop and John Murray for being the best companions and friends I could have hoped to meet.

To Marella Gayla and Bethany Garrett, under whose editorial care two of the essays in this book originally came to life.

To the librarians and archivists whose care, curiosity and above-and-beyond stewardship were essential to the writing of this book: Allison Foster and George Cooban at the Sainsbury Archive; Philippa and Joshua at the Guardian News & Media Archive; Annabel Valentine at Oxford Brookes; Lucie Whitmore at London Museum; the staff at the Unilever Archives at Port Sunlight, the London

Acknowledgements

Archives, the Wellcome Collection library and the New York Public Library. And enormous thanks to all the staff at the British Library, who not only helped me to find all the materials I needed, but also offered the moments of human warmth that kept me going along the way.